Other Kaplan High School Books

Essential Review: High School Biology

Essential Review: High School Chemistry

Essential Review: High School Mathematics I

Essential Review: High School Mathematics II

High School 411

Essential Review

High School MATHEMATICS III

Ira Ewen, M.S.
Principal, James Madison High School (retired)
Brooklyn, NY

Mark Weinfeld, M.A.
MathWorks
New York, NY

Judith Covington, Ph.D.
Louisiana State University
Shreveport, LA

Simon & Schuster

Kaplan Books
Published by Kaplan Educational Centers and Simon & Schuster
1230 Avenue of the Americas
New York, New York 10020

For bulk sales to schools, colleges, and universities, please contact Vice President of Special Sales, Simon & Schuster Special Markets, 1633 Broadway, 8th Floor, New York, NY 10019.

Project Editors: Eileen Mager, Richard Christiano
Cover Design: Cheung Tai
Production Editor: Maude Spekes
Interior Design and Production: James Stirling
Desktop Publishing Manager: Michael Shevlin
Managing Editor: David Chipps
Executive Editor: Del Franz
Contributing Editors: Gregg Driben and Marti Garlett

Special thanks are extended to Robert Marantz, Larissa Shmailo, and Sara Pearl.

Library of Congress Cataloging-in-Publication data is available.

Manufactured in the United States of America
Published Simultaneously in Canada

The practice tests in this book are reprinted by permission of the University of the State of New York/State Education Department.

The testing strategies in chapter 1, "Test Taking," are excerpted from *Learning Power*, by Cynthia Johnson and Drew Johnson (published by Kaplan and Simon & Schuster), and are used by permission. The information on handling stress in chapter 1 is excerpted from "The Kaplan Advantage™ Stress Management System," by Dr. Ed Newman and Bob Verini, copyright © 1996, Kaplan Educational Centers.

October 1999

10 9 8 7 6 5 4 3 2 1

ISBN 0-684-86824-5

CONTENTS

How to Use This Book

This book is designed to supplement your textbook and your class notes. As a general outline to the material you are studying, it contains the most important facts you'll need to remember to do well on your class tests, midterms, and finals. It's a powerful tool, for the student who can use it correctly. Here's how to make your test scores higher:

Study Tips

The first chapter contains some general strategies for doing well on tests. . . strategies that you may not have learned in school. Read through it and remember the valuable advice it contains.

Diagnostic Test

The first practice test is a diagnostic test—by taking it and checking your answers, you will be able to identify your weak points and begin your work of shoring them up. The answer to every question will point you to the chapter in the book where problems like the one tested in the question are further explained. Consult the relevant chapter in your texbook to further solidify your understanding of each concept.

Content Review

The chapters after the diagnostic test are a comprehensive review of the material you are learning in class. Read these in the order that will help you best. For example, if you're preparing for a final exam, you can hit the chapters you identified as weak points in the diagnostic test first, and then read all of the others later. Or, if you're studying for a weekly test, you can concentrate only on the topics that will be tested. Or, if you have some time on your hands, you can start at the beginning and read straight through to the end. There is no wrong way to read it . . . the most important thing is that you get the information you need to do well.

Practice Tests

This book contains five practice tests (the diagnostic test in the beginning of the book, and four others at the end). These are closer in difficulty to a final exam than they are to an ordinary test, but don't panic: You're the only one who will see your scores, and you have the benefit of filling the gaps in your knowledge before you're tested for real in school. If you can do well on these tests, you're well on the road to mastering this subject!

Part I

Study Tips

Chapter 1

Studying for Success in Mathematics

You are going to pass all of your mathematics tests.

You are going to pass because you will believe in yourself, because you will know the mathematics, and because you will have practiced enough of the problems so that the examination will look familiar and not frightening.

Think about some long-range goals, beyond the mere passing of tests, which are within your reach with some additional effort:

- You can learn the mathematics well enough to carry over the summer break and assist you in doing even better in your next course.

- You can learn the mathematics well enough to be able to apply the *concepts* and *skills* in new contexts such as science, economics, or business.

- You can learn the mathematics well enough to be able to apply what you have learned in unfamiliar settings and to problem situations in which you are not certain how to begin or where you are going. (Such situations, formally called *ill-defined problem situations*, occur continually in life. They occur at home, on the job, in school, and in your interaction with friends.)

- You can learn the mathematics well enough so that you will think of yourself as mathematically able.

Here are some things you can do so that the effort you put into passing your tests will reward you far beyond the grades you get.

Reflect on Your Work

After each problem you do, take a few seconds to think about the problem. What mathematical concepts were involved? Which part of the problem gave you difficulty? What question about the ideas behind the problem could you ask a teacher about?

Reflection is thinking about what you have done, what you have heard, what has happened to you so that you can learn from the experience. Some people reflect on each day in their lives because they want to avoid repeating avoidable mistakes. They want to continue doing the things they did which worked well for them.

Most students rarely or never reflect on what they learn at school. Taking the few seconds needed to ask, "What was the main thing I must remember from that class?" or "from that chapter?" or "from that discussion?" helps your brain to process an experience. You will be astounded at the way reflection helps you to remember what you have heard or have done.

Few students or teachers have reflected on the major concepts of their subject. What are the major concepts of mathematics? Which of these concepts applies to the current problem (or the current lesson, or the current topic)?

For your guidance, here are a few of the concepts central to mathematics:

1. Sameness and equivalence

2. Evidence and certainty

3. Measure and measurement

4. Symbols and meaning

5. Characteristics and representation of data

6. Symmetry

7. Relations and functions

8. Invariance

9. Operations

10. Inference

11. Mathematical systems and models

This is not a complete list, but you might want to reflect on where topics fit on this partial list. *Probability*? Probability is a measure (concept 3) of events; the study of probability is related closely to the study of length, area, and volume. *Statistics*? The mean, median, mode, range, and dozens of other measures (concept 3) are characteristics of data (concept 5).

Graphs and charts are also representations of data (concept 5).

Slope is a measure (concept 3) of a line and an invariant (concept 8) in a set of parallel lines.

When you *solve an equation*, how are you certain (concept 2) that you have all the solutions? When you *solve a pair of simultaneous equations* by addition and subtraction, how do you infer (concept 10) that the solution of the new set of equations is the same as the solution of the set you were given?

The act of thinking about questions such as these is a powerful mode of study. It makes connections, fixes ideas in your long-term memory (the memory that lingers after tomorrow) and it puts you in charge of what you are trying to learn.

Keep a Journal

A simple route to productive reflection is to keep a brief daily mathematics journal with four key elements:

1. The topic of the homework assignment or lesson and the date.

2. The major mathematical concept(s) involved in the assignment or lesson.

3. One question about the lesson or assignment which you would like to have answered to improve your understanding.

4. One application of the lesson or assignment to another subject, topic in mathematics, life situation, or problem which you made up.

If you can discipline yourself to keep such a journal for two weeks, compare your grades on the material covered during those weeks to your usual grades. You will be pleasantly amazed. You may decide that the journal, requiring perhaps five minutes of time each day, is the best investment of time you have ever made to improve your grades and your retention of schoolwork.

Practice New Ideas by Making Up Problems and Solving Them

When you try to make up problems on the current assignment, you might want to begin simply by taking a problem in the book that you have solved successfully and changing the numbers, operations, or variables. The new problem is not very different from the one you solved; nevertheless, it is a start. Soon you'll be making up more powerful problems.

A far richer technique is easily available with any verbal problem. Copy down the data; *omit the question*. Explore several things you might be able to deduce from the data given. Write one or two questions based on the data which you could answer. You will be amazed once again. Often you will figure out for yourself what the question in the problem actually was! On occasion you will have come up with a better question than the one in the book. The resulting problem is yours in a very meaningful way. You are not only reflecting on the problem; you are turning it like a gem in the sunlight to see hidden brilliancy. You are creating mathematics.

Before a test, try to make up five to ten problems that would worry you if you found them on the actual test. Try to solve those problems. If you cannot solve them yourself, enlist a friend, family member, or teacher to help you. If the problem is solvable, reflect on why you had difficulty with it. Was it unfamiliarity with the topic, with a skill related to the topic, with the underlying mathematical concept, or with the thinking skills used in analyzing the problem?

If the problem cannot be solved by you, your friends, or your teacher, you might consider what it is that made this problem so different from those in this book. You might want to investigate problems that cannot be solved at all. Consider the following: find a rational number which is two more than itself. Such a number would satisfy the equation

$$x = x + 2.$$

That could happen if and only if $0 = 2$. Thus, there is no rational number which is two more than itself.

Some of the most successful students in high school and college try to predict the questions that will appear on examinations and to answer those questions. They reflect on the way the writer of the test might be thinking. Whether or not they predict the questions correctly, they are studying for the examination in an effective way which helps them to remember their reading and thinking for a considerable period of time.

Why not try it yourself?

THINKING SKILLS AND PROBLEM SOLVING STRATEGIES

Several strategies exist that are particularly helpful in mathematics (and in many other school and life settings) when dealing with unfamiliar problem situations. Some of the most frequently applicable strategies are:

1. Working backward

2. Finding a pattern

3. Adopting a different point of view

4. Solving a simpler analogous problem

5. Considering extreme cases

6. Using visual representation

7. Making intelligent guesses

Knowing these strategies means that you are way ahead of the game whenever you face something new. Do you know, for example, when it is better to work backward from the goal of a problem to a starting point?

Working Backward

Whenever there are several possible ways to begin and a limited objective, working backward is helpful. Suppose you want to go to law school and you ask your adviser what to take next term. A good adviser will suggest that you work backward from the requirements of several law schools to the courses you will need in college to the courses you will need to get into college and be eligible to take the courses needed for admission to law school. This analysis helps you to pinpoint the courses you should consider taking the following year.

The same situation occurs in mathematics in problems or proofs where it is not clear how to begin. A good example is the proof that $\sqrt{2}$ is irrational. Because we cannot see how to begin a direct proof, we begin backward, saying "Suppose $\sqrt{2}$ were rational." We follow an argument that leads us to a contradiction of the fact that every rational number can be reduced to lowest terms as a quotient of integers. Even when you know this proof very well, you would be hard put to make it into a direct proof.

There are countless situations in mathematics and in life when working backward is advisable. Reflect on the pertinence of this strategy whenever you are stumped on a problem. Make it an active part of your problem solving arsenal.

Finding a Pattern

This strategy applies continually to real life situations. You need to catch a subway at an hour when the trains run infrequently. You do not have access to a train schedule. After a few days you guess at (an informed guess is known as a *conjecture*) the time when the train is supposed to arrive so that you can be in the station a few minutes before.

Another example might occur as a football coach is preparing his high school team for an upcoming game. He notes that the opposing coach has a pattern of running on first and second down and passing on third down whenever his team is in possession of the ball. He prepares a defense based on that pattern.

In mathematics, some challenging problems are easily solved if a pattern is uncovered. A teacher challenges you to count accurately the number of diagonals in a convex 12-sided polygon (which is known to mathematicians as a convex dodecagon). You draw a figure (following strategy 6) and attempt to draw in all the diagonals. You find it difficult to keep track of what you are doing and are not very confident of your result.

Suppose you combined strategies 2 (finding a pattern) and 4 (solving a simpler analogous problem) and began looking at simpler polygons. You make a chart (strategy 6) listing the number of sides in each polygon in the first column and the number of diagonals in the second column. With a little effort you get down to 7-sided polygons (heptagons) and your table looks like this:

number of sides	number of diagonals
3	0
4	2
5	5
6	9
7	14

You don't know *why* this pattern is developing, but you notice that the right hand column increases first by two, then by 3, then by 4, and then by 5. Each time you increase the number of sides by one, the number of diagonals increases by a whole number one greater than the one for the prior increase. You conjecture that the table will continue to follow that pattern:

8	20
9	27
10	35
11	44
12	54

Refer to concept 2 (evidence and certainty): You have made an educated guess based on limited evidence; you are not certain of your answer and you do not know why that pattern developed. Giving your teacher your conjecture and your evidence has a far better chance of getting you recognition than presenting a cluttered diagram with a large number of diagonals in which you are very likely to have missed a few diagonals or miscounted them.

As in the case of working backward, there are countless situations in mathematics and in real life when finding a pattern will lead you to a conjecture that escapes many others. In time you may even become skillful at explaining *why the pattern develops*. If that happens, you will have grown significantly in your ability to prove (or disprove) your own conjectures. In that case you will be functioning much like a professional mathematician.

Adopting a Different Point of View

This saved IBM (International Business Machines) from ruin when management foresaw a day when mechanical calculators would no longer sell. Most of you have probably never seen a mechanical calculator. Mechanical calculators did far less than what your electronic calculator can do and it weighed fifteen pounds or more. The decision to get into the business of developing and marketing computers made IBM one of the great companies of modern times.

How could this strategy apply to mathematics? Suppose you are having difficulty understanding why the textbook has defined $x^0 = 1$, for $x \neq 0$. Instead of merely stewing about it, you decide to change your point of view and look for a pattern that might help you to understand the definition. You note that in order to get from x^4 to x^3, you divide by x. To get from x^3 to x^2, you divide by x. To get from x^2 to x^1, you divide by x, getting $x^1 = x$. You conjecture that in order to get from x^1 to x^0, you might expect to have to divide by x. Since $x \div x = 1$ (for $x \neq 0$), you can now accept the definition $x^0 = 1$ more easily.

Many startling solutions to mathematical problems arise from changing a point of view. Some geometry problems are far easier to solve algebraically once you have learned how. Keep looking for chances to spin gold from straw by changing your own point of view.

Solving a Simpler Analogous Problem

You already saw this strategy applied in combination with strategy 2 in our analysis of the number of diagonals in a polygon.

When you are first learning to make a budget, would you begin by budgeting a multibillion dollar national budget or your five dollar allowance? It seems silly to ask. Remember this extreme case (strategy 5) whenever a problem seems too complicated for you to address directly.

You are asked to determine the change in the product xy from the case when $x = y$ to the case when x is increased by 7 and y is decreased by 7. You decide to use simpler (smaller) numbers and make a chart (strategy 6) when 1 is the increase/decrease instead of 7. You write:

Original value of x	Original value of xy	Final value of xy
1	$1 \cdot 1 = 1$	$2 \cdot 0 = 0$
2	$2 \cdot 2 = 4$	$3 \cdot 1 = 3$
3	$3 \cdot 3 = 9$	$4 \cdot 2 = 8$
4	$4 \cdot 4 = 16$	$5 \cdot 3 = 15$
5	$5 \cdot 5 = 25$	$6 \cdot 4 = 24$

In each of these five cases the product has decreased by 1. Based on the observed pattern (strategy 2), you conjecture that when the increase/decrease is 1, the product always decreases by 1.

You now make a chart for the increase/decrease 2.

Original value of x	Original value of xy	Final value of xy
1	$1 \cdot 1 = 1$	$3 \cdot (-1) = -3$
2	$2 \cdot 2 = 4$	$4 \cdot 0 = 0$
3	$3 \cdot 3 = 9$	$5 \cdot 1 = 5$
4	$4 \cdot 4 = 16$	$6 \cdot 2 = 12$
5	$5 \cdot 5 = 25$	$7 \cdot 3 = 21$

In each of these five cases the product has decreased by 4. Based on the observed pattern (strategy 2), you conjecture that when the increase/decrease is 2, the product always decreases by 4.

You now make charts for the increase/decrease 3, for 4, and for 5. You make another chart showing your results.

Increase/Decrease	Change in Product
1	Decreases by 1
2	Decreases by 4
3	Decreases by 9
4	Decreases by 16
5	Decreases by 25

Based on the observed pattern (strategy 2), you conjecture that for any increase/decrease, the product will always decrease by its *square.* For the case when the increase/decrease is 7, you expect the product to decrease by 49.

When you reflect on this, you see that you might have simply compared x^2 to $(x + 7)(x - 7)$. You have learned that $(x + 7)(x - 7) = x^2 - 49$. The point of this strategy was to give you something to look at and think about if you could not see the easier way immediately.

People often do not immediately see the easiest way to do something. Solving a simpler analogous problem can lead you to a simple or to a complicated answer in easy steps which you will be able to construct and understand.

Considering Extreme Cases

You saw in the discussion of strategy 4 the "trick" of being asked to compare the budgeting of a multibillion dollar national budget to the budgeting of a five dollar allowance. By having you consider extreme cases, you were led to think about the value of purposely looking for simpler analogous problems.

Speakers often use extreme cases to make a point. Sometimes the extreme cases provide a useful analogy; sometimes they do not. When you use this strategy you must be aware that the extreme cases may give insight or they may lead to incorrect conjectures. So long as you reflect on what you do, you can benefit from the insights and reject the incorrect conjectures.

Let's look at a really difficult problem. You may or may not be asked to learn a formula expressing what we are about to discuss, and you will probably never see anything as complicated as this discussion on your tests—at least not in high school. Reading through a difficult discussion (even one that you can barely follow) helps you to master the material easily at a later time. It helps your brain to create pathways (called synapses), which make future learning easier.

Suppose, in geometry, you are asked to test a conjecture about regular polygons such as the suggestion that the area of any regular polygon is one-half the product of its perimeter and the length of the perpendicular line segment from its center to a side. You then panic because you don't have a clue where to begin.

What are the extreme cases of a regular polygon? You need some knowledge and intuition to recognize that the extremes are the equilateral triangle and the circle. (Yes, the circle is not technically a polygon at all. It doesn't have sides which are straight line segments. However, if you drew a regular polygon with a million sides [don't try it!], it would look just like a circle until you put it under a microscope.)

Because equilateral triangles (as, in fact, all regular polygons and all circles) have a lot of symmetries (central concept 6), the triangle's altitudes are the same as its medians. You learn in geometry that the distance from the point where the medians intersect to the midpoint of a side is one-third the length of the median to that side. Thus, in the equilateral triangle, the distance from the center (where medians, altitudes, and angle bisectors all meet in any equilateral triangle because they are all the same line segments) to a side is one-third the length of the altitude.

We learn that the length of a altitude of an equilateral triangle with side s is $\frac{s\sqrt{3}}{2}$. Thus, the length of the segment from the center perpendicular to a side is $\frac{s\sqrt{3}}{6}$. The perimeter of the equilateral triangle is $3s$. Half the product of those quantities is $\frac{1}{2} \cdot \frac{s\sqrt{3}}{6} \cdot 3s = \frac{s^2\sqrt{3}}{4}$, exactly the formula for the area of an equilateral triangle with side s. The complicated conjecture works in the case of the simplest regular polygon!

What about the biggest "regular polygon" (which isn't *really* a polygon at all)? In a circle, the line segment from the center to a side is just a radius. The perimeter of the circle is its circumference. If the radius is r, the circumference is $2\pi r$.

Half the product of the radius and the circumference is $\frac{1}{2} \cdot r \cdot 2\pi r$, which simplifies to πr^2, the familiar formula for the area of a circle. The complicated conjecture works in the case of the largest "regular polygon" as well!

If something like this works in the extreme cases, it shouldn't surprise you at all if it always works. You have not seen a proof, but the conjecture has gained a lot of believability.

If someone tells you that a formula works for all numbers, test the formula for 0 and for 1 (the simplest cases) and for some random number such as 1,739. If the formula checks out in those three cases, although you have not proved it *always* works, it now has some real credibility.

Remember to *examine* the extremes, but never *depend unthinkingly* on them.

Using Visual Representation

You have already been exposed to charts as a help in exploring problem situations. You have experienced the value of diagrams in geometry and logic (Venn diagrams), the value of graphs in analyzing data in algebra and in statistics, the value of a diagram as you attempt to assemble a bicycle for your kid sister, and the value of pictures in textbooks. You also will find diagrams helpful in setting up many of the verbal problems in algebra.

Sometimes a picture helps you to solve a very tricky problem.

A jogger leaves home at 6 A.M. and jogs at an irregular pace along a narrow path, arriving at his destination at 7 A.M. that morning. He spends 23 hours at his destination. The next day he reverses his path and jogs at an irregular pace back home, leaving for home at 6 A.M. and arriving at 7 A.M. Under what conditions must there have been a place in the road which he reached at *exactly the same time* both days?

Believe it or not, there always must be such a place somewhere along his route. If it's not obvious, draw a pair of graphs on the same axes, labeling the x-axis with time and the y-axis with distance from his home. For simplicity (strategy 4) we say the distance from his home to his destination is 10 miles. One graph is an irregular curve rising and moving right and extending from (6, 0) to (7, 10). The second graph is an irregular curve falling and moving right and extending from (6, 10) to (7, 0).

Somewhere, the two curves cross each other. At the time and place represented by that intersection, the jogger was in exactly the same place at exactly the same time on the two days.

Making Intelligent Guesses

On a short answer test, it is often advisable to take a shortcut to an answer by smart guessing and testing.

Consider the following problem: Find three consecutive integers with product 5,814.

Setting up algebraic equations is time-consuming and difficult. You think: if the three numbers were the same, they would be the cube root of 5,814. Take out your handy calculator and compute $\sqrt[3]{5814}$. The calculator gives you 17.98146. You guess that 18 is the middle number and the three numbers are 17, 18, and 19. You again use your calculator to check. Sure enough, $17 \cdot 18 \cdot 19 = 5814$.

Suppose we need to solve the inequality $x^2 + 5x + 6 < 0$. We solve the equation $x^2 + 5x + 6 = 0$ and obtain the solution set $\{-2, -3\}$. We expect the answer to the inequality to be either the "inner interval" $\{x|\ -3 < x < -2\}$ or the union of the two "outer intervals," $\{x|\ x < -3 \text{ or } x > -2\}$. We test $x = -2.5$.

$(-2.5)^2 + 5 \cdot (-2.5) + 6 = 6.25 - 12.5 + 6 = 12.25 - 12.5 = -.25.$

We now guess the solution set to the inequality to be $\{x|\ -3 < x < -2\}$.

Of course, we could have had a simpler time testing $x = 0$ and $x = -10$, mentally getting two positive results again causing us to reject the outside intervals and to select the inner.

Guessing has gotten a bad reputation because of two major difficulties: (1) teachers want students to do a problem a certain way and discourage shortcuts; (2) students tend to guess rather randomly, saying almost anything. When you make an intelligent guess, you must have a reason for your guess—it must be based on knowledge and sound intuition.

Using This Book

You will derive maximum benefit from this book by playing with the problems throughout. Reflect on them, change them, find the central concepts they illustrate. See if you can solve each problem in more than one way, perhaps by using a different thinking strategy. When you find more than one way to do a problem, think about when you would use each approach.

Keep a "tough" file of problems that you found extremely difficult. Talk to friends and teachers about the problem and include repeated attacks on the problems in your tough file in your study plan. Nothing builds confidence as much as gaining a thorough understanding of a problem that initially stumped you.

Following the suggestions made in this section will help you to do well on your mathematics tests. And you might just find the next math course you take will be easier and more fun than any you've taken before.

Part II

Diagnostic Test

Practice Test 1: Diagnostic Test

Part I

Answer 30 questions from this part. Each correct answer will receive 2 credits. No partial credit will be allowed. Write your answers in the spaces provided on the separate answer sheet. Where applicable, answers may be left in terms of π or in radical form.   [60]

1 Solve for the *negative* value of w:
$$|7 + 4w| = 13$$

2 Express $140°$ in radian measure.

3 Under a dilation with center P and scale factor k, A' is the image of A. Find k if $PA = 7$ and $PA' = 28$.

4 If $f(x) = x^2 + 3x$ and $g(x) = x + 3$, for what positive value of x does $f(x) = g(x)$?

5 Evaluate: $\displaystyle\sum_{k=1}^{4} (k^2 + 2)$

6 Evaluate $x^{\frac{3}{4}} - x^0$ if $x = 16$.

7 Express in simplest form: $\dfrac{x - \frac{4}{x}}{1 + \frac{2}{x}}$

8 In the accompanying diagram, chords $\overline{AB}$ and $\overline{CD}$ intersect in the circle at E. If $m\widehat{BC} = 60$ and $m\widehat{AD} = 80$, find $m\angle AEC$.

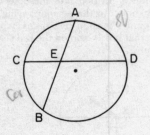

9 If $\tan \theta = 0.1988$, find θ to the *nearest minute*.

10 A translation maps $(1,4)$ onto $(7,-3)$. Write the image of $(5,10)$ under the same translation.

11 What is the value of $\cos \left(\text{Arc sin } \frac{\sqrt{3}}{2}\right)$?

12 Express as a fraction with a rational denominator:
$$\frac{5}{5 - \sqrt{7}}$$

13 Find the value of x if $\log_2 x = 3$.

14 In $\triangle ABC$, $a = \sqrt{2}$, $b = 1$, and $m\angle A = 90$. Find the measure of $\angle B$.

15 In the accompanying diagram, $\overrightarrow{PC}$ is tangent to circle O at C and $\overrightarrow{PAB}$ is a secant. If $PC = 8$ and $PA = 4$, find AB.

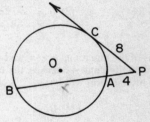

16 In right triangle ABC, $\overline{AB}$ is the hypotenuse. If $AC = 5$ and $BC = 12$, express $\dfrac{\sin B}{\tan B}$ as a fraction in lowest terms.

17 If $m\angle A = 40$, $a = 6$, and $b = 8$, how many distinct triangles can be constructed?

Directions (18–35): For *each* question chosen, write on the separate answer sheet the *numeral* preceding the word or expression that best completes the statement or answers the question.

18 When expressed in scientific notation, the number $0.0000000364 = 3.64 \times 10^n$. The value of n is
(1) 8   (3) –10
(2) 10   (4) –8

19 What is the image of $P(-4,6)$ under the composite $r_{x=2} \circ r_{y\text{-axis}}$?
(1) $(-8,6)$　　　　(3) $(6,0)$
(2) $(4,-2)$　　　　(4) $(0,6)$

20 The sum of $\sqrt{-8}$ and $2\sqrt{-50}$ is
(1) $12\sqrt{2}$　　　　(3) $12i\sqrt{2}$
(2) $-12\sqrt{2}$　　　(4) $-12i\sqrt{2}$

21 Which is an equation of the graph shown below?

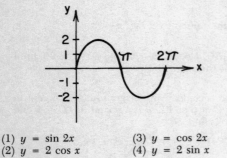

(1) $y = \sin 2x$　　　(3) $y = \cos 2x$
(2) $y = 2\cos x$　　　(4) $y = 2\sin x$

22 If the graphs of the equations $y = x^2$ and $y = -2$ are sketched on the same set of axes, the number of points of intersection will be
(1) 1　　　　(3) 3
(2) 2　　　　(4) 0

23 What are the roots of the equation $x^2 - x + 1 = 0$?
(1) $\dfrac{1 \pm \sqrt{3}}{2}$　　　(3) $\dfrac{1 \pm i\sqrt{3}}{2}$

(2) $\dfrac{1 \pm \sqrt{5}}{2}$　　　(4) $\dfrac{1 \pm i\sqrt{5}}{2}$

24 Which geometric figure has $72°$ rotational symmetry?
(1) square　　　　　(3) rhombus
(2) regular pentagon　(4) regular hexagon

25 If the discriminant of an equation is 10, then the roots are
(1) real, rational, and unequal
(2) real, irrational, and unequal
(3) real, rational, and equal
(4) imaginary

26 The multiplicative inverse of $\sin^2 90° + \cos^2 90°$ equals
(1) 1　　　　(3) -1
(2) 0　　　　(4) ∞

27 In $\triangle ABC$, if $a = 5$, $b = 6$, and $m\angle C = 60$, the value of c is
(1) 1　　　　(3) $\sqrt{41}$
(2) $\sqrt{31}$　　(4) $\sqrt{51}$

28 Which is the solution set for the inequality $|2x - 1| < 3$?

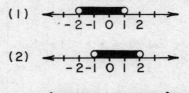

29 What is the value of x in the interval $90° \le x \le 180°$ that satisfies the equation $\sin x + \sin^2 x = 0$?
(1) $90°$　　　　(3) $180°$
(2) $135°$　　　(4) $270°$

30 A circular region is divided into three sections and labeled as shown in the accompanying diagram. If the spinner is spun five times, what is the probability that it will land on the red section *exactly* two times?

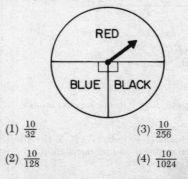

(1) $\dfrac{10}{32}$　　　　(3) $\dfrac{10}{256}$

(2) $\dfrac{10}{128}$　　　(4) $\dfrac{10}{1024}$

31 The value of sin (−210°) is

(1) $\frac{\sqrt{3}}{2}$

(3) $\frac{1}{2}$

(2) $-\frac{\sqrt{3}}{2}$

(4) $-\frac{1}{2}$

32 If cos $A = \frac{1}{3}$, then the positive value of tan $\frac{1}{2}A$ is

(1) $\sqrt{2}$

(3) $\frac{\sqrt{3}}{3}$

(2) $\sqrt{3}$

(4) $\frac{\sqrt{2}}{2}$

33 The third term in the expansion of $(a - \sqrt{2})^5$ is

(1) $20a^3$

(3) $-20a^2\sqrt{2}$

(2) $20a^2\sqrt{2}$

(4) $40a^3$

34 If sin $\theta = -\frac{3}{5}$ and cos $\theta < 0$, then θ terminates in Quadrant

(1) I

(3) III

(2) II

(4) IV

35 What is the domain of the function $f(x) = \sqrt{3x + 7}$?

(1) $\left\{ x \mid x \geq -\frac{3}{7} \right\}$

(3) $\left\{ x \mid x \geq \frac{3}{7} \right\}$

(2) $\left\{ x \mid x \geq -\frac{7}{3} \right\}$

(4) $\left\{ x \mid x \geq \frac{7}{3} \right\}$

Answers to the following questions are to be written on paper provided by the school.

Part II

Answer four questions from this part. Show all work unless otherwise directed. [40]

36 *a* On the same set of axes, sketch and label the graphs of the equations $y = \tan x$ and $y = 2 \cos x$ in the interval $0 \le x \le 2\pi$. [8]

   b Using the graphs drawn in part *a*, find the number of values of x in the interval $0 \le x \le 2\pi$ that satisfy the equation $\tan x = 2 \cos x$. [2]

37 *a* Combine and express in simplest form:

$$\frac{y - 20}{y^2 - 16} + \frac{2}{y - 4} \qquad [4]$$

   b Find all values of θ in the interval $0° \le \theta < 360°$ that satisfy the equation $\sin \theta + 1 = 2 \cos^2 \theta$. [6]

38 *a* Using logarithms, find $\sqrt[5]{87}$ to the *nearest tenth*. [4]

   b For all values of θ for which the expressions are defined, prove that the following is an identity:

$$\frac{\tan \theta + \cot \theta}{\cos \theta \sin \theta} = \sec^2 \theta \csc^2 \theta \qquad [6]$$

39 In $\triangle ABC$, $a = 30$, $c = 27$, and $m\angle A = 34° 20'$.

   a Find the measure of $\angle C$ to the *nearest ten minutes*. [6]

   b Using the answer obtained in part *a*, find the area of $\triangle ABC$ to the *nearest square unit*. [4]

40 *a* Sketch and label the graph of the equation $y = 2^x$. [2]

   b Reflect the graph of the equation $y = 2^x$ in the x-axis. Label your answer *b*. [3]

   c Reflect the graph of the equation $y = 2^x$ in the line $y = x$. Label your answer *c*. [3]

   d Write an equation of the graph drawn in part *c*. [2]

41 In the accompanying diagram, $\overline{AOD}$ is a diameter of circle O, secant $\overline{CFB}$ is parallel to $\overline{DA}$, $\overline{CD}$ is tangent to circle O at D, chords $\overline{AF}$ and $\overline{BD}$ intersect at E, and $m\angle BAF = 20$.

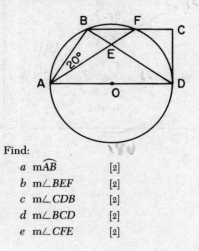

Find:

   a $m\widehat{AB}$ [2]

   b $m\angle BEF$ [2]

   c $m\angle CDB$ [2]

   d $m\angle BCD$ [2]

   e $m\angle CFE$ [2]

42 The table below shows the frequency of the average daily temperatures during the month of June.

Temperature (x_i)	Frequency (f_i)
63	5
70	3
78	4
79	3
80	6
84	4
96	5

   a Using this set of data, find
   (1) the mode [1]
   (2) the median [1]

   b The mean, $\bar{x}$, for these data is 79. Find the standard deviation to the *nearest tenth*. [8]

Practice Test 1

Answers

1. The correct answer is $w = -5$.

   Two possible values will occur, one when $7 + 4w = -13$ and one when $7 + 4w = 13$.

$7 + 4w = -13$	$7 + 4w = 13$

   $$7 + 4w - 7 = -13 - 7 \qquad 7 + 4w - 7 = 13 - 7$$
   $$\text{Subtract 7 from both sides.}$$

$4w = -20$	$4w = 6$

   $$\text{Divide both sides by 4.}$$

$w = -5$	$w = \dfrac{6}{4} = \dfrac{3}{2}$

   You can review absolute value in chapter 2, "The Complex Number System."

2. The correct answer is $\dfrac{7\pi}{9}$.

   Set up a ratio using the fact that $180° = \pi$ radians.

   $$\frac{140}{x} = \frac{180}{\pi} \qquad \text{Cross multiply.}$$

   $$140\pi = 180x \qquad \text{Divide by 180.}$$

   $$\frac{140\pi}{180} = x$$

   $$\frac{7\pi}{9} = x$$

   See chapter 6, "Trigonometric Functions and Their Inverses," for a review of radians.

3. The correct answer is 4.

   Since the length of $PA' = 28$ and $PA = 7$ then PA' is four times as long as PA. Thus, the scale factor is 4.

   You can review images and dilations in chapter 3, "Transformations."

4. The correct answer is $x = 1$.

   Set the two functions equal to each other.

   $$x^2 + 3x = x + 3 \qquad \text{Subtract } x + 3 \text{ from both sides.}$$

   $$x^2 + 3x - x - 3 = x + 3 - x - 3$$

   $$x^2 + 2x - 3 = 0 \qquad \text{Factor the left side.}$$

   $$(x + 3)(x - 1) = 0 \qquad \text{Set each factor equal to zero.}$$

$x + 3 = 0$	$x - 1 = 0$
$x = -3$	$x = 1$

   Functions are covered in chapter 4, "Relations and Functions."

5. The correct answer is 38.

   Substitute 1, 2, 3, and 4 for k. Add the values

   $$[(1)^2 + 2] + [(2)^2 + 2] + [(3)^2 + 2] + [(4)^2 + 2]$$

   $$= (1 + 2) + (4 + 2) + (9 + 2) + (16 + 2)$$

$= 3 + 6 + 11 + 18$

$= 38$

You can review summation notation in chapter 10, "Statistics."

6. The correct answer is 7.

    $(16)^{\frac{3}{4}} = (16^{\frac{1}{4}})^3 = (\sqrt[4]{16})^3 = 2^3 = 8$

    Anything to the zero power is 1, so $16^0 = 1$

    $(16)^{\frac{3}{4}} - (16)^0 = 8 - 1 = 7$

    See chapter 2, "The Complex Number System," for a review of algebraic substitution.

7. The correct answer is $x - 2$.

    $$\dfrac{x - \frac{4}{x}}{1 + \frac{2}{x}}$$

    Multiply numerator and denominator by least common denominator, which is x.

    $$\dfrac{x\left(x - \frac{4}{x}\right)}{x\left(1 + \frac{2}{x}\right)} \qquad \text{Distribute}$$

    $$= \dfrac{x \cdot x - \cancel{x} \cdot \frac{4}{\cancel{x}}}{x \cdot 1 + \cancel{x} \cdot \frac{2}{\cancel{x}}} = \dfrac{x^2 - 4}{x + 2}$$

    $$= \dfrac{(x - 2)\cancel{(x + 2)}}{\cancel{(x + 2)}} \qquad \begin{array}{l}\text{Cancel the common} \\ \text{factor } x + 2.\end{array}$$

    $= x - 2$

    For more on solving fractional equations, see chapter 2, "The Complex Number System."

8. The correct answer is $m\angle AEC = 110$.

    $m\overset{\frown}{AC} + m\overset{\frown}{BD} = 360 - (60 + 80) = 220$

    Then, $m\angle AEC = \frac{1}{2}(220) = 110$

    Circles are covered in chapter 5, "Circles."

9. The correct answer is $11°15'$.

    $\tan \theta = .1988$. Using the $\tan^{-1}$ key on a calculator $\theta = 11.24380673$. Thus we have $11°$. Subtract 11 and multiply by 60 to get minutes. The result is 14.628, which rounds to 15 minutes.

    To review tangent, see chapter 6, "Trigonometric Functions and Their Inverses."

10. The correct answer is $(11, 3)$.

    If the translation maps $(1, 4)$ onto $(7, -3)$, it changes the x-value by $7 - 1 = 6$ and it changes the y-value by $-3 - 4 = -7$. Thus, $(5, 10)$ maps to $(5 + 6, 10 - 7)$ or $(11, 3)$.

    See chapter 3, "Transformations," for a review of translations.

11. The correct answer is $\frac{1}{2}$.

    $\arcsin \dfrac{\sqrt{3}}{2} = 60°$ since $60°$ is the angle that has a sin of $\dfrac{\sqrt{3}}{2}$.

    $\cos\left(\arcsin \dfrac{\sqrt{3}}{2}\right) = \cos(60°) = \dfrac{1}{2}$

    Trigonometric functions are reviewed in chapter 6, "Trigonometric Functions and Their Inverses."

12. The correct answer is $\dfrac{5(5 + \sqrt{7})}{18}$.

    To obtain a rational denominator, multiply the numerator and denominator of $\dfrac{5}{5 - \sqrt{7}}$

    by the conjugate of $5 - \sqrt{7}, 5 + \sqrt{7}$.

    $$\dfrac{5(5 + \sqrt{7})}{(5 - \sqrt{7})(5 + \sqrt{7})} = \dfrac{5(5 + \sqrt{7})}{25 - 7} = $$

    $$\dfrac{5(5 + \sqrt{7})}{18}$$

    Irrational numbers are covered in chapter 2, "The Complex Number System."

13. The correct answer is 8.

    $\log_2 x = 3$ translates to $2^3 = x$, so $x = 8$

    See chapter 4, "Relations and Functions," for more on logarithms.

14. The correct answer is 45°.

    Using the law of sines, $\dfrac{\sin A}{a} = \dfrac{\sin B}{b}$ so,

    $$\dfrac{\sin 90}{\sqrt{2}} = \dfrac{\sin B}{1}$$

    $$\dfrac{1}{\sqrt{2}} = \sin B$$

    Since $\dfrac{1}{\sqrt{2}} = \dfrac{\sqrt{2}}{2}$ and the angle whose sine is

    $\dfrac{\sqrt{2}}{2}$ is 45°, m$\angle B = 45°$.

    See chapter 8, "Trigonometry—Triangle Solution," for a review of trigonometric triangle solutions.

15. The correct answer is 12.

    $(\overline{PC})^2 = (\overline{PA})(\overline{PB})$ The length of the tangent segment squared is equal to the product of the lengths of PA and PB

    $$64 = 4(PB)$$

    $$16 = PB$$

    So, $AB = 16 - 4 = 12$.

    See chapter 5, "Circles," for a review of circles.

16. The correct answer is $\dfrac{12}{13}$.

    If $\overline{AB}$ is the hypotenuse then $\angle C$ is a right angle.

    $$\sin B = \dfrac{\text{opposite side}}{\text{hypotenuse}} = \dfrac{AC}{AB} = \dfrac{5}{AB}$$

    $$\tan B = \dfrac{\text{opposite side}}{\text{adjacent side}} = \dfrac{AC}{BC} = \dfrac{5}{12}$$

    To find AB use the Pythagorean Theorem.

    $$(AC)^2 + (BC)^2 = (AB)^2$$

    $$(5)^2 + (12)^2 = 25 + 144 = 169$$

    Since $(AB)^2 = 169$, $AB = 13$

    Thus $\sin B = \dfrac{5}{13}$ and $\tan B = \dfrac{5}{12}$.

    $$\dfrac{\sin B}{\tan B} = \dfrac{\frac{5}{13}}{\frac{5}{12}} = \dfrac{5}{13} \times \dfrac{12}{5} = \dfrac{12}{13}$$

    Trigonometric triangle solutions are covered in chapter 8, "Trigonometry—Triangle Solution."

17. The correct answer is 2.

    Since we are given an acute angle and the side opposite, this is an ambiguous case. Find $\sin B$.

$$\text{Sin } B = \frac{b \sin A}{a} = \frac{8 \sin 40}{6} = 0.857$$

Since sin $B < 1$, two triangles could occur, one obtuse and one acute.

Trigonometric triangle solutions are covered in chapter 8, "Trigonometry—Triangle Solution."

18. The correct answer is (4).

    Since the decimal in 3.64 must be moved to the left 8 places to obtain the original number, $n = -8$.

    See chapter 2, "The Complex Number System," for more on scientific notation.

19. The correct answer is (4), (0, 6).

    Reflect $(-4, 6)$ about the y-axis to obtain $(4, 6)$.

    Reflect $(4, 6)$ about $x = 2$, the result is $(0, 6)$.

    Since 4 is two units to the right of 2 it will reflect to 2 units to the left of 2 which is 0.

    Images are covered in chapter 3, "Transformations,"

20. The correct answer is (3), $12i\sqrt{2}$

    $$\sqrt{-8} + 2\sqrt{-50}$$
    $$= \sqrt{-4} \cdot \sqrt{2} + 2\sqrt{-25} \cdot \sqrt{2}$$
    $$= 2i\sqrt{2} + 2(5i)\sqrt{2}$$
    $$= 2i\sqrt{2} + 10i\sqrt{2} = 12i\sqrt{2}$$

    To review radicals, see chapter 2, "The Complex Number System."

21. The correct answer is (4).

    The graph has the shape of sin x, but the high and low points are twice as high.

    The graphs of trigonometric functions are reviewed in chapter 6, "Trigonometric Functions and Their Inverses."

22. The correct answer is (4).

    There will be no intersection since there are no real solutions to the equation $x^2 = -2$.

23. The correct answer is (3).

    Using the quadratic formula with $a = 1$, $b = -1$, and $c = 1$

    $$x = \frac{1 \pm \sqrt{(-1)^2 - 4(1)(1)}}{2(1)} = \frac{1 \pm \sqrt{1 - 4}}{2}$$
    $$= \frac{1 \pm \sqrt{-3}}{2} = \frac{1 \pm i\sqrt{3}}{2}$$

    If you want to review quadratic equations, see chapter (2), "The Complex Number System."

24. The correct answer is (2).

    Each angle of a regular pentagon meaures 108°.

    $$108° + 72° = 180°$$

    You can review symmetry in chapter 3, "Transformations,"

25. The correct answer is (2).

    $\sqrt{10}$ is real and irrational.

    There will be 2 distinct roots since $\sqrt{10} \neq 0$.

    Roots are covered in chapter 2, "The Complex Number System."

26. The correct answer is (1).

$\sin^2 90 + \cos^2 90 = 1$ and the multiplicative inverse of 1 is 1.

This and other trigonometric identities are reviewed in chapter 7, "Trigonometric Identities and Equations."

27. The correct answer is (2).

Using the law of cosines, $c^2 = a^2 + b^2 - 2ab \cos C$.

$c^2 = (5)^2 + (6)^2 - 2(5)(6) \cos 60°$

$c^2 = 25 + 36 - 2(5)(6)(.5)$

$c^2 = 61 - 2(5)(3)$

$c^2 = 61 - 30$

$c^2 = 31$

$c = \sqrt{31}$

See chapter 8, "Trigonometry—Triangle Solution," for a review of trigonometric triangle solutions.

28. The correct answer is (2).

In order for $|2x - 1| < 3$, then

$-3 < 2x - 1 < 3$ Add 1 to all three sides.

$-3 + 1 < 2x - 1 + 1 < 3 + 1$

$-2 < 2x < 4$ Divide by 2.

$-1 < x < 2$

You can review inequalities in chapter 2, "The Complex Number System."

29. The correct answer is (3).

$\sin^2 x + \sin x = 0$ Factor.

$\sin x(\sin x + 1) = 0$.   Set each factor equal to zero.

$\sin x = 0$ $\sin x + 1 = 0$

$\sin x = -1$

If $\sin x = 0$, $x = 0°$ or $180°$. If $\sin x = -1$, $x = 270°$.

The value of the given interval is $180°$.

See chapter 7, "Trigonometric Identities and Equations," for a review of trigonometric equations.

30. The correct answer is (1).

The probability that the spinner lands on red on each spin is $\frac{1}{2}$. The probability that exactly 2 landings on red occurs in 5 spins is

$_5C_2\left(\frac{1}{2}\right)^2\left(1 - \frac{1}{2}\right)^{5-2} = {_5C_2}\left(\frac{1}{2}\right)^5$

$= \frac{5!}{2!3!} \cdot \frac{1}{32} = \frac{5 \cdot 4}{2} \cdot \frac{1}{32} = \frac{10}{32}$

Probability is covered in chapter 9, "Probability."

31. The correct answer is (3), $\frac{1}{2}$

$\sin(-210°) = \frac{1}{2}$

$-210°$ has the same sine as $150°$ and $150°$ has the same sine as $30°$.

You can review trigonometric functions in chapter 6, "Trigonometric Functions and Their Inverses."

32. The correct answer is (4).

$$\tan \frac{1}{2} A = \pm \sqrt{\frac{1 - \cos A}{1 + \cos A}}$$

$$= \pm \sqrt{\frac{1 - \frac{1}{3}}{1 + \frac{1}{3}}}$$

$$= \pm \sqrt{\frac{\frac{2}{3}}{\frac{4}{3}}} = \sqrt{\frac{2}{3} \times \frac{3}{4}} = \pm \sqrt{\frac{1}{2}}$$

The positive value is $\sqrt{\frac{1}{2}} = \frac{\sqrt{1}}{\sqrt{2}} = \frac{1}{\sqrt{2}} = \frac{\sqrt{2}}{2}$.

See chapter 7, "Trigonometric Identities and Equations," for a review of functions of the half-angle.

33. The correct answer is (1).

The third term will be $10a^3(-\sqrt{2})^2$ which is $10a^3 \cdot 2 = 20a^3$

You can review expansions in chapter 9, "Probability."

34. The correct answer is (3).

Since sin and cos are both negative, θ must terminate in the third quadrant.

Trigonometric functions are covered in chapter 6, "Trigonometric Functions and Their Inverses."

35. The correct answer is (2).

$3x + 7 \geq 0$	In order for the result to be real.
$3x + 7 - 7 \geq 0 - 7$	Subtract 7 from both sides.
$3x \geq -7$	Divide by 3.

$$x \geq -\frac{7}{3}$$

You can review functions in chapter 4, "Relations and Functions."

36. a.

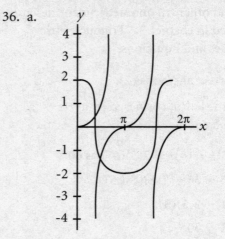

b. It is seen that there are 2 values of x in the interval $0 \leq x \leq 2\pi$ that satisfy the equation $\tan x = 2 \cos x$.

See chapter 6, "Trigonometric Functions and Their Inverses," for a review of graphing trigonometric functions.

37. a. The correct answer is $\frac{3}{y + 4}$.

$$\frac{y - 20}{y^2 - 16} + \frac{2}{y - 4}$$

$$= \frac{y - 20}{(y - 4)(y + 4)} + \frac{2}{y - 4}$$

$$= \frac{y - 20}{(y - 4)(y + 4)} + \frac{2}{y - 4} \times \frac{y + 4}{y + 4}$$

$$= \frac{y - 20}{(y - 4)(y + 4)} + \frac{2(y + 4)}{(y - 4)(y + 4)}$$

$$= \frac{(y - 20) + 2(y + 4)}{(y - 4)(y + 4)}$$

$$= \frac{y - 20 + 2y + 8}{(y - 4)(y + 4)}$$

$$= \frac{3y - 12}{(y - 4)(y + 4)}$$

$$= \frac{3(y - 4)}{(y - 4)(y + 4)}$$

$$= \frac{3}{y + 4}$$

Simplifying fractional expressions is reviewed in chapter 2, "The Complex Number System."

b. The correct answer is 30°, 150°, and 270°.

$\sin \theta + 1 = 2 \cos^2 \theta$

$\sin \theta + 1 = 2(1 - \sin^2 \theta)$

$\sin \theta + 1 = 2 - 2 \sin^2 \theta$

$2 \sin^2 \theta + \sin \theta - 1 = 0$

$(\sin \theta + 1)(2 \sin \theta - 1) = 0$

When the product of a group of numbers is 0, at least one of the numbers must be 0. So either $\sin \theta + 1 = 0$ or $2 \sin \theta - 1 = 0$. If $\sin \theta + 1 = 0$, then $\sin \theta = -1$, so $\theta = 270°$. If $2 \sin \theta - 1 = 0$, then $2 \sin \theta = 1$, so $\sin \theta = \frac{1}{2}$. So $\theta = 30°$ or $\theta = 150°$. So all the values of θ are 30°, 150°, 270°.

See chapter 7, "Trigonometric Identities and Equations," for a review of trigonometric equations.

38. a. The correct answer is 2.4.

Note: When this test was given, the use of calculators was not permitted. This test was given when one had to use a logarithm table given on paper.

Today, if you want to find $\sqrt[3]{87}$ to the nearest tenth, you do not need to use logarithms. You just used your calculator to find

that $\sqrt[3]{87}$ is approximately 2.4428897, and then you round 2.4428897 off to the nearest tenth, which is 2.4. Thus, to the nearest tenth $\sqrt[3]{87}$ is 2.4.

See chapter 4, "Relations and Functions," for more on logarithms.

b.
$$\frac{\tan \theta + \cot \theta}{\cos \theta \sin \theta}$$

$$= \frac{\dfrac{\sin \theta}{\cos \theta} + \dfrac{\cos \theta}{\sin \theta}}{\cos \theta \sin \theta}$$

$$= \frac{\dfrac{\sin \theta}{\cos \theta} \times \dfrac{\sin \theta}{\sin \theta} + \dfrac{\cos \theta}{\sin \theta} \times \dfrac{\cos \theta}{\cos \theta}}{\cos \theta \sin \theta}$$

$$= \frac{\dfrac{\sin^2 \theta}{\cos \theta \sin \theta} + \dfrac{\cos^2 \theta}{\cos \theta \sin \theta}}{\cos \theta \sin \theta}$$

$$= \frac{\left(\dfrac{\sin^2 \theta + \cos^2 \theta}{\cos \theta \sin \theta} \right)}{\cos \theta \sin \theta}$$

$$= \frac{\left(\dfrac{1}{\cos \theta \sin \theta} \right)}{\cos \theta \sin \theta}$$

$$= \frac{1}{\cos^2 \theta \sin^2 \theta}$$

$$= \frac{1}{\cos^2 \theta} \times \frac{1}{\sin^2 \theta}$$

$$= \sec^2 \theta \csc^2 \theta$$

Trigonometric identities are reviewed in chapter 7, "Trigonometric Identities and Equations."

39. a. The correct answer is 30°30'.

$$\frac{a}{\sin A} = \frac{c}{\sin C}$$

$$\frac{30}{\sin 34°20'} = \frac{27}{\sin C}$$

29

Cross-multiplying, 30 sin C = 27(sin 34°20').

Then sin C = $\dfrac{27\,(\sin 34°20')}{30}$

Now convert 34°20' to a decimal number of degrees. Do this by converting 20' to a decimal number of degrees. Using your calculator, divide 20 by 60 because there are 60 minutes in a degree, obtaining approximately 0.333333. Thus 20' is approximately 0.3333333 of a degree.

So 34°20' ≈ 34.333333°.

So sin C = $\dfrac{27(\sin 34.333333°)}{30}$.

Next, use your calculator to evaluate the right side of the equation

sin C = $\dfrac{27(\sin 34.333333°)}{30}$. You find that

sin C = 0.5076059. Next, use the sin^{-1} key on your calculator to find that C = Arc sin 0.5076059 = 30.504491°. You need to find the number of minutes. On your calculator, subtract 30 from 30.504491, to obtain 0.504491. Next, because there are 60 minutes in a degree, multiply 0.504491 by 60 on your calculator to get the number of minutes. 0.504491 × 60 = 30.269459. That is, 0.504491° = 30.269459'. To the nearest 10 minutes, this is 30 minutes. So to the nearest 10 minutes, C = 30°30'.

b. The correct answer is 367.

The area of triangle ABC is $\frac{1}{2}ac$ sin B. We need the measure of angle B. $\angle A$ = 34°20', and from part a, $\angle C$ ≈ 30°30'. The sum of the measures of the interior angles of any triangle is 180°. Here, $\angle A$ + $\angle B$ + $\angle C$ = 180°. 34°20' + $\angle B$ + 30°30' = 180°, 64°54' + $\angle B$ = 180, so $\angle B$ = 115°10'. The area is

equal to $\frac{1}{2}ac$ sin B = $\frac{1}{2}$(30)(27) sin 115°10'.

Now convert 115°10' to a decimal number of degrees. Do this by converting 10' to a decimal number of degrees. Using you calculator, divide 10 by 60 because there are 60 minutes in a degree, obtaining approximately 0.16667. Thus 10' is approximately 0.16667 of a degree. So 115°10 ≈ 115.16667°. Next, multiply this out on your calculator, and find that $\frac{1}{2}$(30)(27) sin 115.16667° ≈ 366.55521. To the nearest square unit this is 367.

Trigonometric triangle solutions are covered in chapter 8, "Trigonometry—Triangle Solution."

40. a.

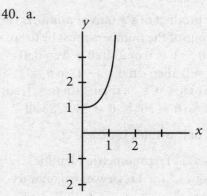

b.

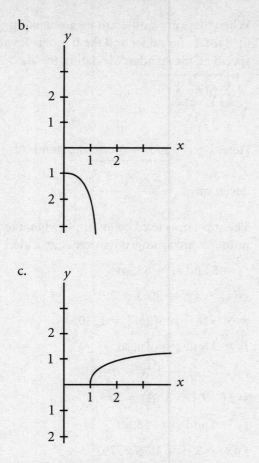

c.

d. The correct answer is $x = 2y$.

The equation of the graph resulting from reflecting the graph with the equation $y = 2x$ about the line with the equation $y = x$ is the equation resulting from interchanging the x and the y in $y = 2x$. So the equation of the reflected graph is $x = 2y$.

See chapter 3, "Transformations," for a review of reflections.

41. a. The correct answer is 70.

Since CFB is parallel to DA, m∠BFA =

m∠DAF. Since ∠BFA intercepts minor arc AB and ∠DAF intercepts minor arc FD, the measure of minor arc AB is equal to the measure of minor arc FD. Angle BAF intercepts minor arc BF. Since m∠$BAF = 20$, 20 must be $\frac{1}{2}$ the measure of minor arc BF. So the measure of minor arc BF is 40. Let the measure of minor arc AB be called x. Then minor arc FD also has measure x. Minor arcs AB, BF, and FD together make up semicircle $ABFD$ because AD is a diameter, so the sum of the measures of minor arcs AB, BF, and FD is 180. So $x + 40 + x = 180$, $2x + 40 = 180$, $2x = 140$, $x = 70$. The measure of minor arc AB is 70.

b. The correct answer is 110.

From part a, we know that the measure of arc AB is 70 and that the measure of minor arc AB is equal to the measure of minor arc FD. So the measure of minor arc FD is also equal to 70. Now look at triangle BFE. m∠$AFB = \frac{1}{2}$m(minor arc AB), so m∠$EFB = \frac{1}{2}(70) = 35$. Similarly, m∠$DBF = \frac{1}{2}$m(minor arc FD), so m∠$EBF = \frac{1}{2}(70) = 35$. Now in triangle

BFE, m∠EFB + m∠EBF + m∠$BEF = 180$. So $35 + 35 + $ m∠$BEF = 180$, $70 + $ m∠$BEF = 180$, so m∠$BEF = 110$.

c. The correct answer is 55.

∠CDB = ∠CDA − ∠BDA

m∠$CDA = 90$ because CD is tangent to the circle. From part a, m(minor arc AB) $= 70$.

So m$\angle BDA = \frac{1}{2}(70) = 35$. So m$\angle CDB$
$$= 90 - 35 = 55.$$

d. The correct answer is 90.

CFB is parallel to *DA* and m$\angle CDA = 90$.
Now m$\angle CDA +$ m$\angle BCD = 180$, $90 +$
m$\angle BCD = 180$, and m$\angle BCD = 90$.

e. The correct answer is 145.

From part b, m$\angle EFB = 35$. Now angle *CFE*
is supplementary to angle *EFB*. So m$\angle CFE$
$180 - 35 = 145$.

You can review this topic in chapter 5,
Circles."

42. a. (1) The correct answer is 80.

The mode is the item occurring most often.
Here, 80 occures 6 times, and no other tem-
perature occurs that often. So the mode is 80.

a. (2) The correct answer is 79.5.

Here there are $5 + 3 + 4 + 3 + 6 + 4 +$
$5 = 30$ terms. When there are an even number of terms, the median is the average of the
two middle terms. Here, when the terms are
arranged in increasing order, the 15th term
is 79 and the 16th term is 80. So the median
is the average of 79 and 80. Thus the median
is $\frac{79 + 80}{2} = \frac{159}{2} = 79\frac{1}{2}$ or 79.5.

b. The correct answer is 10.1.

The general formula for standard deviation
is $\sqrt{\dfrac{\sum_{i=1}^{n} (x_i - \bar{x})^2}{n}}$ which equals $\sqrt{\dfrac{\sum_{i=1}^{n} x_i}{n} - \bar{x}^2}$.

When there are k different values making
up a total of n values and the frequencies are
specified, the standard deviation equals

$$\sqrt{\dfrac{\sum_{i=1}^{k} f_i(x_i - \bar{x})^2}{n}}.$$

Here, $k = 7$ and $n = 30$. So the standard

deviation is $\sqrt{\dfrac{\sum_{i=1}^{7} f_i(x_i - \bar{x})^2}{30}}$.

The subscripts used below apply when the
numbers are arranged in increasing order.

$f_1 = 5$ and $x_1 = 63$, so

$f_1(x_1 - \bar{x})^2 = 5(63 - 79)^2$

$= 5(-16)^2 = 5(256) = 1280.$

$f_2 = 3$ and $x_2 = 70$, so

$f_2(x_2 - x)^2 = 3(70 - 79)^2$

$= 3(-9)^2 = 3(81) = 243.$

$f_3 = 4$ and $x_3 = 78$, so

$f_3(x_3 - \bar{x})^2 = 4(78 - 79)^2$

$= 4(-1)^2 = 4(1) = 4.$

$f_4 = 3$ and $x_4 = 79$, so

$f_4(x_1 - \bar{x})^2 = 3(79 - 79)^2$

$= 3(0)^2 = 3(0) = 0.$

$f_5 = 6$ and $x_5 = 80$, so

$f_5(x_5 - \bar{x})^2 = 6(80 - 79)^2$

$= 6(1)^2 = 6(1) = 6.$

$f_6 = 4$ and $x_6 = 84$, so

$f_6(x_6 - \bar{x})^2 = 4(84 - 79)^2$

$= 4(5)^2 = 4(25) = 100$.

$f_7 = 5$ and $x_7 = 96$, so

$f_7(x_7 - \bar{x})^2 = 5(96 - 79)^2$.

$= 5(17)^2 = 5(289) = 1445$.

So the standard deviation equals

$$\sqrt{\frac{1280 + 243 + 4 + 0 + 6 + 100 + 1445}{30}}$$

$$= \sqrt{\frac{3078}{30}} = \sqrt{\frac{1026}{10}} = \sqrt{102.6}.$$

Using your calculator you find that $\sqrt{102.6} \approx 10.129166$.

To the nearest tenth the standard deviation is 10.1.

See chapter 10, "Statistics," to review mean, median, mode, and standard deviation.

Part III

Math III Review

Chapter 2

The Complex Number System

A. Review of the Real Numbers

    1. Basic Set Theory

        a. Definitions

            Set: Any collection of objects.

            Element: Each object in a set is called an *element* or a member of the set.

            Notation: A set is generally designated by a capital letter, such as A, B, or R, and an element of the set is designated by a lowercase letter, such as a, b, or r.

            The symbol $\in$: $\in$ is used to indicate that a particular element belongs to a set. The symbol $\notin$ is used to indicate that an element does not belong to a set. If a is an element of set A, and b is not an element of the set, we write $a \in A$, $b \notin A$.

        b. Set Notation

            Enumeration: The set containing the numbers 3, 6, and 9 is written {3, 6, 9}.

            The set containing all of the even numbers from 2 to 200 can be written {2, 4, 6, 8, 10, ..., 198, 200}.

            Set-builder notation: The set of all even numbers from 2 to 200 could be written $\{x \mid x = 2n, n = 1, 2, 3, ..., 100\}$. This is read, "The set of all x such that $x = 2n$ where $n = 1, 2, 3, ..., 100$.

        c. Subsets, Union, and Intersection

            Subset: If every element in set B is also an element of set A, then set B is called a *subset* of A. Notation: $B \subset A$.

            Null Set: A set that contains no elements is called an *empty* or *null* set. Notation: {} or $\varnothing$.

Union: If A and B are two sets, the union of the two sets is the set containing all of the elements in either A or B. Notation: $A \cup B$.

Intersection: If A and B are two sets, the *intersection* of the two sets is the set containing all of the elements that are in both A and B. Notation: $A \cap B$.

Example: If $A = \{2, 4, 6\}$ and $B = \{2, 3, 4\}$, $A \cup B = \{2, 3, 4, 6\}$, and $A \cap B = \{2, 4\}$.

2. Subsets of the Real Numbers

The set of *natural numbers,* or *positive integers,* is the set $N = \{1, 2, 3, 4, 5, 6, \ldots\}$.

The set of *whole numbers* is the set $W = \{0, 1, 2, 3, 4, 5, \ldots\}$.

The set of *integers* is the set $I = \{\ldots, -3, -2, -1, 0, 1, 2, 3, \ldots\}$.

The set of *rational numbers* is the set $Q = \{\frac{p}{q} \mid p$ and q are integers, $q \neq 0\}$.

The set of *irrational numbers* contains numbers that cannot be expressed as the quotient of integers. Examples of irrational numbers are $\sqrt{3}, \sqrt{5}, \pi$.

The set of *real numbers* is obtained by combining the rational and irrational numbers. If we use the letter H to denote the set of irrational numbers and the letter R to denote the set of real numbers, then we have $R = Q \cup H$. Also, note that $Q \subset R$ and $H \subset R$.

3. The Properties of a Field

a. Definitions

Closure: If for any $a, b \in A$, $a + b \in A$, we say A is closed under addition. The definition is analogous for multiplication and other operations.

Identity Element: Because, for any real number r, the number 0 has the property that $r + 0 = 0 + r = r$, we call the number 0 the *identity element* for the real numbers under the operation of addition. Similarly, because $r(1) = (1)r = r$, the number 1 is called the identity element for the reals under the operation of multiplication

Inverse Element: For any $r \in R$, there is a number, called $-r$, with the property that $r + (-r) = 0$, the identity element for addition. Thus, we say that for each element r in the set R, there exists an *inverse element,* $-r$, under the operation of addition. Similarly, for any $r \in R$, there is a number, called $\frac{1}{r}$, with the property that $r\left(\frac{1}{r}\right) = \left(\frac{1}{r}\right)r = 1$, the identity element for multiplication. Thus, we say that for each element r in the set R, there exists an *inverse element*, $\frac{1}{r}$, under the operation of multiplication.

b. Definition of a Field

A *field* is a mathematical system consisting of a set together with two operations, usually addition and multiplication, which has the following properties:

a. closure with respect to both operations

b. associative with respect to both operations

c. commutative with respect to both operations

d. existence of an identity element with respect to both operations

e. existence of an inverse for each element under both operations (excluding 0 for multiplication)

f. distributive with respect to multiplication over addition

g. The identity element with respect to one operation, usually addition, is different than the identity element with respect to the other operation, usually multiplication.

Example: The set of real numbers is a field under the operations of addition and multiplication. It is clearly closed with respect to both operations, has 0 as an identity element for addition and 1 as an identity element for multiplication, and has $-a$ as the inverse of a for addition and $\frac{1}{a}$ as the inverse for multiplication. Further, the associative laws hold for both operations, $a + (b + c) = (a + b) + c$ and $a(bc) = (ab)c$, as do the commutative laws, $a + b = b + a$ and $ab = ba$. Finally multiplication distributes over addition, $a(b + c) = ab + ac$. However, not all of the subsets of the real number system are fields.

B. The Operations of Algebra

1. Factoring

   a. Removing a Common Monomial Factor

      The Rule: $AB + AC = A(B + C)$

      Example: $5x^5 - 15x^3 = 5x^3(x^2 - 3)$

   b. Factoring Trinomials

      The Difference of Two Squares: $x^2 - y^2 = (x - y)(x + y)$

      Perfect Square Trinomial: $x^2 + 2xy + y^2 = (x + y)^2$

      Perfect Square Trinomial: $x^2 - 2xy + y^2 = (x - y)^2$

      A Quadratic Expression: $acx^2 + (ad + bc)x + bd = (ax + b)(cx + d)$

      Example: $2x^2 - 7x - 15 = (2x + 3)(x - 5)$

2. Laws of Exponents

   a. Definitions

      Power: A power is a base raised to an exponent.

      x raised to the nth power: For any real number x and any positive integer n, the symbol x^n is read "x raised to the exponent n," or more briefly "x to the nth," and represents the product of n factors of x. Thus, $x^n = x \cdot x \cdot x \ldots \cdot x$, where there are n factors of x.

      Exponent: The number n in the expression above is called the exponent of x. We'll see that exponents do not always have to be positive integers.

      Base: The number x in the expression above is called the base.

   b. Integral Exponents

      x to a negative power: For any positive integer n, we define $x^{-n} = \dfrac{1}{x^n}$ $(x \neq 0)$

      x to the power of 0: For any nonzero base x, we define $x^0 = 1$

   c. The Laws of Exponents

      Rule 1: $x^a \cdot x^b = x^{a + b}$

Rule 2: $\dfrac{x^a}{x^b} = x^{a-b}\ (x \neq 0)$

Rule 3: $(x^a)^b = x^{ab}$

Rule 4: $(xy)^a = x^a\, y^a$

Rule 5: $\left(\dfrac{x}{y}\right)^a = \dfrac{x^a}{y^a}$

3. Simplifying Radical Expressions

   a. Definitions

   Square Root: If, for any nonnegative real number x we have $r^2 = x$, then we say that r is a square root of x. For example, 16 has two square roots, 4 and -4, since $4^2 = 16$ and $(-4)^2 = 16$. For $x \geq 0$, $\sqrt{x}$ always means the nonnegative square root of x.

   Radical and Radicand: The expression $\sqrt{x}$ is called a radical, and x is called the radicand.

   Like Radicals: Square roots that have the same expression under the square root sign are called like radicals.

   Unlike Radicals: Radicals that are not alike are unlike.

   b. Simplifying Square Roots

   Step 1: Express the radicand as the product of two factors, one of which is a perfect square.

   Step 2: Using the property $\sqrt{a} \times \sqrt{b} = \sqrt{a \times b}$, write the square root of the product as the product of the square roots.

   Step 3: Compute the square root of the perfect square factor.

   Step 4: Repeat the above process until all perfect square factors have been removed from under the radical sign.

   c. The Arithmetic of Radicals

   Addition and Subtraction: Only like square roots can be added and subtracted. To add or subtract like square roots, simply add or subtract their coefficients. Unlike square roots cannot be combined. However, sometimes, when simplified, unlike roots may be changed into like roots.

Multiplication: The product of two square roots is equal to the square root of the product, $\sqrt{a} \times \sqrt{b} = \sqrt{a \times b}$.

Division: The quotient of two square roots is equal to the square root of the quotient, $\dfrac{\sqrt{a}}{\sqrt{b}} = \sqrt{\dfrac{a}{b}}$.

Rationalizing Denominators: Rationalizing denominators is a technique that enables you to rewrite any fraction that has a square root in the denominator as a fraction with a rational denominator.

Example: $\dfrac{5}{\sqrt{3}} = \dfrac{5}{\sqrt{3}} \times \dfrac{\sqrt{3}}{\sqrt{3}} = \dfrac{5\sqrt{3}}{3}$.

4. Algebraic Fractions

    a. Definitions

    Algebraic Fraction: An algebraic fraction is any fraction that contains variables.

    Complex Fraction: A complex fraction is a fraction that contains at least one fraction in either its numerator or its denominator.

    b. The Arithmetic of Algebraic Fractions

    Simplifying Algebraic Fractions: Rewrite the numerator and denominator in completely factored form. Then divide the numerator and denominator by common factors until no common factors remain.

    Adding and Subtracting Like Algebraic Fractions: If the algebraic fractions have the same denominator, add or subtract the numerators, and place the result over the common denominator.

    Adding and Subtracting Unlike Algebraic Fractions: If the algebraic fractions have different denominators, first change them to fractions with the same denominator, then add or subtract the numerators, and place the result over the common denominator. The simplest way to obtain a common denominator is to multiply the given denominators.

    Multiplying Algebraic Fractions: Multiply the numerators together, then multiply the denominators together. If the numerators and denominators contain common factors, they can be cancelled before multiplying.

Dividing Algebraic Fractions: First invert the divisor (the number after the division sign), then multiply as discussed above.

Simplifying Complex Fractions: Multiply every fraction in the complex fraction by the common denominator of all the fractions contained within the complex fraction.

C. Solving Equations

   1. Absolute Value Equations

      a. Notation and Definition

         The Notation for Absolute Value: The absolute value of a real number r is written $|r|$.

         Meaning of Absolute Value: The symbol $|r|$ represents the nonnegative number of the pair r and $-r$. Intuitively, the absolute value of a number can be thought of as the number without regard to its sign. Also, $|r|$ is the distance of the number r on the number line from 0.

         Formal Definition of Absolute Value: If r is a real number, then $|r| = r$ if $r \geq 0$, and $-r$ if $r < 0$.

         Examples: $|-6| = 6$, $|-4-7| = |-11| = 11$, $|0| = 0$, $-|-5| = -(5) = -5$

      b. Solving Absolute Value Equations

         Concept: Absolute value equations can be solved by applying the definition given above. There may be more than one solution.

         Example: Solve $|5x - 2| = 3$.

         By the definition of absolute value, we have

$$(5x - 2) = 3 \quad \text{or} \quad -(5x - 2) = 3$$

$$5x - 2 = 3 \quad \text{or} \quad -5x + 2 = 3$$

$$5x = 5 \quad \text{or} \quad -5x = 1$$

$$x = 1 \quad \text{or} \quad x = -\frac{1}{5}$$

2. Quadratic Equations

a. Definition

Quadratic Equation: A quadratic equation is any equation that can be expressed in the form $ax^2 + bx + c = 0$, with a, b, and c real numbers, $a \neq 0$.

b. Solving Quadratic Equations

Solutions by Factoring: The easiest way to solve a quadratic equation, when possible, is by factoring. Write the equation in the form $ax^2 + bx + c = 0$, factor the left hand side, set each factor equal to 0, and solve. Note that, in general, quadratic equations will have two solutions.

Example: $2x^2 - 6x = 8$

Write in the form $ax^2 + bx + c = 0$.

$2x^2 - 6x - 8 = 0$　　　Factor the left hand side.

$2(x^2 - 3x - 4) = 0$

$2(x - 4)(x + 1) = 0$

$x - 4 = 0 \text{ or } x + 1 = 0$

$x = 4, \ x = -1$

Solutions Using the Quadratic Formula: The quadratic formula can be used to solve all quadratic equations, including those that cannot be factored. The quadratic formula tells us that $x = \dfrac{-b \pm \sqrt{b^2 - 4ac}}{2a}$.

Example: Solve $x^2 - x - 3 = 0$.

In this equation $a = 1$, $b = -1$, and $c = -3$. Thus,

$$x = \frac{-b \pm \sqrt{b^2 - 4ac}}{2a} = \frac{-(-1) \pm \sqrt{(-1)^2 - 4\,(1)(-3)}}{2(1)} = \frac{1 \pm \sqrt{1 + 12}}{2}$$

$$= \frac{1 \pm \sqrt{13}}{2}.$$

Thus, the solutions are $\dfrac{1 + \sqrt{13}}{2}$ and $\dfrac{1 - \sqrt{13}}{2}$.

3. Systems of Equations

   a. Definitions

      Linear Equation: A linear equation is an equation of the form $ax + b = 0$, $a \neq 0$.

      System of Equations: A system of equations consists of a number of equations for which we are interested in finding a common solution.

   b. Solving a System of Two Linear Equations

      Addition Method: In this method, the two equations are added together in such a way that one of the variables cancels out. The resulting equation is then solved for the remaining variable, and the result substituted into one of the original equations to find the value of the other variable.

      Example: Find the common solution of the system:

      $3x + 2y = 11$
      $5x - 4y = 11$

      First, multiply the top equation by 2:

      $2(3x + 2y) = (11)2$
      $\quad 5x - 4y = 11$

      or

      $6x + 4y = 22$
      $5x - 4y = 11$ Now, add the two equations together:

      $6x + 4y = 22$
      $\underline{5x - 4y = 11}$
      $11x = \quad\quad 33$ Thus, $x = 3$. Substitute this number into the first equation:

      $\quad\quad 3x + 2y = 11$
      $\quad 3(3) + 2y = 11$
      $\quad\quad 9 + 2y = 11$
      $\quad\quad\quad 2y = 2$
      $\quad\quad\quad\; y = 1$ The common solution is $(3, 1)$.

Substitution Method: In this method, one equation is solved for one of the unknowns, and the resulting equation is substituted into the second equation, which can then be solved.

Example: Find the common solution of the following:

$3x - y = 0$

$x + 2y = 14$

Write the first equation as $y = 3x$. Substitute this into the second equation:

$x + 2(3x) = 14$ or

$x + 6x = 14$

$7x = 14$

$x = 2$. Then, since $y = 3x$, $y = 3(2) = 6$. The common solution is $(2, 6)$.

c. Solving a System Containing a Linear and a Quadratic Equation

Substitution Method: This is usually the best technique to use. Solve the linear equation for one of the unknowns, and substitute into the quadratic equation.

Example: Solve the following system of equations:

$y = x^2 - 5$

$y = 4x$

Substitute $4x$ into the first equation and solve the resulting quadratic equation.

$4x = x^2 - 5$

$x^2 - 4x - 5 = 0$

$(x - 5)(x + 1) = 0$

$x = 5, x = -1$

When $x = 5$, $y = 4(5) = 20$, and when $x = -1$, $y = -4$.

The common solutions are $(5, 20)$, $(-1, -4)$.

4. Fractional Equations

a. Definition

Fractional Equation: A fractional equation is an equation that contains algebraic fractions.

b. Solving Fractional Equations

LCD Method: The easiest way to solve such an equation is to determine the LCD of all of the fractions and multiply both sides of the equation by this expression. The resulting expression will contain no fractions and can thus be solved using techniques already discussed. Be careful to check all answers to insure that the fractions are defined for the answers obtained.

Example: $\dfrac{12}{x-3} + \dfrac{12}{x+4} = 1$

Multiply both sides by $(x-3)(x+4)$:

$$\frac{12(x-3)(x+4)}{x-3} + \frac{12(x-3)(x+4)}{x+4} = (x-3)(x+4)$$

$$\frac{12\cancel{(x-3)}(x+4)}{\cancel{x-3}} + \frac{12(x-3)\cancel{(x+4)}}{\cancel{x+4}} = (x-3)(x+4)$$

$$12(x+4) + 12(x-3) = (x-3)(x+4)$$

$$12x + 48 + 12x - 36 = x^2 + x - 12$$

$$24x + 12 = x^2 + x - 12$$

$$x^2 - 23x - 24 = 0$$

$$(x-24)(x+1) = 0$$

$$x = 24, -1$$

Note that the original equation is defined for both solutions, so both 24 and -1 solve the equation.

5. Solving Radical Equations

a. Definition

A *radical equation* is an equation in which the variable appears under a radical sign.

b. Solving Radical Equations

To solve a radical equation, begin by isolating the radical on one side of the equation. Then, square both sides to eliminate the radical, and solve using the techniques discussed above. Be sure to check all answers, as the squaring process sometimes leads to extraneous solutions—solutions that do not actually solve the given equation.

Example:

Solve $\sqrt{3x + 1} = 4$.
$$(\sqrt{3x + 1})^2 = 4^2$$
$$3x + 1 = 16$$
$$3x = 15$$
$$x = 5$$

D. Solutions of Inequalities

1. Linear Inequalities

a. Definitions

Inequality Symbols: The symbol for "less than" is "$<$." The symbol for "greater than" is "$>$." The symbol "$\leq$" means "less than or equal to," and the symbol "$\geq$" means "greater than or equal to."

Strict and Weak Inequalities: Inequalities using the symbols "$<$" or "$>$" are called strict inequalities; inequalities using the symbols "$\leq$" or "$\geq$" are called weak inequalities.

Linear Inequality: Recall that a linear equation is an equation that can be put in the form $ax + b = 0$, $a \neq 0$. A linear inequality has the same form as a linear equation, except that the equal sign is replaced by one of the symbols: $<$, $>$, $\leq$, or $\geq$.

b. Solving Linear Inequalities

Linear inequalities can be solved using the same techniques which are used to solve linear equations, with one important difference—if you multiply or divide both sides by a negative number, the inequality sign must be reversed.

Example: Solve the inequality $5x + 9 < 2(x - 2)$.

$5x + 9 < 2(x - 2)$ Distribute.

$5x + 9 < 2x - 4$ Subtract $2x$, subtract 9.

$3x < -13$ Divide by 3.

$x < -\dfrac{13}{3}$

Example: Solve the inequality $-3y \le 21$.

$-3y \le 21$ Divide by -3, reverse the inequality sign:

$y \ge -7$

c.   Graphing Linear Inequalities

Graphing Inequalities on a Number Line: To graph a linear inequality on a real number line means to indicate those points on the number line that are in the solution set of the inequality. For strict inequalities, place an open circle at the endpoint to indicate that the endpoint is excluded. For weak inequalities, place a closed circle at the endpoint to indicate that the endpoint is included.

Examples: Graph the following inequalities on the number line:

a. $x < -\dfrac{13}{3}$

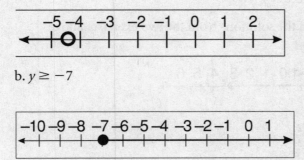

b. $y \ge -7$

2.   Absolute Value Inequalities

a.   Solving Absolute Value Inequalities

Absolute value inequalities are handled in much the same way as absolute value equations. Typically, you rewrite the inequality as two inequalities that do not involve absolute value signs, solve the new inequalities, and combine the results.

Example: Solve $\left|2x - 1\right| < 5$.

If $2x - 1 > 0$, then $2x - 1 < 5$, and $2x < 6$ or $x < 3$.

If $2x - 1 < 0$, then $-(2x - 1) < 5$, and $-2x + 1 < 5$ or $-2x < 4$, $x > -2$.

Thus, we must have $x < 3$ and $x > -2$, which can be written as $-2 < x < 3$.

Example: Solve $\left|3x - 2\right| > 4$.

Either $3x - 2 > 4$ or $-(3x - 2) > 4$.

If $3x - 2 > 4$, then $3x > 6$ or $x > 2$.

If $-(3x - 2) > 4$, then $3x - 2 < -4$ or $3x < -2$ or $x < -\frac{2}{3}$.

Thus, either $x > 2$ or $x < -\frac{2}{3}$.

These two examples indicate that, in general, for $a > 0$, we have that $\left|x\right| < a$ means $-a < x < a$, and $\left|x\right| > a$ means that $x < -a$ or $x > a$.

b. Graphing Absolute Value Inequalities

The solutions to absolute value inequalities can be graphed on a number line. Sometimes the graphs will yield lines of finite length; sometimes the graphs will have two pieces.

Example: Graph the solutions from the two exercises above.

$-2 < x < 3$

$-5\ -4\ -3\ -2\ -1\ 0\ 1\ 2\ 3\ 4\ 5\ 6$

$x > 2$ or $x < -\frac{2}{3}$

$-3\quad -2\quad -1\quad 0\quad 1\quad 2\quad 3$

3. Solving Quadratic Inequalities

   a. Definitions

   Quadratic Inequality: A quadratic inequality is an inequality that can be written in the form $ax^2 + bx + c < 0$, $ax^2 + bx + c > 0$, $ax^2 + bx + c \geq 0$, or $ax^2 + bx + c \leq 0$.

   b. Solving Quadratic Inequalities

   Begin by factoring the quadratic polynomial in the usual fashion. The solutions of the inequality separate the real numbers into three subsets, and within each subset, the quadratic polynomial will always be positive or always be negative. By considering the sign of the polynomial within each subset, it is possible to solve the inequality. Indicating the signs of each factor on the number line will help in finding the solution.

   Example: Solve the inequality $x^2 - 3x \leq 4$ over the set of real numbers.

   $x^2 - 3x - 4 \leq 0$ Factor the polynomial.

   $(x - 4)(x + 1) \leq 0$ Note that the polynomial is equal to 0 at 4 and -1.

   Now, consider the three sets of numbers $A = \{x \mid x < -1\}$, $B = \{x \mid -1 < x < 4\}$, $C = \{x \mid x > 4\}$.

   Note that for $x \in A$, $(x - 4)$ and $(x + 1)$ are negative, so their product is positive. Also note that for $x \in C$, $(x - 4)$ and $(x + 1)$ are positive, so their product is positive. However, for $x \in B$, $(x - 4)$ is negative and $(x + 1)$ is positive, so the product is negative. Thus, the original inequality is satisfied for all x in the region $-1 \leq x \leq 4$. Using a number line as below helps to keep track of these relationships.

    E. Complex Numbers

      1. Definitions

The Imaginary Unit: The imaginary unit, i, was created to enable us to solve quadratic equations such as $x^2 + 1 = 0$, which have no solutions in the real number system. The symbol i is defined as $i = \sqrt{-1}$. Thus, $i^2 = -1$, and i is the solution to the quadratic equation $x^2 + 1 = 0$.

Imaginary Numbers: A number of the form bi, where b is a real number and i is the imaginary unit.

Complex Numbers: Numbers of the form $a + bi$, where a and b are real numbers and i is the imaginary unit. Note that the real numbers and the imaginary numbers are subsets of the complex numbers. Also note that the complex numbers form a field under the operations of addition and multiplication.

Complex Conjugate: The complex conjugate of the number $a + bi$ is $a - bi$.

      2. Simplifying Square Roots with Negative Radicands

The definition of i makes it possible to simplify square roots of negative numbers. Note that for any real number $n > 0$, $\sqrt{-n} = \sqrt{(-1)n} = \sqrt{(-1)}\sqrt{n} = i\sqrt{n}$

Example: Simplify $\sqrt{-72}$.

$$\sqrt{-72} = \sqrt{(-1)(9)(4)(2)} = (3)(2)i\sqrt{2} = 6i\sqrt{2}$$

      3. Powers of i

Note that when you raise i to successive powers, you end up with values repeating in cycles of four, in the pattern $i, -1, -i, 1$. That is,

$$i^1 = i$$
$$i^2 = -1$$
$$i^3 = (-1)i = -i$$
$$i^4 = (-1)(-1) = 1$$
$$i^5 = (i^4)i = (1)i = i$$

$i^6 = (i^4)i^2 = (1)i^2 = -1$

$i^7 = (i^4)i^3 = (1)i^3 = -i$

$i^8 = (i^4)i^4 = (1)(1) = 1$, etcetera

4. **Operations with Complex Numbers**

    Addition: $(a + bi) + (c + di) = (a + c) + (b + d)i$

    Subtraction: $(a + bi) - (c + di) = (a - c) + (b - d)i$

    Multiplication: $(a + bi)(c + di)$ Multiply as you would ordinary binomials.

    $(a + bi)(c + di) = ac + adi + bci + bdi^2 = ac + (ad + bc)i + bd(-1) = (ac - bd) + (ad + bc)i$

    Division: Division by an imaginary number (a number of the form bi) is accomplished by writing the division as a fraction and multiplying both the numerator and the denominator by i. Division by a complex number (a number of the form $a + bi$) is accomplished by writing the division as a fraction and multiplying both the numerator and the denominator by the complex conjugate of the denominator:

    $$\frac{4}{3i} = \frac{4}{3i} \times \frac{i}{i} = \frac{4i}{3i^2} = \frac{4i}{-3} = -\frac{4}{3}i$$

    $$\frac{a + bi}{c + di} = \frac{a + bi}{c + di} \times \frac{c - di}{c - di} = \frac{ac - adi + bci - bdi^2}{c^2 - d^2 i^2} = \frac{(ac + bd) + (bc - ad)i}{c^2 + d^2}$$

5. **Solving Quadratic Equations**

    Recall that a quadratic equation is an equation of the form $ax^2 + bx + c = 0$, where a, b, and c are real numbers and $a \neq 0$. It is possible for a quadratic equation to have complex roots, as shown by the following example.

    Example: Solve for x: $x^2 + x + 30 = 0$.

    In this equation, $a = 1$, $b = 1$, and $c = 30$. Thus, via the quadratic formula:

    $$x = \frac{-b \pm \sqrt{b^2 - 4ac}}{2a} = \frac{-1 \pm \sqrt{1 - 4(1)(30)}}{2} = \frac{-1 \pm \sqrt{-119}}{2} = \frac{-1 \pm i\sqrt{119}}{2}$$

53

6. The Nature of the Roots of a Quadratic Equation

    The expression $b^2 - 4ac$ from the quadratic formula is called the *discriminant*. The discriminant indicates the nature of the roots of a quadratic equation. In particular, in a quadratic equation with real coefficients, the equation has two different real roots if $b^2 - 4ac > 0$, one double real root if $b^2 - 4ac = 0$, and two imaginary complex conjugate roots if $b^2 - 4ac < 0$. Further, a quadratic equation with rational coefficients will have rational roots if and only if its discriminant is the square of a rational number.

    Example: Without actually solving the equation, determine the nature of the roots of $3x^2 + 2x - 4 = 0$.

    In this equation, $a = 3$, $b = 2$, and $c = -4$. Thus, $b^2 - 4ac = 4 - 4(3)(-4)$ $= 4 + 48 = 52$.

    Since the discriminant is positive, there are two different real roots. Since 52 is not a perfect square, these roots are irrational.

7. The Graph of a Quadratic Equation

    There is a relationship between the nature of the roots of a quadratic equation and its graph. Recall that the graph of a quadratic equation of the form $y = ax^2 + bx + c$ is always a parabola that opens either up or down. If the roots are complex, this parabola will not cross the x-axis. If the two roots are real and different, the graph will cross the x-axis in two places. If the two roots are equal real numbers, the graph touches the x-axis in one point; that is, the vertex of the parabola touches the x-axis. The following three graphs illustrate this relationship.

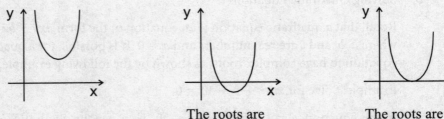

The roots are complex   The roots are real and different   The roots are real and equal

8. The Relationship Between the Roots and the Coefficients of a Quadratic Equation

If r_1 and r_2 are the roots of the equation $ax^2 + bx + c = 0$, $a \neq 0$, then $r_1 + r_2 = -\dfrac{b}{a}$ and $r_1 r_2 = \dfrac{c}{a}$. This result makes it possible to write a quadratic equation whose roots are known.

Example: What is the quadratic equation whose roots are $1 + i$ and $1 - i$?

The sum of the roots is $(1 + i) + (1 - i) = 2$, so $2 = \dfrac{-b}{a}$.

The product of the roots is $(1 + i)(1 - i) = 1 - i^2 = 1 - (-1) = 2$, so $2 = \dfrac{c}{a}$. If a, for example, is equal to 1, then $b = -2$, and $c = 2$. Thus, the desired equation would be $x^2 - 2x + 2 = 0$.

Questions

Real Numbers

1. If $A = \{1, 2, 3, 4, 5\}$, $B = \{1, 3, 5\}$ and $C = \{2, 4, 6\}$, find $A \cup B$, $A \cap B$, $A \cup C$, $A \cap C$, and $B \cap C$.

2. List all of the elements of the set $\{x \mid x$ is an integer and $0 < x < 7\}$.

3. Consider the sets of positive integers, integers, rational numbers, irrational numbers, and real numbers. To which of these sets does each of the numbers below belong?

   a. -5

   b. $\dfrac{1}{2}$

   c. $\sqrt{64}$

   d. $\sqrt{65}$

   e. $0.33333\ldots..$

4. Give an example to show that subtraction on the set of real numbers is not commutative.

5. Give an example to show that the operation of multiplication on the set of irrational numbers is not closed.

6. Is the set of integers a field? If not, which of the field properties does it not possess?

7. Is the set of rational numbers a field? If not, which of the field properties does it not possess?

The Operations of Algebra

1. Factor the following expressions completely:

   a. $4x^3 - 12x^7$

   b. $2a^2b + 4abc$

2. Factor the following expressions completely:

   a. $9x^2 - 4y^2$

   b. $x^2 + 10x + 25$

   c. $x^2 + 5x - 6$

3. Find the value of the indicated numbers:

   a. 3^{-4}

   b. $(-10)^0$

4. Eliminate the negative exponents and simplify:

   a. $(-5x^3y^4)(3xy^{-2})$

   b. $(4x^3y^{-5})^4$

5. Perform the indicated operations:

   a. $6\sqrt{45} + 7\sqrt{125}$

   b. $(3\sqrt{2})(5\sqrt{32})$

   c. $\dfrac{15\sqrt{75}}{5\sqrt{3}}$

6. Rationalize the denominator of $\dfrac{2}{3 - \sqrt{5}}$.

7. Perform the indicated operation:

   $\dfrac{2}{x + 3} + \dfrac{5}{x - 3}$

Solving Equations

Solve the following equations for the variables indicated:

1. $\left|9 + 3a\right| = 6$

2. $y^2 - 3y - 10 = 0$

3. $6x^2 - 5x = 2$

4. $\dfrac{5}{2x + 1} - \dfrac{4}{x - 4} = 3$

5. $\sqrt{3x - 12} + 4 = 7$

Solve the following systems of equations for a common solution:

6. $2x + y = 3$

   $x + y = 2$

Solutions of Inequalities

In problems 1 and 2, solve the given linear inequality, and graph the solution on a number line.

1. $3x + 5 > 2x + 3$

2. $\left(\dfrac{5x}{3}\right) - 3 \leq 7$

In problems 3 and 4, solve the given absolute value inequality, and graph the solution on a number line.

3. $\left|x - 5\right| < 3$

4. $\left|6 - 3x\right| \geq 12$

In problems 5 and 6, solve the given quadratic inequality, and graph the solution on a number line.

5. $x^2 - 9 \leq 0$

6. $2x^2 + x \geq 1$

Complex Numbers

1. Simplify $\sqrt{-27} + 2\sqrt{-45}$.

2. What is the value of i^{73}?

In problems 3 through 6, perform the indicated operations:

3. $(3 + 4i) + (5 - 6i)$

4. $(6 + 9i) - (3 - 2i)$

5. $(3 - 7i)^2$

6. $\dfrac{7 - 4i}{2 + i}$

7. Solve for x: $3x^2 + 2x + 5 = 0$.

In problems 8 and 9, determine the nature of the roots of the equations without actually solving.

8. $x^2 + x + 12 = 0$

9. $x^2 - x - 12 = 0$

10. Write a quadratic equation whose roots are $2 + 5i$ and $2 - 5i$.

Answers

Real Numbers

1. $A \cup B = \{1, 2, 3, 4, 5\}, A \cap B = \{1, 3, 5\},$
   $A \cup C = \{1, 2, 3, 4, 5, 6\}, A \cap C = \{2, 4\},$
   $B \cap C = \varnothing$

2. $\{1, 2, 3, 4, 5, 6\}$

3. a. -5 belongs to the integers, rational numbers, and real numbers.

   b. $\frac{1}{2}$ belongs to the rational numbers and real numbers.

   c. $\sqrt{64} = 8$. 8 belongs to the positive integers, integers, rationals, and reals.

   d. $\sqrt{65}$ belongs to the irrationals and reals.

   e. $0.3333\ldots = \frac{1}{3} \cdot \frac{1}{3}$ belongs to the rational numbers and real numbers.

4. $4 - 5 \neq 5 - 4$

5. $\sqrt{2} \times \sqrt{2} = 2$, and $2 \notin$ the irrational numbers.

6. The integers are not a field since the set does not contain multiplicative inverses for each nonzero number.

7. The rational numbers do form a field.

The Operations of Algebra

1. a. $4x^3 - 12x^7 = 4x^3(1 - 3x^4)$

b. $2a^2b + 4abc = 2ab(a + 2c)$

2. a. $9x^2 - 4y^2 = (3x - 2y)(3x + 2y)$

   b. $x^2 + 10x + 25 = (x + 5)^2$

   c. $x^2 + 5x - 6 = (x + 6)(x - 1)$

3. a. $3^{-4} = \frac{1}{3^4} = \frac{1}{81}$

   b. $(-10)^0 = 1$

4. a. $(-5x^3y^4)(3xy^{-2}) = -15x^4y^2$

   b. $(4x^3y^{-5})^4 = 256x^{12}y^{-20} = \frac{256x^{12}}{y^{20}}$

5. a. $\quad 6\sqrt{45} + 7\sqrt{125}$
   $= 6\sqrt{9 \times 5} + 7\sqrt{25 \times 5}$
   $= 6\sqrt{9} \times \sqrt{5} + 7\sqrt{25} \times \sqrt{5}$
   $= 6 \times 3\sqrt{5} + 7 \times 5\sqrt{5}$
   $= 18\sqrt{5} + 35\sqrt{5} = 53\sqrt{5}$

   b. $(3\sqrt{2})(5\sqrt{32}) = 15\sqrt{64} = 15 \times 8$
   $= 120$

   c. $\frac{15\sqrt{75}}{5\sqrt{3}} = \left(\frac{15}{5}\right)\left(\frac{\sqrt{75}}{\sqrt{3}}\right) = 3\sqrt{25} =$
   $3 \times 5 = 15$

6. $\frac{2}{3 - \sqrt{5}} = \frac{2}{3 - \sqrt{5}} \times \frac{3 + \sqrt{5}}{3 + \sqrt{5}} = \frac{6 + 2\sqrt{5}}{9 - 5} =$
   $\frac{6 + 2\sqrt{5}}{4} = \frac{3 + \sqrt{5}}{2}$

7. $\dfrac{2}{x+3} + \dfrac{5}{x-3} = \dfrac{2(x-3)}{(x+3)(x-3)} +$

$\dfrac{5(x+3)}{(x+3)(x-3)} =$

$\dfrac{2x-6+5x+15}{(x+3)(x-3)} = \dfrac{7x+9}{x^2-9}$

Solving Equations

1. $|9+3a| = 6$

$9+3a=6$	or	$-(9+3a)=6$
$3a=-3$	or	$-9-3a=6$
$a=-1$	or	$-3a=15$
$a=-1$	or	$a=-5$

2. $y^2 - 3y - 10 = 0$

The left side of this equation can be factored:
$(y-5)(y+2) = 0$
$y - 5 = 0$ or $y + 2 = 0$
$y = 5$ or -2

3. $6x^2 - 5x = 2$

Then $6x^2 - 5x - 2 = 0$. We must use the quadratic formula for this equation, with $a = 6, b = -5, c = -2$.

$x = \dfrac{-b \pm \sqrt{b^2 - 4ac}}{2a} =$

$\dfrac{-(-5) \pm \sqrt{(-5)2 - 4\,(6)(-2)}}{2(6)} =$

$\dfrac{5 \pm \sqrt{25 + 48}}{12} = \dfrac{5 \pm \sqrt{73}}{12}$

Thus, the roots are $\dfrac{5 + \sqrt{73}}{12}$ and

$\dfrac{5 - \sqrt{73}}{12}$.

4. $\dfrac{5}{2x+1} - \dfrac{4}{x-4} = 3$

Multiply both sides by $(2x+1)(x-4)$

$\dfrac{5(2x+1)(x-4)}{(2x+1)} - \dfrac{4(2x+1)(x-4)}{(x-4)}$

$= 3(2x+1)(x-4)$
$5(x-4) - 4(2x+1) = 3(2x^2 - 7x - 4)$
$5x - 20 - 8x - 4 = 6x^2 - 21x - 12$
$6x^2 - 18x + 12 = 0$
$6(x^2 - 3x + 2) = 0$
$6(x-2)(x-1) = 0$
$x = 2$ or 1

5. $\sqrt{3x-12} + 4 = 7$

$\sqrt{3x-12} = 3$
$(\sqrt{3x-12})^2 = 3^2$
$3x - 12 = 9$
$3x = 21$
$x = 7$

6. $2x + y = 3$
$\ \ x + y = 2$

Multiply the bottom equation by -1.

$2x + y = 3$
$(-1)(x+y) = 2(-1)$ so
$2x + y = 3$
$\underline{-x - y = -2}$ $\qquad$ Add.
$x \quad = 1$ $\qquad$ If $x = 1$, then $y = 1$. The common solution is $(1, 1)$.

59

Solutions of Inequalities

1. $3x + 5 > 2x + 3$

   Subtract $2x$ from both sides; subtract 5 from both sides.

   $x > -2$

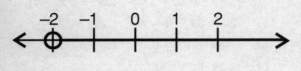

2. $\frac{5x}{3} - 3 \leq = 7$ Add 3 to both sides.

   $\frac{5x}{3} \leq 10$ Multiply both sides by 3.

   $5x \leq 30$ Divide both sides by 5.

   $x \leq 6$

3. $|x - 5| < 3$

   Either $x - 5 < 3$, or $-(x - 5) < 3$.

   If $x - 5 < 3$, then $x < 8$.

   If $-(x - 5) < 3$, then $x - 5 > -3$ or $x > 2$.

   Thus, the solution set is $2 < x < 8$.

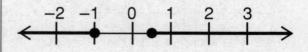

4. $|6 - 3x| \geq 12$

   Either $6 - 3x \geq 12$ or $-(6 - 3x) \geq 12$.

   If $6 - 3x \geq 12$, then $-3x \geq 6$ or $x \leq -2$.

   If $-(6 - 3x) \geq 12$, then $6 - 3x \leq -12$, so $-3x \leq -18$ or $x \geq 6$.

   Thus, either $x \geq 6$ or $x \leq -2$.

5. $x^2 - 9 \leq 0$ Factor the left hand side.

   $(x + 3)(x - 3) \leq 0$

   Note that for $x < -3$, both factors are negative, so the product is positive. Further, for $x > 3$, both factors are positive, so the product is positive. However, for $-3 < x < 3$, $(x + 3)$ is positive but $(x - 3)$ is negative, so the product is negative. Thus the solution set is $-3 \leq x \leq 3$.

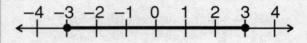

6. $2x^2 + x \geq 1$

   $2x^2 + x - 1 \geq 0$

   $(2x - 1)(x + 1) \geq 0$

   The quadratic expression on the left side is thus equal to 0 when $x = -1$ or $x = \frac{1}{2}$. For $x < -1$, both factors are negative, so the product is positive. For $-1 < x < \frac{1}{2}$, $(2x - 1)$ is negative, but $x + 1$ is positive, so the product is negative. Finally, for $x > \frac{1}{2}$, both factors are positive, and so is the product. Thus, the inequality is true whenever $x \leq -1$ or $x \geq \frac{1}{2}$.

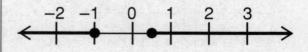

Complex Numbers

1. $\sqrt{-27} + 2\sqrt{-45} = 3i\sqrt{3} + (2)(3)i\sqrt{5} = 3i\sqrt{3} + 6i\sqrt{5}$

2. $i^{73} = (i^4)^{18}(i) = (1)^{18}(i) = i$

3. $(3 + 4i) + (5 - 6i) = 8 - 2i$

4. $(6 + 9i) - (3 - 2i) = 3 + 11i$

5. $(3 - 7i)^2 = (3 - 7i)(3 - 7i) = 9 - 21i - 21i + 49i^2 = 9 - 42i - 49 = -40 - 42i$

6. $\dfrac{7 - 4i}{2 + i} = \dfrac{7 - 4i}{2 + i} \times \dfrac{2 - i}{2 - i} =$

   $\dfrac{14 - 7i - 8i + 4i^2}{4 - i^2} = \dfrac{14 - 15i - 4}{4 + 1} =$

   $\dfrac{10 - 15i}{5} = 2 - 3i$

7. Solve for x: $3x^2 + 2x + 5 = 0$

   In this equation, $a = 3$, $b = 2$, and $c = 5$.

   $x = \dfrac{-b \pm \sqrt{b^2 - 4ac}}{2a} = \dfrac{-2 \pm \sqrt{4 - 4(3)(5)}}{6}$

   $= \dfrac{-2 \pm \sqrt{-56}}{2} = \dfrac{-2 \pm i\sqrt{56}}{6} =$

   $\dfrac{-2 \pm 2i\sqrt{14}}{6} = \dfrac{-1 \pm i\sqrt{14}}{3}$

8. $x^2 + x + 12 = 0$

   In this equation, $a = 1$, $b = 1$, and $c = 12$. Thus, $b^2 - 4ac = 1 - 4(1)(12) = -47$. Thus, the equation has two complex conjugate roots.

9. $x^2 - x - 12 = 0$

   In this equation, $a = 1$, $b = -1$, and $c = -12$. Thus, $b^2 - 4ac = 1 - 4(1)(-12) = 49$. Since 49 is a perfect square, the equation has two different rational roots.

10. Write a quadratic equation whose roots are $2 + 5i$ and $2 - 5i$.

    The sum of the roots is

    $(2 + 5i) + (2 - 5i) = 4$, so $4 = -\dfrac{b}{a}$.

    The product of the roots is $(2 + 5i)(2 - 5i)$

    $= 4 - 25i^2 = 4 - (-25) = 29$, so $29 = \dfrac{c}{a}$. If a, for example, is equal to 1, then $b = -4$, and $c = 29$. Thus, the desired equation would be $x^2 - 4x + 29 = 0$.

Chapter 3

Transformations

A. Review of Concepts

1. Basic Definitions

Transformational Geometry: Transformational geometry is the study of what happens to geometric figures as they change position.

Transformation: A *transformation of the coordinate plane* is a rule that assigns each point in the coordinate plane to a different point or possibly to the same point. Under a transformation, every point in the plane is assigned to only one point. If point *A* is assigned to point *B*, then point *B* is called the *image* of point *A*, and *A* is called the *pre-image* of point *B*.

Fixed Points: Any point that is mapped onto itself by a transformation is called a *fixed point*.

Preserved Properties: When all geometric figures that possess a certain property (such as parallelism or distance) retain that property under a particular type of transformation, the transformation is said to *preserve* that property.

There are four fundamental types of transformation that we will study in this section.

2. Line Reflections

a. Definition

A *reflection in line ℓ* is a transformation that maps every point *P* of the plane into a point *Q* such that the line segment *PQ* is perpendicular to ℓ and the distance from *P* to ℓ is the same as the distance from *Q* to ℓ. Note that every point on the line ℓ is mapped onto itself. Thus, the points on the line ℓ are fixed points.

The following diagram illustrates point *P* being mapped onto point *Q* under a reflection in line ℓ.

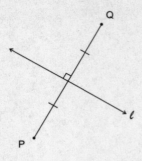

b. Notation

A reflection in line ℓ is typically written as r_ℓ.

c. Properties of Line Reflection

Once again, look at the diagram above. Notice that the distance from point P to the line ℓ is the same as the distance from point Q to line ℓ. Thus, distance is preserved under a line reflection.

Angle measure is also preserved under line reflection. For example, in the diagram below, triangle ABC is reflected in the x-axis to its image triangle $A'\,B'\,C'$. Note that the measure of angle ABC appears to be the same as the measure of angle $A'\,B'\,C'$. This property will hold for all other reflections as well.

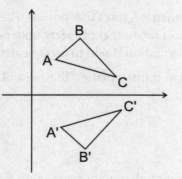

Other properties that are preserved under line reflection include parallelism (if a figure has two parallel sides, the reflected image will also have two parallel sides), betweeness (if point C is between points A and B, the image of C will be between the images of A and B), and collinearity (if A, B, and C are on the same line, the images of A, B, and C will also be on the same line). However, the property of order (or orientation) is not preserved. Consider, as an example, three points A, B, and C, which lie in the second quadrant and are on the same horizontal line, in the order A, B, C from left to right. If the horizontal line is reflected in the y-axis, the point C becomes the leftmost of the three points, while the point A becomes the rightmost. Thus, the points are no longer in the same order.

3. Reflections in the axes and in the Line $x = y$

    If any point (x, y) is reflected in the x-axis, its image is $(x, -y)$.

    If any point (x, y) is reflected in the y-axis, its image is $(-x, y)$.

    If any point (x, y) is reflected in the line $x = y$, its image is (y, x).

4. Rotations

    a. Definition

        A *rotation* about a center C through an angle θ is a transformation that leaves point C fixed, and rotates all of the other points in the plane through an angle θ with point C the vertex of the angle. For example, the diagram below shows the point A rotated about C through the angle θ.

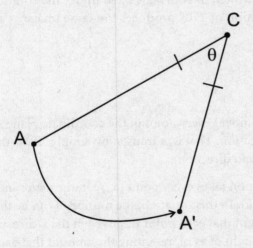

        By convention, a positive value for θ indicates that the rotation is counter-clockwise. Similarly, a negative value for θ indicates that the motion is clockwise.

   b. Notation

A rotation about center C through an angle of θ is typically written $R_{C,\theta}$.

   c. Properties of Rotations

The properties that rotations preserve are distance, angle measure, parallelism, and collinearity. Similar to reflection, however, order is not preserved.

   d. Special Rotations

A $90°$ rotation about the origin maps all points (x, y) into $(-y, x)$.

A $180°$ rotation about the origin maps all points (x, y) into $(-x, -y)$. Such a rotation is called a *half-turn*.

A $270°$ rotation about the origin maps all points (x, y) into $(y, -x)$.

A $360°$ rotation about the origin maps all points (x, y) into themselves. Such a rotation is called a *full turn*.

Note that the above statements apply to all points on the coordinate plane except the origin itself, which, of course, is fixed under the rotations. Further note that a rotation of $270°$ produces the same image as a rotation of $-90°$.

5. Translations

   a. Definition

Intuitively, a *translation* moves every point in the coordinate plane the same distance in the same direction. That is, a translation simply "lifts" the plane a certain distance in a certain direction.

More formally, a translation takes every point (x, y) in the plane and moves it to the point $(x + a, y + b)$. In this situation, the number a can be thought of as representing the amount that each point is moved in the x-direction, and the number b can be thought of as representing the amount that each point moves in the y-direction.

Another way to think about this is to say that the translation $(x, y) \Rightarrow (x + a, y + b)$ shifts every point by a distance $\sqrt{a^2 + b^2}$ along the line with slope $\frac{b}{a}$, $a \neq 0$. If $a = 0$, the translation moves each point vertically a distance of b.

b. Notation

The translation $(x, y) \Rightarrow (x + a, y + b)$ is symbolized $T_{(a, b)}$. The following diagram shows a square transformed under the translation $T_{(2, 1)}$.

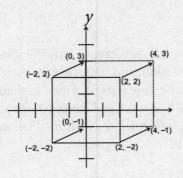

c. Properties of Translations

Translations preserve distance, angle measure, parallelism, collinearity, and order.

6. Dilations

a. Definition

In this section, we shall only consider a specific subset of all possible dilations: a dilation with its center at the origin. Then, a *dilation* with its center at the origin and *scale factor k* is a transformation that maps every point A to an image point A' on the ray OA such that OA' is equal to $k(OA)$.

A more intuitive way to think of this definition is that a dilation with center at the origin and scale factor k is a transformation that maps every point (x, y) to the point (kx, ky).

b. Notation

A dilation with center at the origin and scale factor k is written D_k.

c. Properties of Dilations

Dilations clearly do not preserve distance but do preserve angle measure, parallelism, collinearity, and order.

7. Properties of Figures that are Preserved Under Transformation

We have already considered some of the properties preserved by individual transformations. We now look at properties preserved by transformations in a bit more depth.

a. Congruence

Two geometrical figures are *congruent* if they have exactly the same size and shape. Images under translation, rotation, and reflection are congruent to their pre-images. Images under dilation are not congruent to their pre-images, unless the dilation factor is 1 or -1. The dilation D_1 maps every point on the plane onto itself and is therefore called the identity dilation; the dilation D_{-1} is equivalent to a half-turn.

b. Isometries

An *isometry* is a transformation that preserves distance. Since images under translation, rotation, and reflection are congruent to their pre-images, they are isometries. Since distance is preserved, recall that other properties, such as parallelism, angle measure, and collinearity are also preserved.

c. Direct Isometries

A *direct isometry* is an isometry that preserves orientation, or order. Orientation preservation means that if several noncollinear points are oriented in a particular direction (clockwise or counterclockwise, for example), they are still oriented in this direction after transformation. Translations and rotations are direct isometries; reflections and dilations are not.

d. Nondirect (Opposite) Isometries

As the name implies, an *opposite isometry* is one that changes the orientation of points from either counterclockwise to clockwise or from clockwise to counterclockwise. Reflections are opposite isometries.

B. Compositions of Transformations

1. Definitions and Concepts

Intuitively, the composition of two transformations refers to one transformation being applied after another one. That is, the composition of two transformations is the result of a second transformation performed on the image of the first.

The symbol $\circ$ is used to symbolize composition. Thus, for example, a reflection in line ℓ followed by a dilation about the origin with scale factor 7 would be written $D_7 \circ R_\ell$. Notice that, in this notation, transformations are performed from right to left.

Example: What is the image of $(2, 3)$ under a reflection about the line $x = y$, followed by a 90° rotation about the origin?

When $(2, 3)$ is reflected about the line $x = y$, it becomes $(3, 2)$. A 90° rotation maps this point to $(-2, 3)$.

Using the notation introduced above, we would write

$$R_{O,\,90°} \circ R_{x\,=\,y}(2, 3) = R_{O,\,90°}(3, 2) = (-2, 3).$$

2. Compositions of Line Reflections

a. Compositions of Line Reflections with Parallel Lines

The composition of two line reflections, where the two lines are parallel, is the same as a translation.

In general, any translation can be written as the composition of two reflections in parallel lines. The two lines used are not unique but must be perpendicular to the direction of the translation. Further, it can be shown that the distance between the two lines is one half of the distance between any point A and its image A' under the translation.

Example: Find the image of the point $(5, 7)$ if it is first reflected through the y-axis and then through the line $x = 2$.

As the following graph indicates, the point $(5, 7)$, when reflected through the y-axis becomes $(-5, 7)$. Then, reflecting $(-5, 7)$ through the line $x = 2$ yields

(9, 7). Note that the composition of these two reflections is equivalent to the transformation $T_{(4, 0)}$.

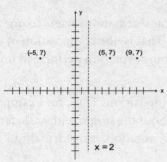

b. Compositions of Line Reflections with Intersecting Lines

The composition of two line reflections, where the two lines intersect, is the same as a rotation, with the point of intersection used as the fixed point for the rotation.

In general, any rotation can be written as the composition of two reflections in intersecting lines. The two lines used to express the rotation are not unique, but it can be shown that the measure of the angle between the two lines must equal one-half of the measure of the angle of rotation.

Example: Find the image of the point (4, 7) if it is first reflected through the x-axis and then through the line $x = y$.

As the following graph indicates, the point (4, 7), when reflected through the x-axis, becomes (4, −7). When (4, −7) is reflected through the line $x = y$, the image is (−7, 4). Note that the composition of these two reflections is equivalent to a rotation of 90° about the origin.

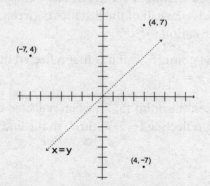

3. Compositions of Rotations

   It should be intuitively obvious that the composition of two rotations about the same center is also a rotation and that the center of the two rotations is the center of the composition. Further, the measure of the composition is simply the sum of the measures of the two rotations. Thus, for example, a rotation about the origin of 30°, followed by a rotation about the origin of 150°, is the same as a rotation about the origin of 180°, that is to say, a half-turn.

4. Compositions of Translations

   It should be intuitively clear that the composition of two translations is also a translation. In fact, in general, if $T_{(a, b)}$ and $T_{(c, d)}$ are two translations, then it follows that $T_{(c, d)} \circ T_{(a, b)} = T_{(a+c, b+d)}$.

5. The Composition of a Line Reflection and a Translation

   The composition of a line reflection and a translation in a direction parallel to the line of reflection is called a glide reflection. Intuitively, then, a glide reflection is a transformation that reflects a set of points in a line and then "glides" or moves this image in a direction parallel to the line of reflection.

   We have already seen that a translation can be viewed as the composition of two line reflections in parallel lines; thus, a glide reflection can be viewed as the composition of three line reflections.

C. Applications to Graphing

   1. Definitions and Concepts

      In upcoming chapters, we will be sketching the graphs of various equations. When we do so, it will be very helpful to make use of any symmetries possessed by the graph.

      Symmetry with respect to the y-axis: A graph is symmetric with respect to the y-axis if, for any point (x, y) on the graph the point $(-x, y)$ is also on the graph. To test if a graph is symmetric with respect to the y-axis, substitute $-x$ for x in the equation of the graph. If the new equation, when simplified, is the same as the original equation, then the graph is symmetric with respect to the y-axis.

A graph that is symmetric with respect to the y-axis can be divided symmetrically into a part to the left of the y-axis and a part to the right of the y-axis. If the graph is "folded" along the y-axis, then the parts to the left and the right will coincide. In other words, the part to the left of the y-axis can be obtained from the right part by "reflecting" it across the y-axis.

Example: Demonstrate that the graph of $y = x^4$ is symmetric with respect to the y-axis.

Taking the equation $y = x^4$ and substituting $-x$ for x, we obtain $y = (-x)^4 = x^4$. The equation is thus unchanged, and therefore, the graph is symmetric with respect to the y-axis.

The graph of this equation is shown below.

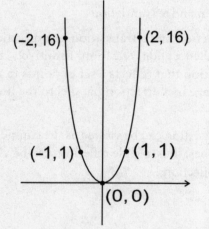

In the future, when we are asked to sketch a graph that is symmetric with respect to the y-axis, we simply need to, for example, sketch the portion to the left of the y-axis and then reflect it across the y-axis.

Symmetry with respect to the x-axis: A graph is symmetric with respect to the x-axis if, for any point (x, y) on the graph, the point $(x, -y)$ is also on the graph. To test if a graph is symmetric with respect to the x-axis, substitute $-y$ for y in the equation of the graph. If the new equation, when simplified, is the same as the original equation, then the graph is symmetric with respect to the x-axis.

Example: Demonstrate that the graph of $x = y^2$ is symmetric with respect to the x-axis.

Taking the equation $x = y^2$ and substituting $-y$ for y, we obtain $x = (-y)^2$ $= y^2$. The equation is thus unchanged, and therefore, is symmetric with respect to the x-axis.

The graph of this equation is shown on the following page.

In the future, when we are asked to sketch a graph that is symmetric with respect to the x-axis, we simply need to, for example, sketch the portion above the x-axis and then reflect it across the x-axis.

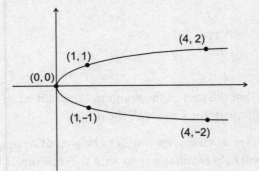

Symmetry with respect to the origin: A graph is symmetric with respect to the origin if, for any point (x, y) on the graph, the point $(-x, -y)$ is also on the graph. To test if a graph is symmetric with respect to the origin, substitute $-x$ for x and $-y$ for y in the equation of the graph. If the new equation, when simplified, is the same as the original equation, then the graph is symmetric with respect to the origin. If a graph is symmetric with respect to the origin, the portion in the first quadrant can be reflected pointwise across the origin to obtain the portion in the third quadrant. Similarly, the portion in the second quadrant can be reflected pointwise across the origin to obtain the portion in the fourth quadrant.

Example: Demonstrate that the graph of $y = x^3$ is symmetric with respect to the origin.

Taking the equation $y = x^3$ and substituting $-x$ for x and $-y$ for y, we obtain $-y = (-x)^3$. This can be simplified into $-y = -x^3$ or $y = x^3$. The equation is thus unchanged, and therefore, is symmetric with respect to the origin. The graph of this equation is shown below.

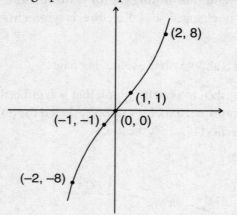

Note that the part of the graph in quadrant 3 can be obtained by reflecting the part in quadrant 1 through the origin.

Later, we will use symmetries to help us draw graphs. The exercises that follow will help familiarize you with the techniques to be used.

Questions

Basic Properties of Transformations

1. Find the image of the point $(7, -4)$ if it is
   a. reflected in the x-axis
   b. reflected in the y-axis
   c. reflected in the line $x = y$

2. Find the image of the point $(3, 5)$ if it is
   a. reflected in the line $y = 3$
   b. reflected in the line $x = 1$
   c. reflected in the line $y = 3$ and then in the line $x = 1$

3. Consider the triangle graphed below.

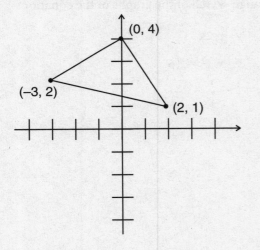

   Find the reflection of this triangle in the x-axis.

4. If point P has coordinates $(4, 7)$, find
   a. $R_{O, 90°}(P)$
   b. $R_{O, 180°}(P)$
   c. $R_{O, 270°}(P)$
   d. $R_{O, 360°}(P)$

5. Consider the line segment AB where $A = (3, 7)$ and $B = (-2, 4)$. Find the image of AB under a rotation of $180°$ about the origin.

6. Find the image of the point $(5, 8)$ under the following translations
   a. $T_{(-3, 4)}$
   b. $T_{(0, 7)}$

7. Find the image of the triangle with vertices $(1, 2)$, $(-3, 7)$, and $(-7, 0)$ under the translation $T_{(-3, -4)}$.

8. Find the image of the triangle in problem 7 under the dilation D_2.

9. Find the image of the triangle in problem 7 under the dilation $D_{\frac{1}{3}}$.

10. A particular dilation maps the point $(16, 0)$ into the point $(4, 0)$. What is the value of the scale factor k?

Compositions of Transformations

1. Find the image of the point $(2, 3)$ if it is first reflected through the line $y = 5$, and then reflected through the x-axis.

2. Which translation will map the point $(2, 3)$ into the same point that it is mapped by the two reflections above?

3. Find the image of the point $(2, 3)$ if it is first reflected through the y-axis, and then reflected through the x-axis.

75

4. Which rotation will map the point $(2, 3)$ into the same point that it is mapped by the two reflections above?

5. A rotation about the origin of $150°$ followed by a rotation about the origin of $-70°$ is equivalent to which single rotation?

6. Consider the square with coordinates $(0, 0)$, $(4, 0)$, $(4, 4)$, and $(0, 4)$. Find the image of the square if it is first translated $T_{(1, 2)}$ and then translated $T_{(-7, -3)}$.

7. Give a single translation that will move the square in problem 6 to the same location as it is moved by the two translations in problem 6.

8. Find the image of the line segment connecting the points $(8, 4)$ and $(4, 2)$ if it is first dilated $D_{\frac{1}{2}}$ and then D_4.

9. Give a single dilation that has the same net effect as the composition of dilations given in problem 8.

10. The vertices of triangle ABC are $A(5, 2)$, $B(8, 10)$, and $C(2, 4)$. Find the coordinates of the image of the triangle under the composition $D_2 \circ T_{(3, -5)} \circ r_{x = y}$.

Applications to Graphing

In problems 1 through 5 below, check each equation for symmetry with respect to the x-axis, the y-axis, and the origin.

1. $y = 12x^6 + 17$

2. $y = 3x^3 - 1$

3. $y^2 = 2x$

4. $y^2 + x^2 = 16$

5. $x = \dfrac{1}{y}$

In problems 6 through 8 below, use the observations you made about symmetries to make a rough sketch of the graphs of the equations.

6. $y^2 = 2x$

7. $y^2 + x^2 = 16$

8. $x = \dfrac{1}{y}$

Answers

Basic Properties of Transformations

1. As the graph below shows, the image of $(7, -4)$ reflected in the x-axis is $(7, 4)$, the image of $(7, -4)$ reflected in the y-axis is $(-7, -4)$, and the image of $(7, -4)$ reflected in the line $x = y$ is $(-4, 7)$.

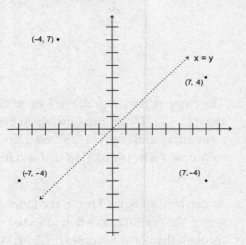

2. As the graph below shows, the image of $(3, 5)$ reflected in the line $y = 3$ is $(3, 1)$, the image of $(3, 5)$ reflected in the line $x = 1$ is $(-1, 5)$, and the image of $(3, 5)$ reflected in the line $y = 3$, then the line $x = 1$ is $(-1, 1)$.

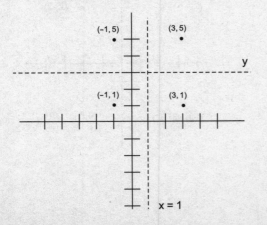

3. As the following graph shows, the reflection of triangle ABC in the x-axis is another triangle $A'B'C'$ with vertices $(-3, -2)$, $(0, -4)$, and $(2, -1)$.

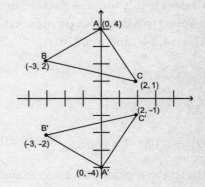

4. a. $R_{O, 90°}(4, 7) = (-7, 4)$
   b. $R_{O, 180°}(4, 7) = (-4, -7)$
   c. $R_{O, 270°}(4, 7) = (7, -4)$
   d. $R_{O, 360°}(4, 7) = (4, 7)$

5. Under a rotation of $180°$ about the origin, $(3, 7)$ is mapped to $(-3, -7)$ and $(-2, 4)$ is mapped to $(2, -4)$. Thus, the image of the line segment AB is a new line segment with endpoints $(-3, -7)$ and $(2, -4)$.

6. a. $T_{(-3, 4)}(5, 8) = (5 + (-3), 8 + 4) = (2, 12)$

   b. $T_{(0, 7)}(5, 8) = (5 + 0, 8 + 7) = (5, 15)$

7. $T_{(-3, -4)}(1, 2) = (1 + (-3), 2 + (-4)) = (-2, -2)$

   $T_{(-3, -4)}(-3, 7) = (-3 + (-3), 7 + (-4)) = (-6, 3)$

   $T_{(-3, -4)}(-7, 0) = (-7 + (-3), 0 + (-4)) = (-10, -4)$

Thus, the image is another triangle with vertices of $(-2, -2)$, $(-6, 3)$, and $(-10, -4)$.

8. $D_2(1, 2) = (2, 4)$

   $D_2(-3, 7) = (-6, 14)$

   $D_2(-7, 0) = (-14, 0)$

   Under the dilation, the given triangle is mapped to a new triangle with vertices $(2, 4)$, $(-6, 14)$, and $(-14, 0)$.

9. $D_{\frac{1}{3}}(1, 2) = \left(\frac{1}{3}, \frac{2}{3}\right)$

   $D_{\frac{1}{3}}(-3, 7) = \left(-1, \frac{7}{3}\right)$

   $D_{\frac{1}{3}}(-7, 0) = \left(-\frac{7}{3}, 0\right)$

   Under the dilation, the given triangle is mapped to a new triangle with vertices $\left(\frac{1}{3}, \frac{2}{3}\right)$, $\left(-1, \frac{7}{3}\right)$, and $\left(-\frac{7}{3}, 0\right)$.

10. A scale factor of $k = \frac{1}{4}$ will map $(16, 0)$ into $(4, 0)$.

Compositions of Transformations

1. As the following graph shows, the point $(2, 3)$ when reflected through the line $y = 5$ becomes $(2, 7)$. When $(2, 7)$ is reflected through the x-axis, its image is $(2, -7)$.

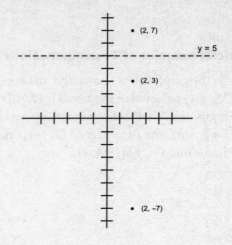

2. The composition in problem 1 maps $(2, 3)$ into $(2, -7)$. The translation which has the same effect must move $(2, 3)$ ten units vertically down. The translation that will do this is $T_{(0, -10)}$.

3. As can be seen by looking at the following graph, the point $(2, 3)$ when reflected through the y-axis becomes $(-2, 3)$. When $(-2, 3)$ is reflected through the x-axis, its image is $(-2, -3)$.

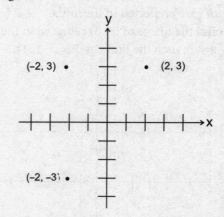

4. The composition in problem 3 maps $(2, 3)$ into $(-2, -3)$. This is the same as a $180°$ rotation about the origin. The equivalent rotation, therefore, is $R_{O,\,180°}$.

5. A rotation of $150°$ about the origin rotates any geometric figure $150°$ in a counterclockwise direction. A rotation of $-70°$ rotates the figure back $70°$ clockwise. The net effect is a counterclockwise rotation of $80°$. Thus, the desired rotation is $R_{O,\,80°}$.

6. Begin by applying the first translation to the vertices of the square.

   $T_{(1,\,2)}(0, 0) = (1, 2)$

   $T_{(1,\,2)}(4, 0) = (5, 2)$

   $T_{(1,\,2)}(4, 4) = (5, 6)$

   $T_{(1,\,2)}(0, 4) = (1, 6)$

   Now apply the second translation to the image vertices.

   $T_{(-7,\,-3)}(1, 2) = (-6, -1)$

   $T_{(-7,\,-3)}(5, 2) = (-2, -1)$

   $T_{(-7,\,-3)}(5, 6) = (-2, 3)$

   $T_{(-7,\,-3)}(1, 6) = (-6, 3)$

   Thus, the new square has vertices $(-6, -1)$, $(-2, -1)$, $(-2, 3)$, and $(-6, 3)$.

7. $T_{(-7,\,-3)} \circ T_{(1,\,2)} = T_{((-7+1),\,(-3+2))} = T_{(-6,\,-1)}$.

8. $D_4 \circ D_{\frac{1}{2}}(8, 4) = D_4(4, 2) = (16, 8)$

   $D_4 \circ D_{\frac{1}{2}}(4, 2) = D_4(2, 1) = (8, 4)$

   The new line segment has endpoints $(16, 8)$ and $(8, 4)$.

9. $D_4 \circ D_{\frac{1}{2}} = D_{(4 \times \frac{1}{2})} = D_2$

10. $D_2 \circ T_{(3,\,-5)} \circ r_{x\,=\,y}(5, 2) =$
    $D_2 \circ T_{(3,\,-5)}(2, 5) = D_2(5, 0) = (10, 0)$

    $D_2 \circ T_{(3,\,-5)} \circ r_{x\,=\,y}(8, 10) = D_2 \circ T_{(3,\,-5)}(10, 8) = D_2(13, 3) = (26, 6)$

    $D_2 \circ T_{(3,\,-5)} \circ r_{x\,=\,y}(2, 4) = D_2 \circ T_{(3,\,-5)}(4, 2) = D_2(7, -3) = (14, -6)$

    The vertices of the image triangle are $(10, 0)$, $(26, 6)$, and $(14, -6)$.

Applications to Graphing

1. $y = 12x^6 + 17$

   First substitute $-x$ for x

   $y = 12(-x)^6 + 17 = 12x^6 + 17$. Thus, the graph is symmetric with respect to the y-axis. No other symmetries hold.

2. $y = 3x^3 - 1$

   It is easy to show that this graph is not symmetric with respect to either axis. Further, if we substitute $-x$ for x and $-y$ for y, we obtain $-y = 3(-x)^3 - 1$, or $-y = -3x^3 - 1$. This is not the same as the original equation, so this graph exhibits none of the three symmetries discussed.

3. $y^2 = 2x$

   In this equation, when y is replaced with $-y$, we obtain the same equation. Thus, the graph is symmetric with respect to the x-axis.

4. $y^2 + x^2 = 16$

   Since $(-y)^2 = y^2$ and $(-x)^2 = x^2$, this graph exhibits all three types of symmetry discussed.

5. $x = \dfrac{1}{y}$

   While this graph is clearly not symmetric with respect to either axis, note that we do obtain the original equation when we replace x with $-x$ and y with $-y$. Thus, it is symmetric with respect to the origin.

6. $y^2 = 2x$

   Since this graph is symmetric with respect to the x-axis, let us sketch the portion above the x-axis and reflect the result across the x-axis.

   In order to draw the graph, we pick a few values for y, and determine the corresponding values for x. It is easy to see, for example, that the following points are on the graph: $(0, 0)$, $(\frac{1}{2}, 1)$, $(2, 2)$, $(8, 4)$. Thus, the portion of the graph above the x-axis looks like:

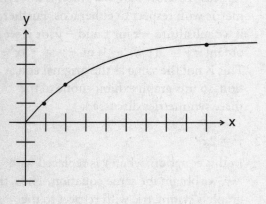

The full graph, then, is

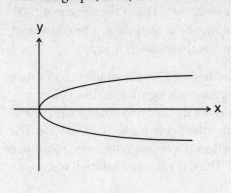

7. $y^2 + x^2 = 16$

   Since this graph exhibits all three types of symmetry, we simply need to sketch the portion in the first quadrant and reflect it through the x- and y-axes and the origin to obtain the full graph. Some points in the first quadrant and on the positive portions of the axis are $(0, 4)$, $(4, 0)$, $(2, 2\sqrt{3})$, and $(2\sqrt{3}, 2)$. The graph in the first quadrant thus appears to have the shape shown below:

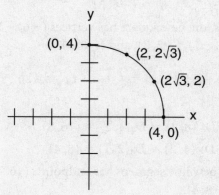

The full graph looks like:

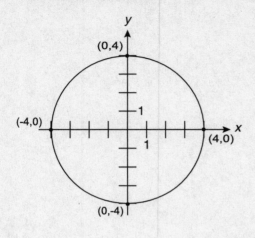

Thus, the portion of the graph in the first quadrant looks like this:

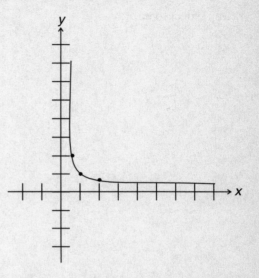

8. $x = \dfrac{1}{y}$

Note, first of all, that this graph only has points in the first quadrant (x and y are both positive) and the third quadrant (x and y are both negative). Since the graph is symmetrical with respect to the origin, let's draw the first quadrant portion and then reflect it through the origin.

First, we need some points in the first quadrant: $(1, 1)$, $(2, \frac{1}{2})$, $(\frac{1}{2}, 2)$, $(4, \frac{1}{4})$, $(\frac{1}{4}, 4)$, $(10, \frac{1}{10})$, and $(\frac{1}{10}, 10)$.

Reflecting this through the origin gives us the entire graph:

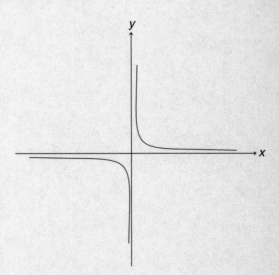

Chapter 4

Relations and Functions

A. Relations

  1. Definitions

Relations: A relation is a correspondence between two sets where to each element of the first set is associated one or more elements of the second set. A relation, thus, is really just a rule that tells us how to match up elements from the first set with elements from the second. The relation may be specified by either listing all elements from the first set alongside the associated elements from the second set, or by giving a rule through which elements from the first set can have elements from the second set associated with them.

Domain: The first set discussed above is called the domain.

Range: The second set discussed above is called the range.

  2. Examples of Relations:

Example 1:

Player		Batting Average
John Linnell	————————	.367
John Flansbergh	————————	.322
Alex Butter	————————	.303
Howard Krauser	————————	.297

The relation shown above describes the assignment of player names to batting averages. The domain is the set of names {John Linnell, John Flansbergh, Alex Butter, Howard Krauser}, and the range is the set of numbers assigned to the names {.367, .322, .303, .297}. The relation is the assignment of the names to the numbers as indicated by the table above.

Example 2:

Name (Domain)		Phone Number (Range)
Jim	———————	555-2736
Peter		
Dan	———————	555-2093
Richard	———————	555-0385
		555-2917

This relation describes the assignment of names to telephone numbers. Note that Richard has two telephone numbers, and Peter and Dan share the same number. This indicates that a relation can have several elements of the domain assigned to the same member of the range, and that a single domain member can be assigned to several range members.

Example 3:

Consider the rule of association $R = \{(x, y) \mid y = x^2 + 1\}$. By convention, if the domain of a relation is not specified, it is assumed to be the largest subset of the reals for which the range contains only real numbers. In this case, since $x^2 + 1$ is never undefined, the domain is the entire set of real numbers. The range is all of the real numbers that can result from substituting domain values into $x^2 + 1$. It is easy to see, then, that the range is the set of all real numbers greater than or equal to 1. Domain values can be indicated along with their related range values by using ordered pair notation. When using this notation, the domain value is listed first, and the range value second. Thus, some of the ordered pairs that are specified by the rule above are $(0, 1)$, $(5, 26)$, and $(-5, 26)$.

This problem motivates the following alternate definition of relation.

3. Definition of Relation as an Ordered Pair

    A relation is a set of *ordered pairs*, (x, y). The set of x values is called the domain, and the set of y values is called the range.

    Example 1: The set of ordered pairs $R = \{(9, 3), (7, -2), (6, 8), (6, -2)\}$ represents the relation between the domain $\{6, 7, 9\}$, and the range $\{-2, 3, 8\}$. The relation assigns 3 to 9, -2 to 7, and both 8 and -2 to 6.

    As Example 1 indicates, if the domain and range are finite, we can express the relation by writing out all of the ordered pairs. If the domain and range are infinite, we can use set builder notation to write the relation.

Example 2: $W = \{(x, y) \mid y = 3x\}$ is a relation with both domain and range equal to the set of real numbers. Each x (domain) value is assigned a y (range) value that is three times the domain value. Frequently, we drop the set notation and simply write the relation as $y = 3x$.

B. Functions

1. Definitions

Function: A function is a correspondence between two sets such that to each element in the first set (which is called the domain) is associated *exactly one* element of the second set (the range). Thus, for a relation to be a function, the rule of correspondence cannot assign more than one element of the range to an element of the domain. However, a function *can* assign an element of the range to more than one element of the domain.

Examples:

The relation

1 ———— 5
3 ———— 7
8 ———— 8

is a function since each element of the domain is assigned to only one element of the range.

The relation

is also a function. Even though two domain elements are assigned to one range element, to each element of the domain only one element of the range is assigned.

Finally, the relation

1 ———— 5
3 ———— 7

is not a function since to the domain value 3 two different range values, 5 and

7, are assigned.

Remember, a function is a special type of relation for which each value in the domain is assigned to only one value in the range.

Independent variable, dependent variable: The letter x is typically used to represent a value of the domain, and the letter y is used to represent a value of the range. Because the value of x determines the value of y, x is called the independent variable and y is called the dependent variable.

2. Function Notation

   The Symbol f(x): The symbol $f(x)$, which is read "f of x," is often used instead of y to represent the range value of the function. Often the rule that specifies a function is expressed in *function notation.* For example, $f(x) = 2x + 3$ specifies a function that, for each value x in the domain, associates the value $2x + 3$ in the range. For the domain value $x = 5$, we express the corresponding range value as $f(5)$ and compute: $f(5) = 2(5) + 3 = 13$.

   Example:

   If $f(x) = 2x - 5$, find $f(3)$ and $f(0)$.

   $f(3) = 2(3) - 5 = 6 - 5 = 1$

   $f(0) = -5$

3. Arithmetic of Functions:

   Let $f(x)$ and $g(x)$ represent two functions. Then, we define the following four functions:

   The sum function: $(f + g)(x) = f(x) + g(x)$

   The difference function: $(f - g)(x) = f(x) - g(x)$

   The product function: $(fg)(x) = f(x)g(x)$

   The quotient function: $\dfrac{f}{g}(x) = \dfrac{f(x)}{g(x)}$ (defined when $g(x) \neq 0$)

   Example:

   Let f and g be functions defined by the rules $f(x) = 3x + 2$ and $g(x) = x - 5$. Find $(f + g)(x)$, $(f - g)(x)$, $(fg)(x)$, $\left(\dfrac{f}{g}\right)(x)$, and $\left(\dfrac{g}{f}\right)(x)$

   $(f + g)(x) = (3x + 2) + (x - 5) = 4x - 3$

$(f - g)(x) = (3x + 2) - (x - 5) = 2x + 7$

$(fg)(x) = (3x + 2)(x - 5) = 3x^2 - 13x - 10$

$\left(\dfrac{f}{g}\right)(x) = \dfrac{3x + 2}{x - 5}$ Note that the domain of this function is all real

numbers except 5.

$\left(\dfrac{g}{f}\right)(x) = \dfrac{x - 5}{3x + 2}$ Note that the domain is all real numbers except $-\dfrac{2}{3}$.

Composition of Functions: The composite function is defined as $f \circ g = f(g(x))$. It can be thought of as representing a chain reaction, where a domain value is first associated with a range value by the rule g, and then this range value is treated as if it were a domain value for f and is associated with a range value for f.

Example:

For the functions $f(x) = 3x + 2$ and $g(x) = x - 5$, find $f \circ g$, $g \circ f$, and $f \circ f$.

$f \circ g = f(g(x)) = f(x - 5) = 3(x - 5) + 2 = 3x - 13$

$g \circ f = g(f(x)) = g(3x + 2) = (3x + 2) - 5 = 3x - 3$

$f \circ f = f(f(x)) = f(3x + 2) = 3(3x + 2) + 2 = 9x + 8$

4. The Vertical Line Test

A quick way to determine if a relation is a function is to graph the relation. If there is a vertical line that intersects the graph of the function in more than one point, then the relation is not a function.

Example: Visually determine which of the following relations are functions by the vertical line test:

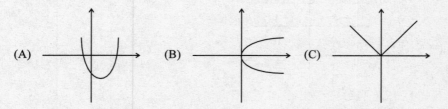

A and *C* are functions, *B* is not.

5. Inverse Variation and the Hyperbola

Inverse Variation: The statement "*y varies inversely as x*" means that there is a constant c, $c \neq 0$, with the property that $y = \dfrac{c}{x}$.

The Constant of Variation: The letter c in the formula above is called the constant of variation. Note that $y = \dfrac{c}{x}$ can be written as $xy = c$. Thus, two variables vary inversely if their product is constant.

The Hyperbola: Let x and y vary inversely, with constant of variation equal to 8, that is, $xy = 8$ or $y = \dfrac{8}{x}$. It can be seen that the definition of inverse variation produces a function that can be written as $f(x) = \dfrac{8}{x}$. The graph of the function is a hyperbola.

Example: Sketch the graph of $xy = 8$.

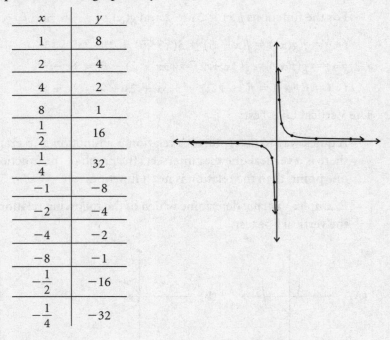

x	y
1	8
2	4
4	2
8	1
$\frac{1}{2}$	16
$\frac{1}{4}$	32
-1	-8
-2	-4
-4	-2
-8	-1
$-\frac{1}{2}$	-16
$-\frac{1}{4}$	-32

6. One-to-One Functions

One-to-one functions: A function is called a one-to-one function if to two different domain members different range numbers are assigned. Thus, for a relation to be a function, each x must be assigned a unique y, and for a function to be one-to-one, different x's must have different y's associated with them.

Examples: Recall the following two examples from above:

The relation

```
1 ——— 5
3 ——— 7
8 ——— −8
```

is a function since to each element of the domain only one element of the range is assigned. It is also one-to-one.

The relation

```
1 ——— 5
3 ╱
8 ——— −8
```

is a function; however, it is not a one-to-one function, since two different x values are associated with the number 5.

Horizontal Line Test: A quick way to determine if a function is one-to-one is to sketch the graph of the function. If a horizontal line intersects the graph of the function at more than one point, the function is *not* a one-to-one function.

C. Inverse Functions

1. Definitions

Inverse Relations: If we switch the domain and the range of a relation and reverse the rule of correspondence, we obtain the inverse relation. That is, if R is a relation, the inverse of R, which is denoted R^{-1}, consists of all ordered pairs (y, x), where (x, y) belongs to R.

Example: If R is the relation $\{(1, 2), (2, 3), (5, 4)\}$, then $R^{-1} = \{(2, 1), (3, 2), (4, 5)\}$.

Inverse Functions: The best way to understand the concept of the inverse function is by example. Consider the relation $\{(1, 2), (3, 5), (7, 2)\}$. This relation is a function since each domain value has only one range value. However, if we find the inverse of this relation, we obtain $\{(2, 1), (5, 3), (2, 7)\}$. Note that this is not a function, since with the domain value of 2 two different range values are associated. Thus, the inverse of a function is not necessarily a function. Note, however, that the initial relation (function) that was given, that is, $\{(1, 2), (3, 5), (7, 2)\}$, is not one-to-one. In order for us to be able to guarantee that the inverse of a function is also a function, the initial function *must* be one-to-one.

Inverse Function Notation: If $f(x)$ is a one-to-one function, we define its inverse, which is denoted by $f^{-1}(x)$, as the function that we obtain by switching the roles of the domain and range values.

2. Determining Inverse Functions

   Whenever we are given a one-to-one function defined by a particular formula, we can find the inverse function by switching x and y and solving for y.

   Example: Find the inverse of the function $f(x) = 3x + 2$

   For convenience, write the function as $y = 3x + 2$. Switch x and y to obtain $x = 3y + 2$. Solve for y to obtain $y = \dfrac{x - 2}{3}$. Thus, $f^{-1}(x) = \dfrac{x - 2}{3}$.

3. Graphing Inverse Relations

   The graph of an inverse relation can be obtained by reflecting the graph of the original relation through the line $x = y$. The drawing below illustrates the relationship between the graph of a relation and its inverse.

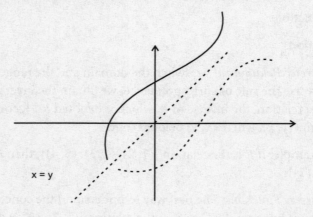

$x = y$

If a function is not one-to-one, its inverse is not a function. One way to make the inverse a function is to restrict the domain of the function so as to make it one-to-one. For example, consider the function $f(x) = x^2$. The graph of this function is shown below.

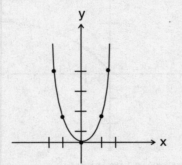

Note that this function fails the horizontal line test and thus is not one-to-one. In fact, the graph of the inverse, found by reflecting the original graph through $x = y$, is shown below.

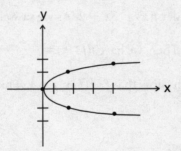

Since this graph fails the vertical line test, it is clear that the inverse is not a function. If, however, we restrict the domain of the function to $x > 0$, the function becomes one-to-one. Note that the graph below passes the vertical line test.

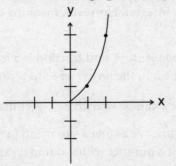

Then, the inverse is a function, as the following graph shows. This technique will be used later to produce an inverse function when the original function is not one-to-one.

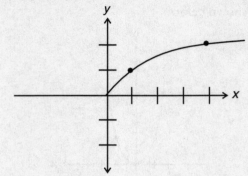

4. Composition of a Function and its Inverse

Intuitively, a function and its inverse "undo" each other. That is, for any function $f(x)$ and its inverse $f^{-1}(x)$, we have $f(f^{-1}(x)) = f^{-1}(f(x)) = x$.

Example: Consider $f(x) = 3x + 2$. As we saw above,

$f^{-1}(x) = \frac{x-2}{3}$. Then, we have $f(f^{-1}x) = \frac{x-2}{3} = 3\left(\frac{x-2}{3}\right) + 2 = x - 2 + 2 = x$.

Similarly, we can show that $f^{-1}(f(x)) = x$. Thus, since $f(3) = 11$, we have $f^{-1}(11) = 3$.

D. The Exponential Function

1. Rational Exponents

When we discussed exponents in the first chapter, all of the exponents we considered were integral. However, meaning can also be given to all fractional exponents.

Unit Fraction Exponents: A unit fraction is a fraction whose numerator is 1. In general, we define a to the power of $\frac{1}{n}$ to represent the nth root of a. That is,

$a^{\frac{1}{n}} = \sqrt[n]{a}$. Thus, 2 can be written as $2^{\frac{1}{2}}$. Similarly, $\sqrt[3]{7} = 7^{\frac{1}{3}}$.

Rational Exponents: We define $a^{\frac{m}{n}}$ to mean $(a^{\frac{1}{n}})^m$, for $a > 0$, $n \neq 0$. Therefore, when you look at a number with a rational exponent, the numerator represents the power to which the number is to be raised, and the denominator represents the root to which it is taken.

Examples:

$$9^{\frac{1}{2}} = \sqrt{9} = 3$$

$$9^{-\frac{1}{2}} = \frac{1}{\sqrt{9}} = \frac{1}{3}$$

$$3^{-\frac{5}{2}} = (3^{-5})^{\frac{1}{2}} = \left(\frac{1}{3^5}\right)^{\frac{1}{2}} = \left(\frac{1}{243}\right)^{\frac{1}{2}} = \frac{1}{\sqrt{243}} \approx .064$$

2. Scientific Notation

    Scientific Notation: Any number can be written as the product of a number between 1 and 10 and some power of 10. (Here, a power of 10 means 10 raised to an exponent). A number written this way is said to be written in scientific notation. The easiest way to understand how to write a number in scientific notation is to look at some examples.

    Example: Write the following numbers in scientific notation:

    a. 820,000

    b. 2,749,697

    a. In writing this number as 8.2, the decimal point is moved 5 places to the left. Thus, $820,000 = 8.2 \times 10^5$.

    b. 2,749,697

    To change this number to 2.749697, the decimal point needs to be moved 6 places to the left. Thus, $2,749,697 = 2.749697 \times 10^6$.

    Example:

    Write the following numbers without scientific notation:

    a. 2.45×10^3

    b. 7.6×10^{-4}

    a. Since $10^3 = 1000$, we see that $2.45 \times 10^3 = 2.45 \times 1,000 = 2,450$.

    b. Since $10^{-4} = .0001$, $7.6 \times 10^{-4} = 7.6 \times .0001 = .00076$.

3. The Exponential Function

Exponential Function: A function of the form $f(x) = a^x$, where $a > 0$ and $a \neq 1$, is called an exponential function.

Example: Sketch the graph of $f(x) = 3^x$.

x	$f(x)$
-3	$\dfrac{1}{27}$
-2	$\dfrac{1}{9}$
-1	$\dfrac{1}{3}$
0	1
1	3
2	9
3	27

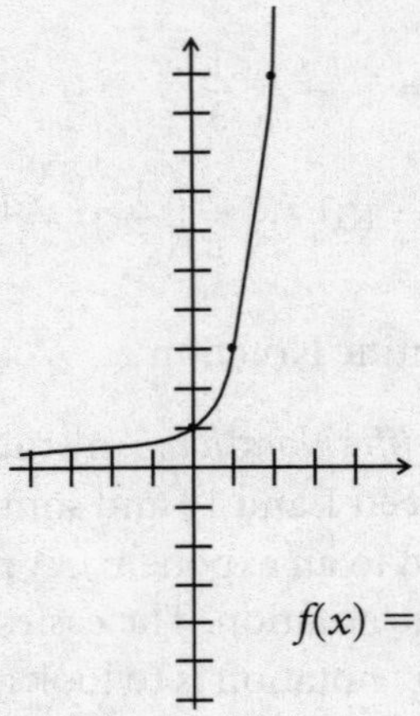

$f(x) = 3^x$

Notice that as x takes on smaller and smaller values, the value of y gets closer and closer to 0. The graph will continue to get closer and closer to the x-axis without ever touching it.

If we graph an exponential function with a base larger than 3, the graph will have the same shape as the one above, but it will rise more sharply.

What if the base is between 0 and 1? Consider $f(x) = \left(\dfrac{1}{3}\right)^x$. Notice that $f(x) = \left(\dfrac{1}{3}\right)^x = 3^{-x}$. Thus, the graph of $f(x) = \left(\dfrac{1}{3}\right)^x$ has exactly the same shape as the graph of $f(x) = 3^x$ but is reflected through the y-axis. This is indicated by the following graph.

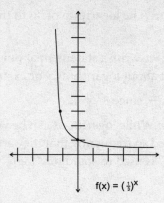

$f(x) = \left(\tfrac{1}{3}\right)^x$

4. Properties of the Exponential Function

   1. The domain of the exponential function is the set of real numbers.

   2. The range of the exponential function is the set of positive real numbers.

   3. Because $a^0 = 1$ for all $a \neq 0$, the graph of an exponential function always passes through the point (0, 1).

   4. The graph of an exponential function rises if $a > 1$, and falls if $0 < a < 1$.

E. The Logarithmic Function

1. Definitions

   The Inverse of the Exponential Function: Recall that the exponential function, $y = a^x$, is a one-to-one function, and therefore, has an inverse. In order to find any inverse function, we typically begin by flipping x and y, and then solve for y. If we flip x and y in the equation $y = a^x$, we obtain $x = a^y$. Note that we do not yet have any technique that would enable us to solve for y. Thus, we need to create a new notation.

   The Logarithmic Function: We write $y = \log_a x$ to mean $x = a^y$, where $a > 0$ and $a \neq 1$. The expression $y = \log_a x$ is read "y is equal to the logarithm of x to the base a."

2. Computing Logarithms

   Background: The logarithm of a number is the power to which a given base must be raised to produce the number. For example, the logarithm of 36 to the base 6 is 2, since 6 must be raised to the exponent 2 to produce the number 36. The statement "The logarithm of 36 to the base 6 is 2," is written as $\log_6 36 = 2$.

Note that every time we write a statement about exponents, we can write an equivalent statement about logarithms. For example, $\log_3 27 = 3$ since $3^3 = 27$, and $\log_8 4 = \frac{2}{3}$, since $8^{\frac{2}{3}} = 4$.

Common Logarithms: While logarithms can be written to any base, logarithms to the base 10 are used so frequently that they are called common logarithms, and the symbol "log" is used to stand for "$\log_{10}$".

Examples:

1. Write logarithmic equivalents to the following statements about exponents:

a. $2^6 = 64$
b. $15^0 = 1$

The statement $2^6 = 64$ is equivalent to $\log_2 64 = 6$

The statement $15^0 = 1$ is equivalent to $\log_{15} 1 = 0$

2. Use the definition of logarithm to evaluate the following:

a. $\log_5 125$
b. $\log_4\left(\dfrac{1}{64}\right)$
$\log_5 125 = 3$, since $5^3 = 125$.
$\log_4\left(\dfrac{1}{64}\right) = -3$ since $4^{-3} = \dfrac{1}{64}$.

3. Properties of Logarithms

Since logarithms are exponents, they follow the rules for combining exponents previously discussed.

Rule 1: $\log_a xy = \log_a x + \log_a y$
Rule 2: $\log_a\left(\dfrac{x}{y}\right) = \log_a x - \log_a y$
Rule 3: $\log_a x^b = b\log_a x$

These rules enable us to simplify the logarithms of arithmetic expressions down into the sums and differences of logarithms of smaller numbers.

Examples:

Rule 1. $\log_3 21 = \log_3 (7 \cdot 3) = \log_3 7 + \log_3 3$

Rule 2. $\log\left(\dfrac{17}{5}\right) = \log 17 - \log 5$

Rule 3. $\log_7 \sqrt{11} = \log_7 (11^{\frac{1}{2}}) = \left(\dfrac{1}{2}\right)\log_7 11$

By combining these rules, we can see, for example, that

$\log\left(\dfrac{17b}{7}\right) = \log 17 + \log b - \log 7.$

Note 1: In most cases, the numerical values of logarithms are irrational, and can be looked up in logarithmic tables, or found by using a scientific calculator.

Note 2: Observe that we cannot determine values for $\log_a x$ if x is either zero or a negative number. For example, if $\log_7 0 = b$, then $7^b = 0$, but there is no exponent satisfying this property. Similarly, if $\log_2(-16) = b$, then $2^b = -16$, and there is no exponent satisfying this property.

4. The Graph of the Logarithmic Function

   In order to graph $y = \log_2 x$, recall that this function is the inverse of $y = 2^x$. Thus, if we graph $y = 2^x$, and reflect this graph through the line $x = y$, we will obtain the graph of $y = \log_2 x$. Just like the graph of the exponential function, the graphs of all logarithmic functions have approximately the same shape.

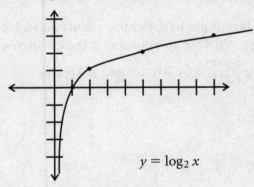

$y = \log_2 x$

5. Properties of the Logarithmic Function

   1. The domain of the logarithmic function is $\{x \mid x > 0\}$.

   2. The range of the logarithmic function is the set of all real numbers.

   3. The graph of all logarithmic functions contains the point $(1, 0)$.

6. Solving Exponential Equations

Exponential Equations: An equation in which an unknown appears in an exponent is called an exponential equation. Most of the time it is necessary to use logarithms to solve exponential equations.

Example: Solve for x: $5^x = 3^{x+2}$.

Take the logarithm of both sides of the equation.

$\log(5^x) = \log(3^{x+2})$	Apply Rule 3.
$x \log 5 = (x + 2) \log 3$	Distribute.
$x \log 5 = x \log 3 + 2 \log 3$	Combine like terms.
$x \log 5 - x \log = 2 \log 3$	
$x(\log 5 - \log 3) = 2 \log 3.$	
Since $2 \log 3 = \log 3^2 = \log 9,$	we have
$x(\log 5 - \log 3) = \log 9$	or

$$x = \frac{\log 9}{\log 5 - \log 3}.$$

Now, from the table of logarithms or a scientific calculator, we look up $\log 9 = 0.9542$, $\log 5 = 0.6990$, and $\log 3 = 0.4771$. Substituting in these values, we obtain:

$$x = \frac{0.9542}{0.6990 - 0.4771} = \frac{0.9542}{0.2219} = 4.300 \text{ to 3 decimal places.}$$

Questions

Relations

Find the domain of the relations indicated.

1. $y = \dfrac{5x}{2x + 1}$

2. $y = x + 7$

3. $y = \sqrt{3x - 9}$

Functions

1. If $f(x) = 4 - 3x$, find $f(-5)$ and $f(13)$.

In problems 2 through 4, state the domain of the given functions:

2. $f(x) = 2x^2 - 4x + 5$

3. $g(x) = \dfrac{2}{x}$

4. $y = \sqrt{x + 3}$

For the problems below, $f(x) = x^2$ and $g(x) = 4x - 2$. Find the following functions:

5. $(f+g)(x)$

6. $(fg)(x)$

7. $(f \circ g)(x)$

8. $(f \circ f)(x)$

In problems 9 and 10, determine if the given relations are functions, and if so, determine if they are one-to-one.

9. $\{(1, 3), (2, 7), (3, 7)\}$

10. $\{(1, 3), (2, 7), (3, 8)\}$

Inverse Functions

In exercises 1 and 2, find the inverses of the given relations.

1. $\{(3, 5), (2, 7), (8, 5)\}$

2. $y = x^2$

In exercises 3 through 6, find the inverse of the given function.

3. $\{(6, -3), (2, -4), (-3, 6)\}$

4. $\{(6, -3), (2, -3), (-3, 6)\}$

5. $f(x) = 5x + 2$

6. $f(x) = x^2 + 7$

Exponential Function

In exercises 1 through 3, write an equivalent exponential form for each radical expression.

1. $\sqrt{11}$

2. $\sqrt[3]{13}$

3. $\sqrt[3]{7^2}$

In exercises 4 through 6, write an equivalent radical expression for each exponential expression.

4. $8^{\frac{1}{5}}$

5. $(x^2)^{\frac{1}{3}}$

6. $\left(\dfrac{x^2}{y^7}\right)^{\frac{1}{5}}$

7. Express the following numbers using scientific notation:

   a. 1,234.56

   b. 0.0876

8. Graph the two equations given below on the same pair of axes:

   $y = 4^x, y = 4^{-x}$

Logarithms

1. Express the following in logarithmic form:

   $7^2 = 49$

2. Express the following in exponential form:

   $\log_8 64 = 2$

3. Solve the following equation for x:

   $125 = 25^{x-1}$

4. Solve $3^{2x} = 4^{x-1}$.

Answers

Relations

1. $y = \dfrac{5x}{2x+1}$.

   The domain will be all real numbers for which the range is defined. The expression $\dfrac{5x}{2x+1}$ is defined for all values of x except for the value $x = -\dfrac{1}{2}$, which would make the denominator equal to 0. Thus the domain is $\{x \mid x \neq -\dfrac{1}{2}\}$.

2. $y = x + 7$

   The domain is all real numbers, since $x + 7$ is defined for all real numbers.

3. $y = \sqrt{3x - 9}$

   Square roots are not defined for negative radicands; thus, $3x - 9$ must be greater than or equal to 0. Therefore,

   $3x - \geq 0$

   $3x \geq 9$

   $x \geq 3$. The domain is $\{x \mid x \geq 3\}$.

Functions

1. $f(-5) = 4 - 3(-5) = 19$

   $f(13) = 4 - 3(13) = 4 - 39 = -35$

2. $f(x) = 2x^2 - 4x + 5$ The domain is all of the real numbers.

3. $g(x) = \dfrac{2}{x}$ The domain is $\{x \mid x \neq 0\}$.

4. $y = \sqrt{x + 3}$ The domain is $\{x \mid x \geq -3\}$.

5. $(f + g)(x) = x^2 + 4x - 2$

6. $(fg)(x) = x^2(4x - 2) = 4x^3 - 2x^2$

7. $(f \circ g)(x) = f(4x - 2) = (4x - 2)^2 = 16x^2 - 16x + 4$

8. $(f \circ f)(x) = (x^2)^2 = x^4$

9. This is a function, but it is not one-to-one since the numbers 2 and 3 both have 7 associated with them.

10. This is a one-to-one function

Inverse Functions

1. The inverse is $\{(5, 3), (7, 2), (5, 8)\}$.

2. The inverse of $y = x^2$ is $y = \pm\sqrt{x}$.

3. The inverse of $\{(6, -3), (2, -4), (-3, 6)\}$ is $\{(-3, 6), (-4, 2), (6, -3)\}$. The inverse is a function.

4. The inverse of $\{(6, -3), (2, -3), (-3, 6)\}$ is $\{(-3, 6), (-3, 2), (6, -3)\}$. This is not a function as the domain value -3 is associated with two range values, 6 and 2.

5. Write $f(x) = 5x + 2$ as $y = 5x + 2$. Switch x and y to get $x = 5y + 2$. Solve for y to get $y = \dfrac{x - 2}{5}$. Thus, $f^{-1}(x) = \dfrac{x - 2}{5}$.

6. Write $f(x) = x^2 + 7$ as $y = x^2 + 7$. Then switch x and y to get $x = y^2 + 7$. Finally, solve for y to get $y = \pm\sqrt{x - 7}$.

   The inverse is not a function. However, if we restrict the domain to $x \geq 0$, the inverse would be $y = \sqrt{x - 7}$, which is a function.

Exponential Function

1. $11^{\frac{1}{2}}$

2. $13^{\frac{1}{3}}$

3. $(7^2)^{\frac{1}{5}}$

4. $\sqrt[5]{8}$

5. $\sqrt[3]{x^2}$

6. $\sqrt[5]{\dfrac{x^2}{y^7}}$

7. a. $1{,}234.56 = 1.23456 \times 10^3$

    b. $0.0876 = 8.76 \times 10^{-2}$

8. Graph the two equations given below on the same axis.

    $y = 4^x, y = 4^{-x}$

    First of all, note that we don't need to make a big table of values to graph these two equations. We know that both pass through $(0, 1)$ and have essentially the same shapes as $y = 3^x$ and $y = 3^{-x}$. Noting that $y = 4^x$ is satisfied by $(1, 4)$ and $(2, 16)$ and that $y = 4^{-x}$ is the reflection of $y = 4^x$ through the y-axis is enough to draw the graphs.

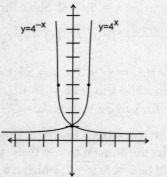

Logarithms

1. $7^2 = 49$ is equivalent to $\log_7 49 = 2$.

2. $\log_8 64 = 2$ is equivalent to $8^2 = 64$.

3. $125 = 25^{x-1}$. Rewrite 125 as 5^3, and 25 as 5^2. Then,

    $$5^3 = 5^{2(x-1)}$$

    Thus it must be true that:

    $3 = 2(x - 1)$, or

    $3 = 2x - 2$

    $5 = 2x$

    $x = \dfrac{5}{2}$

4. $3^{2x} = 4^{x-1}$

    Take the common logarithm of both sides.

    $\log 3^{2x} = \log 4^{x-1}$

    $2x \log 3 = (x - 1) \log 4$

    $2x \log 3 = x \log 4 - \log 4$

    $2x \log 3 - x \log 4 = -\log 4$

    $x(2 \log 3 - \log 4) = -\log 4$

    $x = \dfrac{-\log 4}{2 \log 3 - \log 4}$

    We now need to obtain values for $\log 3$ and $\log 4$. These can be obtained from either a table of logarithms or a scientific calculator. We determine $\log 3 = 0.4771$ and $\log 4 = 0.6021$. Thus

    $$x = -\dfrac{0.6021}{2(0.4771) - 0.6021} =$$

    $$\dfrac{-0.6021}{0.3521} = -1.7100$$

Chapter 5

Circles

A. Angles, Arcs, and Chords

   1. Definitions

      a. Background Definitions

Line Segment: Let ℓ be a line and let P and Q be any two points on the line. Then, the line segment PQ consists of points P and Q along with all of the points that are between P and Q. The notation for the line segment PQ is $\overline{PQ}$. (The entire line that contains the points P and Q is written $\overleftrightarrow{PQ}$). The length of $\overline{PQ}$ is indicated by PQ. The points P and Q are called the endpoints of PQ. The point M is called the midpoint of the segment if M lies between P and Q and the distance from P to M is the same as the distance from Q to M.

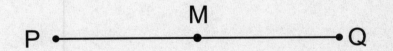

Ray: Let ℓ be a line and let P and Q be any two points on the line. Then, the ray PQ consists of points P and Q along with all of the points that are between P and Q, and all of the points R such that Q is between P and R. Intuitively, then, the ray PQ begins at P and extends on a straight line through Q and then on forever in the same direction.

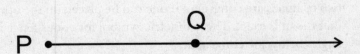

Angle: An angle is the union of two rays that have the same endpoint. The two rays are called the sides of the angle, and the endpoint is called the *vertex*. The notation for angle A is $\angle A$.

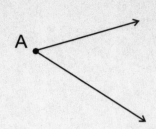

Angle Measure: Typically, angles are measured in degrees with a protractor. By convention, a straight line can be thought of as an angle containing 180°. As the figure below shows, all smaller angles can be assigned measures proportionally. Thus, an angle that is half the size of a straight angle measures 90° and is called a right angle. Also pictured below are several angles of various measures.

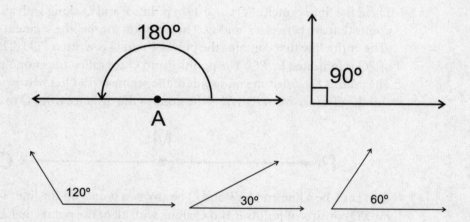

Congruence: Intuitively, any two geometric figures are congruent if they have the same size and shape. Two angles, thus, are congruent if they have the same measure; two line segments are congruent if they have the same length; two triangles are congruent if one can be placed on the other in such a way that the fit is exact. The geometric symbol for congruence is ≅. The three triangles below are congruent.

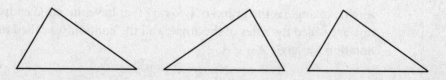

Bisect: Any geometric figure that intersects a segment at its midpoint is said to bisect the segment.

b. Definitions Related to Circles

Circle: A circle is the set of all points in a plane that are the same distance from a point called the *center.* An equivalent way to define circle is to say that, in a plane, a circle is the locus of points equidistant from a fixed point (the center). The figure below is a circle with center O.

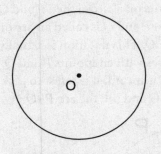

Circumference: The circumference of a circle is the distance around the circle.

Radius: A radius is a line segment that has as one endpoint the center of the circle and as the other endpoint a point on the circle. A circle has an infinite number of radii, and they are all congruent.

Chord: A chord is a line segment that has as its endpoints any two points on the circle.

Diameter: A diameter is a chord that goes through the center of the circle. A diameter is the longest possible chord and is twice the length of a radius.

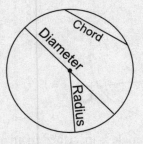

Central Angle: A central angle is an angle formed by two radii. In the figure below, angle *BAC* is a central angle.

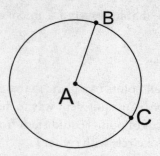

Arc: If P and Q are two points on a circle, then P and Q together with all of the points on the circle between P and Q is called an arc of the circle. The notation for the arc PQ is $\overset{\frown}{PQ}$. This notation is actually ambiguous, for on every circle there are two arcs with endpoints P and Q. If it is not apparent from the context which arc is meant, it is safest to pick another point R somewhere between P and Q and call the arc $\overset{\frown}{PRQ}$.

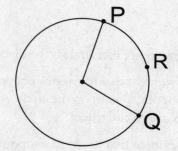

Inscribed Angle: An angle is inscribed in a circle if its vertex is a point of the circle and its two sides are chords of the circle.

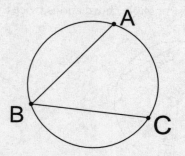

Angle Inscribed in an Arc: An angle is inscribed in an arc if the two end-points of the arc lie on the two sides of the angle, and the vertex of the angle is a point, but not an end point, of the arc.

Intercepted Arc: In addition to the definition above, we say that an angle inter-cepts an arc if the end-points of the arc lie on the angle, each side of the angle contains at least one endpoint of the arc, and, except for its end-points, the arc lies in the interior of the angle. In the figure below, the three inscribed angles *x*, *y*, and *z* all intercept the same arc $\overset{\frown}{PQ}$.

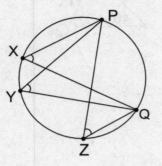

Semicircle: A semicircle is an arc whose endpoints, *P* and *Q*, lie on a diameter of the circle. In other words, a semicircle is an arc equal in length to one half of the circumference of the circle. Since a full circle contains 360°, a semicir-cle contains 180°.

Major Arc, Minor Arc: A major arc is an arc that is greater in length than a semicircle. A minor arc is an arc that is less in length than a semicircle.

The figure below illustrates the definitions above.

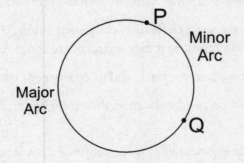

The Degree Measure of an Arc: If $\overset{\frown}{PQ}$ is a minor arc, the degree measure of the arc is the measure of the central angle whose sides contain the endpoints of the arc. In other words, the degree measure of a minor arc is the degree mea-sure of the central angle that intercepts the arc. Thus, in the figure below, we say that the measure of $\overset{\frown}{PRQ}$ is 45°. If $\overset{\frown}{PQ}$ is a major arc, its degree measure is

360° minus the measure of the corresponding minor arc. Thus the measure of $\overset{\frown}{PSQ}$ below is 360° − 45° = 315°.

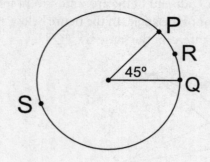

2. Congruence Theorems

Based on the definitions above, a number of theorems pertaining to congruencies within circles can be proved.

Theorem 1: In the same circle or in congruent circles, if two chords are congruent, then so are the corresponding minor arcs.

Theorem 2: In the same circle or in congruent circles, chords equidistant from the center are congruent.

Theorem 3: In the same circle or in congruent circles, if two central angles are congruent, then the chords that they subtend (cut off) are congruent.

Theorem 4: In the same circle or in congruent circles, if two central angles are congruent then the arcs that they intercept are congruent.

Other theorems about the circle and its component parts include:

Theorem 5: Any perpendicular from the center of a circle to a chord bisects the chord.

Theorem 6: The segment joining the center of a circle to the midpoint of a chord is perpendicular to the chord.

Example: A circle has a diameter of 80 inches. A chord is drawn perpendicular to a radius. The distance from the point of intersection of the chord and the radius to the outer end of the radius is 16 inches. Find the length of the chord.

A circle with diameter of 80 inches has a radius of 40 inches. Consider the diagram below:

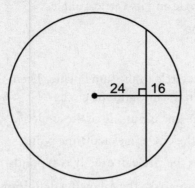

We know from theorem 5 that the radius shown bisects the chord. Now, draw in an additional radius as shown.

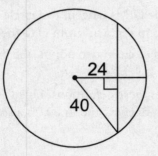

The right triangle formed has a hypotenuse of 40 and one leg of 24. By the Pythagorean Theorem, the remaining leg has a length of 32. Thus, the entire chord must have length 64.

3. Angle Measurement Theorems

Based on the definitions above, a number of theorems pertaining to the measurements of angles within circles can be proved.

Theorem 7: The measure of an inscribed angle is equal to one half of the measure of its intercepted arc.

Following immediately from this theorem are two additional corollaries:

Corollary 7.1: Angles inscribed in the same arc are congruent.

Corollary 7.2: An angle inscribed in a semicircle is a right angle.

Theorem 8: The measure of an angle formed by two chords that intersect within a circle is equal to one-half of the sum of the measures of the arcs intercepted by the angle and its vertical angle.

B. Chords, Secants, and Tangents

1. Definitions:

Consider a line and a circle in the same plane. Then, there are three possible relationships between the line and the circle:

1. Every point on the line is outside of the circle.

2. The line touches the circle in exactly one point.

3. The line intersects the circle in exactly two points.

Based on this result, we make the following definitions:

Tangent: If a line intersects a circle in one point, the line is said to be tangent to the circle, and the point of intersection is called the point of tangency.

Tangent Segment: If the line $\overleftrightarrow{QR}$ is tangent to a circle at R, then the line segment $\overline{QR}$ is called the tangent segment from Q to the circle.

Secant: If a line intersects a circle in two points, the line is called a secant of the circle.

The figure below illustrates these definitions. Line ℓ_1 is tangent to the circle with point T the point of tangency, and line ℓ_2 is a secant line.

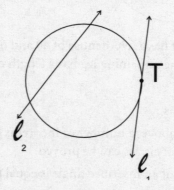

There are a number of results that can be proved concerning chords, tangents, and secants.

2.   Perpendicularity Theorems

In addition to the results (Theorems 5 and 6) given previously, we have the following key facts:

Theorem 9: Every line tangent to a circle is perpendicular to the radius drawn to the point of contact.

Theorem 10: Any line in the same plane as a circle that is perpendicular to a radius of the circle at its outer end is tangent to the circle.

3.   Theorems Related to the Lengths of Chords, Tangents, and Secants

Theorem 11: Two tangent segments drawn to a circle from an external point are congruent and form congruent angles with the line joining the external point to the center of the circle.

Theorem 12: Given a circle and an external point E, line ℓ_1 intersects the circle in points A and B, and line ℓ_2 intersects the circle in points C and D (see the figure below). Then the product of the length of EA and the length of EB is equal to the product of the length of EC and the length of ED.

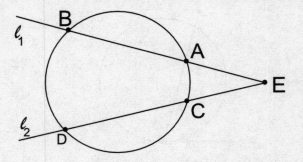

Theorem 13: Given a tangent segment ET to a particular circle, and a secant line through E, intersecting the circle in points A and B (see the following figure). Then, the length of ET squared is equal to the product of the length of EA and the length of EB.

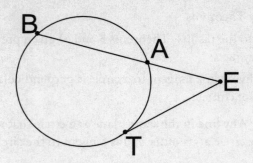

Theorem 14: Consider two chords that intersect within a circle. Then, the product of the lengths of the segments of one chord is equal to the products of the lengths of the segments of the other chord.

4. Theorems Related to Angle Measurement

Theorem 15: Consider an angle whose vertex is a point on a circle and whose sides are formed by a tangent ray and a secant ray (see figure below). Then, the measure of the angle is one-half of the measure of the arc that it intercepts.

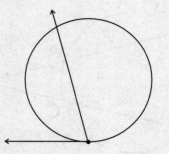

Theorem 16: Consider an angle whose vertex is a point external to a circle and whose sides are formed by two secants (or two tangents or a tangent and a secant) to the circle. Then, the degree measure of the angle is equal to one-half of the difference of the degree measures of the two intercepted arcs.

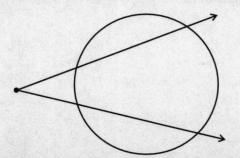

Questions

Arcs, Angles, and Chords

1. Find the measure of the central angle that intercepts an arc of 50°.

2. Find the measure of an inscribed angle that intercepts an arc of 50°.

3. In the figure below, if the measure of arc *RXQ* is 130°, how many degrees are in the measure of angle *PRQ*?

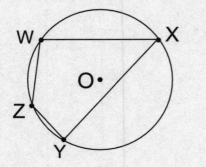

4. Quadrilateral *WXYZ* is inscribed in the circle with center at *O*. If the measure of angle *X* is 55°, what is the measure of angle *Z*?

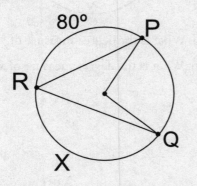

5. In circle *C* (at the top of the next column), *AB* = 80 and chord *BD* has length 48. What is the distance from the center of the circle to *BD*?

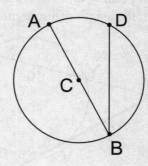

Chords, Secants, and Tangents

1. In the figure below, segment *PR* and rays *PT* and *RS* are tangent to the circle at the points indicated. Explain why it must be true that *PT* + *RS* = *PR*.

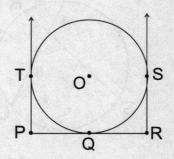

2. Secants *FB* and *FD* intersect a circle as shown below. What is the length of line segment *FC*?

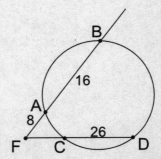

3. In the figure below, *WV* is tangent to the circle at point *V*, and *WZ* is a secant line. What is the length of line segment *WY*?

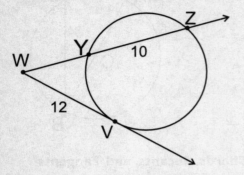

4. Two chords intersect in a circle as shown below. If $RS = 18$, and $x < y$, find x and y.

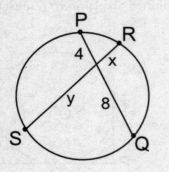

5. In the figure below, triangle *ABC* is inscribed in the circle, and line segment *DC* is tangent to the circle.

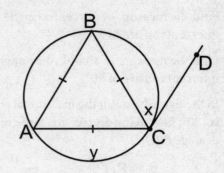

a. What is the degree measure of *y*?

b. What is the degree measure of *x*?

Answers

Arcs, Angles, and Chords

1. The measure of a central angle *is* the measure of its intercepted arc. The angle measures 50°.

2. The measure of an inscribed angle is half the measure of its intercepted arc. The angle measures 25°.

3. The entire circle measures 360°. Since minor arc $\overset{\frown}{RP}$ measures 80°, and arc RXQ measures 130°, the measure of arc $\overset{\frown}{PQ}$ must be 360° − 130° − 80° = 150°. Since the measure of an inscribed angle is half the measure of its intercepted arc, angle $\overset{\frown}{PRQ}$ measures 75°.

4. Consider the diagram below. Angle X intercepts arc $\overset{\frown}{WZY}$, so the measure of this arc must be 110°. Then, the measure of arc $\overset{\frown}{WXY}$ must be 250°. Since angle Z intercepts this arc, its measure must be one half of 250°, or 125°.

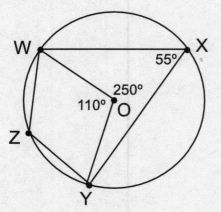

5. AB is a diameter of the circle, so it follows that the radius is 40. Drawing the perpendicular from the center of the circle to the chord (it is this length that we are trying to find) yields the following relationships.

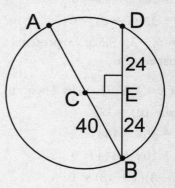

Note that $BE = ED$ by Theorem 5.

Since CBE is a right triangle, we can find the length of CE from the Pythagorean Theorem.

$CE^2 + 24^2 = 40^2$

$CE^2 + 576 = 1600$

$CE^2 = 1024$

$CE = 32$

Then, the distance from the center to the chord is 32.

Chords, Secants, and Tangents

1. Note that PT, PQ, RQ, and RS are all tangent segments to the circle. By Theorem 11, we know that $PT = PQ$ and $RS = RQ$. Adding these equations together, we obtain

$PT + RS = PQ + QR$. Since $PQ + RQ = PR$, we have $PT + RS = PR$.

2. Let $x = FC$. By Theorem 12, we have:

$$8(24) = x(x + 26)$$
$$192 = x^2 + 26x$$
$$x^2 + 26x - 192 = 0$$
$$(x + 32)(x - 6) = 0$$

$x = 6, -32$. Since x represents a length, it must equal 6.

3. Let $x = WY$. Then, by Theorem 13, we have

$$x(x + 10) = 12^2$$
$$x^2 + 10x = 144$$
$$x^2 + 10x - 144 = 0$$
$$(x - 8)(x + 18) = 0$$

$x = 8, -18$. Since x is a length, it must equal 8.

4. From Theorem 14, we have $8 \times 4 = x \times y$.

Now, we know that $x + y = 18$, so

$y = 18 - x$. Therefore,

$$32 = x(18 - x)$$
$$32 = 18x - x^2$$
$$x^2 - 18x + 32 = 0$$
$$(x - 16)(x - 2) = 0$$

$x = 16$ or 2.

Note that if $x = 16$, then $y = 2$ and vice versa. Since we are given $x < y$, we must have $x = 2$ and $y = 16$.

5. a. First of all, note that the inscribed triangle is equilateral. Therefore, each angle of the triangle must measure 60°. Now, note that angle B intercepts minor arc $\overset{\frown}{AC}$. Therefore, arc $\overset{\frown}{AC}$ must measure twice 60°, or 120°.

b. Note that angle $\overset{\frown}{BCD}$ intercepts minor arc $\overset{\frown}{BC}$. Since arc BC measures 120°, by Theorem 16 we have that x measures 60°.

Chapter 6

Trigonometric Functions and Their Inverses

A. Basic Concepts

1. The Geometric (Static) Concept of Angles

In a basic geometry course, an angle is defined as a figure formed by two rays with a common endpoint. As such, the measure of an angle can range between 0° and 360°. Recall that an angle whose measure is less than 90° is called an *acute* angle, an angle whose measure is 90° is called a *right* angle, an angle whose measure is between 90° and 180° is called an *obtuse* angle, a 180° angle is called a *straight* angle, and an angle whose measure is between 180° and 360° is called a *reflex* angle.

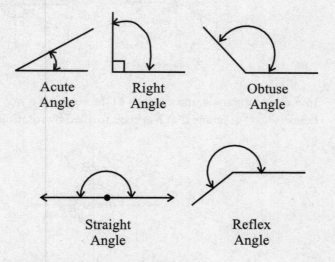

Acute   Right   Obtuse
Angle   Angle   Angle

Straight   Reflex
Angle   Angle

2. The Trigonometric (Dynamic) Concept of Angles

In trigonometry, we define an angle in a more dynamic way. The definition views an angle as the result of a rotation of a ray. Imagine two rays, one of which, *OA*, is called the *initial side* of the angle, and the other of which, *OB*, is called the *terminal side* of the angle. The angle is said to be in *standard position* if the vertex is at the origin and the initial side is along the positive *x*-axis.

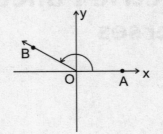

An angle is generated by rotating the initial ray *OA* onto the terminal ray *OB*. The direction of the rotation is indicated by an arrow. An angle is considered to be *positive* if the rotation is in a counterclockwise direction, and *negative* if the rotation is in a clockwise direction. An angle whose terminal side is on either the *x*- or *y*-axis is called a *quadrantal angle*.

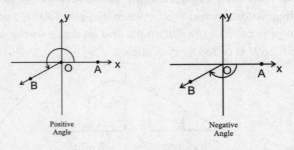

In forming an angle, the amount of the rotation is not restricted. The diagram below shows an angle that has been formed by rotating the ray $2\frac{1}{4}$ times.

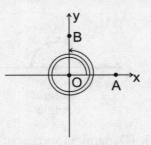

Note that such an angle has its initial side and terminal side in the same position as an angle that has been formed by $1\frac{1}{4}$ rotations, or $\frac{1}{4}$ of a rotation.

Thus, many different angles in standard position can have the same terminal side. Such angles are said to be *co-terminal*.

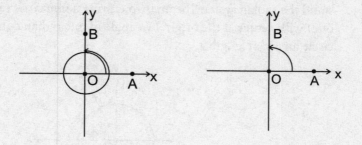

3. Measuring Angles in Degrees

There are two common methods for assigning a measure to an angle. The most familiar way to measure an angle is in *degrees*. In this system, we assign the measure of 360° to the angle formed by one complete counterclockwise rotation. An angle formed by 2 complete counterclockwise rotations, therefore, would measure 720°. An angle formed by one-half of a clockwise rotation would have a measure of −180°. Using such a system, it is possible for any real number to be the measure of an angle. Below are pictured a number of angles measured in degrees.

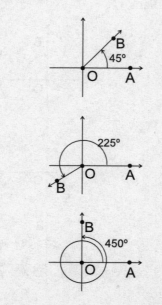

4. Measuring Angles in Radians

The other common unit for measuring angles is called the *radian*. To understand the radian system, begin by picturing a *unit circle* (a circle of radius one) with center at the origin. An angle of one radian cuts off from the unit circle an arc of length 1.

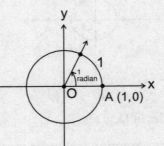

Since the unit circle has a circumference of 2π, one complete rotation is said to measure 2π radians. One-half of a rotation, then, measures π radians, and one-quarter of a rotation (a right angle) measures $\frac{\pi}{2}$ radians. Two complete rotations measure 4π radians and three complete rotations measure 6π radians. In general, the radian measure of an angle θ in standard position is the arc length along the unit circle covered in rotating from the initial side to the terminal side. The following diagram shows several rotations and the resulting angles in radians.

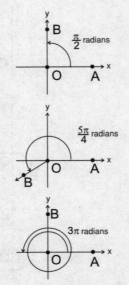

Note that even though we have used the unit circle to define radian, the radian measure is, in truth, independent of the size of the circle used to measure it. Further, the radian measure of an angle is dimensionless and thus may be regarded simply as a real number.

5. Converting Between Degrees and Radians

    We have already seen that $360° = 2\pi$ radians, from which it follows that $1° = \dfrac{\pi}{180}$ radians, and 1 radian $= \dfrac{180°}{\pi}$. The ratio $\dfrac{\pi}{180}$, thus, can be used as a conversion factor to change degrees to radians; the ratio $\dfrac{180}{\pi}$ can be used as a conversion factor to change radians to degrees.

    Example 1:

    a. Express the angle of $45°$ in radians.
    b. Express the angle of $\dfrac{5\pi}{4}$ radians in degrees.

        a. $45° = 45\left(\dfrac{\pi}{180}\right) = \dfrac{\pi}{4}$ radians

        b. $\dfrac{5\pi}{4} = \left(\dfrac{5\pi}{4}\right)\left(\dfrac{180°}{\pi}\right) = 225°$

6. The Sine and Cosine Functions

    Let θ represent a trigonometric angle in standard position. Further, let $P(x, y)$ represent the point of intersection between the terminal side of the angle and the unit circle. The diagram below depicts this situation.

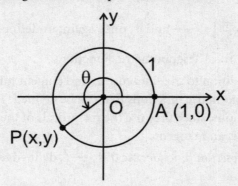

    Then, we define the sine and cosine functions as follows:

    $\sin \theta = y$

    $\cos \theta = x$

$\sin \theta = y$ means that the sine of θ is the directed vertical distance from the x-axis to the y-coordinate of $P(x, y)$. Thus, as θ progresses from 0 radians to $\frac{\pi}{2}$ radians to π radians to $\frac{3\pi}{2}$ radians to 2π radians, the value of $\sin \theta$ goes from 0 to 1 back to 0, to -1 and back to 0. Then, as θ progresses beyond 2π radians, the values of $\sin \theta$ repeat in the same pattern: 0 to 1 to 0 to -1 to 0. Another way to say this is that $\sin 0 = 0$, $\sin\left(\frac{\pi}{2}\right) = 1$, $\sin \pi = 0$

$\sin\left(\frac{3\pi}{2}\right) = -1$, $\sin 2\pi = 0$, etcetera. $\cos \theta = x$ means that the cosine of θ is the directed horizontal distance from the y-axis to the x-coordinate of $P(x, y)$. Thus, as θ progresses from 0 radians to $\frac{\pi}{2}$ radians to π radians to $\frac{3\pi}{2}$ radians to 2π radians, the value of $\cos \theta$ goes from 1 to 0 to -1, back to 0, and then back to 1. Then, as θ progresses beyond 2π radians, the values of $\cos \theta$ repeat in the same pattern: 1 to 0 to -1 to 0 to 1. This means that $\cos 0 = 1$, $\cos\left(\frac{\pi}{2}\right) = 0$, $\cos \pi = -1$, $\cos\left(\frac{3\pi}{2}\right) = 0$, $\cos 2\pi = 1$, etc.

7. The Tangent Function

Using the same definitions for θ and $P(x, y)$ as above, we can define a third trigonometric function, the tangent function, as $\tan \theta = \frac{y}{x}$. As in the section above, let's determine the value of the tangent for the quadrantal angles. First of all, note that $\tan 0 = 0$ since $y = 0$ for an angle of 0 radians. Then, $\tan \frac{\pi}{2} = \frac{1}{0}$, and is thus undefined. Next, the value for $\tan \pi$ is $\frac{0}{-1} = 0$, $\tan\left(\frac{3\pi}{2}\right) = \frac{-1}{0}$ and is, once again, undefined. Finally, $\tan 2\pi = 0$.

8. The Reciprocal Trigonometric Functions

In addition to the sine, cosine, and tangent functions, there are three other trigonometric functions that can be defined. They are called the reciprocal functions, since they use the reciprocals of the function values for sine, cosine, and tangent.

The cosecant function: $\csc \theta = \dfrac{1}{\sin \theta}$, defined for all θ such that $\sin \theta \neq 0$.

The secant function: $\sec \theta = \dfrac{1}{\cos \theta}$, defined for all θ such that $\cos \theta \neq 0$.

The cotangent function: $\cot \theta = \dfrac{1}{\tan \theta}$, defined for all θ such that $\tan \theta \neq 0$.

B. The Eight Fundamental Identities

There are eight trigonometric identities that will be very useful to us when solving problems.

The first three are called the *reciprocal identities*; we encountered them in the previous section.

$$\csc \theta = \frac{1}{\sin \theta}$$

$$\sec \theta = \frac{1}{\cos \theta}$$

$$\cot \theta = \frac{1}{\tan \theta}$$

Now, recall that in the previous section we defined $\sin \theta = y$, $\cos \theta = x$, and $\tan \theta = \frac{y}{x}$. From this, we derive the two quotient identities.

$$\tan \theta = \frac{\sin \theta}{\cos \theta}$$

$$\cot \theta = \frac{\cos \theta}{\sin \theta}$$

Finally, since $P(x, y)$ is on the unit circle, it must be true (via the Pythagorean Theorem) that $x^2 + y^2 = 1$. Thus, we can see that $\sin^2 \theta + \cos^2 \theta = 1$. If we divide both sides of this identity by $\cos^2 \theta$ or by $\sin^2 \theta$ we obtain two alternative forms of this identity:

$$1 + \tan^2 \theta = \sec^2 \theta$$

$$\cot^2 \theta + 1 = \csc^2 \theta$$

Since these three reciprocal identities are derived from the Pythagorean Theorem, they are called the Pythagorean identities.

C. Function Values

1. The Values of the Trigonometric Functions for Special Angles

In general, the values of the trigonometric functions for particular angles must be found by using a trig table or a scientific calculator. However, there are several special angles for which the values of the trigonometric functions can be determined by using the properties of the 30-60-90 triangle and the 45-45-90 triangle. The values for the special angles, 30°, 45°, and 60°, as well as those for 0°, 90°, 180°, and 270° should be memorized. The table below gives the values for sine, cosine, and tangent. The values for the other functions can be determined by using the trigonometric identities.

θ (degrees)	θ (radians)	$\sin \theta$	$\cos \theta$	$\tan \theta$
0°	0	0	1	0
30°	$\dfrac{\pi}{6}$	$\dfrac{1}{2}$	$\dfrac{\sqrt{3}}{2}$	$\dfrac{\sqrt{3}}{3}$
45°	$\dfrac{\pi}{4}$	$\dfrac{\sqrt{2}}{2}$	$\dfrac{\sqrt{2}}{2}$	1
60°	$\dfrac{\pi}{3}$	$\dfrac{\sqrt{3}}{2}$	$\dfrac{1}{2}$	$\sqrt{3}$
90°	$\dfrac{\pi}{2}$	1	0	—
180°	π	0	−1	0
270°	$\dfrac{3\pi}{2}$	−1	0	—

2. Reference Angles

a. Definition

If θ is an angle in the second, third, or fourth quadrant, the values of the trigonometric functions of θ can always be expressed in terms of a *reference angle* in the first quadrant. In general, for any angle θ (except $\dfrac{\pi}{2}$ and $\dfrac{3\pi}{2}$), the measure of the reference angle θ' in the first quadrant is equal to the measure of the acute angle formed by the terminal side of θ and the *x*-axis. The figure below illustrates the reference angles for θ with terminal side in each of the quadrants II, III, and IV respectively.

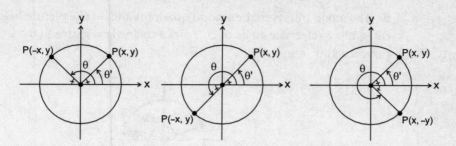

The value of a trigonometric function for a particular angle in the second, third, or fourth quadrant is equal to either plus or minus the value of the function for the first quadrant reference angle. The sign of the value is dependent upon the quadrant that the angle is in.

Examples:

Express each of the following in terms of first quadrant reference angles.

a. sin 330°

b. cos 160°

c. $\tan\left(\dfrac{5\pi}{3}\right)$

a. The angle 330° is in the fourth quadrant and, as the picture below indicates, has a reference angle of 30°. Since sine is negative in the fourth quadrant, sin 330° = −sin 30°.

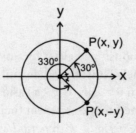

b. The angle 160° is in the second quadrant and, as the picture below indicates, has a reference angle of 20°. Since cosine is negative in the second quadrant, $\cos 160° = -\cos 20°$.

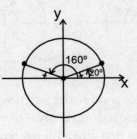

c. The angle $\dfrac{5\pi}{3}$ is in the fourth quadrant, and, as the picture below indicates, has a reference angle of $2\pi - \dfrac{5\pi}{3} = \dfrac{\pi}{3}$. Since tangent is negative in the fourth quadrant, $\tan\left(\dfrac{5\pi}{3}\right) = -\tan\left(\dfrac{\pi}{3}\right)$.

b. **Periodicity**

We have previously seen that for any real number θ, the angles θ and $\theta \pm 2\pi$ are co-terminal. Thus, they determine the same point on the unit circle. This tells us that $\sin\theta = \sin(\theta \pm 2\pi)$ and $\cos\theta = \cos(\theta \pm 2\pi)$. In other words, the sine and cosine functions repeat their values every 2π units. It is said that sine and cosine are *periodic* with *period* 2π.

Similarly, the tangent and cotangent functions can be shown to be periodic with period π and the secant and cosecant functions can be shown to be periodic with period 2π.

The concept of periodicity can be used along with reference angles to express the value of a trigonometric function of any angle in terms of a first quadrant angle.

Examples:

Express each of the following in terms of first quadrant reference angles.

a. $\cos 480°$

b. $\sin \dfrac{20\pi}{3}$

a. Since $480° = 360° + 120°$, $\cos 480° = \cos 120°$. The reference angle for $120°$ is $60°$. Since cosine is negative in the second quadrant, $\cos 120° = -\cos 60°$.

b. Since $\dfrac{20\pi}{3} = 6\pi + \dfrac{2\pi}{3}$, $\sin\left(\dfrac{20\pi}{3}\right) = \sin \dfrac{2\pi}{3}$. The reference angle for $\dfrac{2\pi}{3}$ is $\dfrac{\pi}{3}$, so $\sin\left(\dfrac{20\pi}{3}\right) = \sin\left(\dfrac{\pi}{3}\right)$.

c. Using Trigonometric Tables

There are two ways by which we can determine the values of trigonometric functions for specific angles. One is to use a scientific calculator, and the other is to use a table of values of trigonometric functions.

Since tables typically contain only the values of the sine, cosine, and tangent function for angles whose measures run from 0° to 90°, the first step in evaluating a trigonometric function for a specific angle is to use the techniques discussed above to express the function in terms of a first quadrant reference angle. Then, look up the reference angle in the table. In a typical table, the left-hand column lists angle measures from 0° to 45°, and the right hand column, beginning at the end of the table and reading backwards to the beginning, lists angle measurements from 45° to 90°. Most tables not only contain the values of the trigonometric functions of integral degrees but actually list the measures in multiples of 10′ (10 minutes).

To find the values for the secant, cosecant, and cotangent functions, find the values for the sine, cosine, or tangent and then use the reciprocal identities to find the desired values. Only the reciprocal identities are needed to find the cosecant of an angle when the sine of that angle is known to find the secant of an angle when the cosine of that angle is known, and to find the cotangent of an angle when the tangent of that angle is known.

D. Graphs of the Basic Functions

1. The Graph of the Sine Function

One of the best ways to understand the trigonometric functions is to draw their graphs. Before we draw the graph of $y = \sin \theta$, let us recall some of the properties that the sine function possesses:

1. The function is periodic with period 2π. This tells us that once we draw the graph for values of θ between 0 and 2π, the graph will simply repeat itself in intervals of 2π.

2. The values for $\sin \theta$ are positive for θ in the first and second quadrant and negative for θ in the third and fourth quadrant.

3. The values of $\sin \theta$ lie between -1 and $+1$. In fact, since $\sin 0 = 0$, $\sin\left(\dfrac{\pi}{2}\right) = 1$, $\sin \pi = 0$, $\sin\left(\dfrac{3\pi}{2}\right) = -1$, and $\sin 2\pi = 0$, the curve oscillates from 0 to 1 to 0 to -1 to 0 and then repeats.

Below is the graph of the sine function. Note how clearly it illustrates the properties above. We have used some of the values of special angles summarized above to help draw the graph.

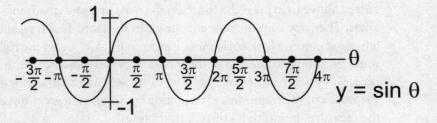

2. The Graph of the Cosine Function

The graph of the cosine function has the same shape as that of the sine function. Before graphing it, let's look at some of its properties.

1. Like the sine function, the cosine function is periodic with period 2π. This tells us that once we draw the graph for values of θ between 0 and 2π, the graph will simply repeat itself in intervals of 2π.

2. The values for $\cos \theta$ are positive for θ in the first and fourth quadrants, and negative for θ in the second and third quadrants.

3. The values of cos θ lie between -1 and $+1$. In fact, since $\cos 0 = 1$, $\cos\left(\dfrac{\pi}{2}\right) = 0$, $\cos \pi = -1$, $\cos\left(\dfrac{3\pi}{2}\right) = 0$, and $\cos 2\pi = 1$, the curve oscillates from 1 to 0 to -1 to 0 to 1 and then repeats.

The graph of the cosine function is shown below.

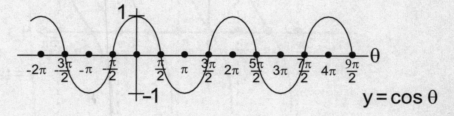

Note that the cosine graph is identical to the sine graph shifted $\dfrac{\pi}{2}$ units to the left. This is a consequence of the property that $\cos \theta = \sin\left(\dfrac{\pi}{2} + \theta\right)$, which will be demonstrated in the next chapter.

3. The Graph of the Tangent Function

The graph of the tangent function is very different in appearance than those of the sine and cosine. Here are some of its properties:

1. The function is periodic with period π. This tells us that once we draw the graph for values of θ between 0 and π, the graph will simply repeat itself in intervals of π.

2. The values for tan θ are positive for θ in the first and third quadrants and negative for θ in the second and fourth quadrants.

3. The value of tan θ can be any real number. In fact, $\tan 0 = 0$, and then the value of the tangent function becomes arbitrarily large as θ approaches $\dfrac{\pi}{2}$. At $\dfrac{\pi}{2}$, tangent is undefined. This fact is indicated by the dotted line through $\theta = \dfrac{\pi}{2}$ in the graph below. On the other side of this dotted line, the tangent function starts out with arbitrarily large negative values, moves up

to a value of 0 at π, and then gets bigger again. At $\dfrac{3\pi}{2}$, tangent is once again undefined. The graph of the tangent function follows.

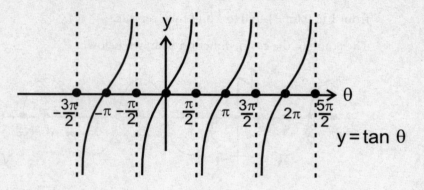

4. Amplitude and Period in the Sine and Cosine Function

Amplitude: Consider the function $y = 2 \sin \theta$. We can obtain the graph of this function by doubling each y value in the graph $y = \sin \theta$. When we do, we obtain the following graph, which is graphed on the same axis as $y = \sin \theta$ for comparison.

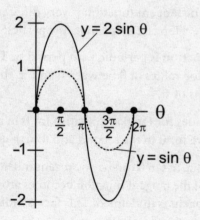

In general, consider the graph of $y = a \sin \theta$ or $y = a \cos \theta$. The number a is called the *amplitude* of these functions, and represents the maximum distance of any point on the graph from the x-axis. The graph of $y = a \sin \theta$ can be obtained by multiplying the y-coordinate of each point on the graph of $\sin \theta$ by the number a. Similar comments apply for the cosine graph.

Example: Draw the graphs of $y = \frac{1}{2} \cos \theta$ and $y = 2 \cos \theta$ in the interval $0 \leq \theta \leq 2\pi$ on the same pair of axes.

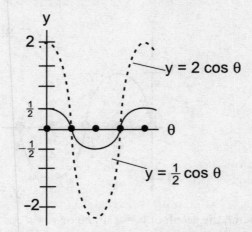

Period: Now consider the graph of $y = \sin b\theta$ for $b > 0$. Remember that the graph of $y = \sin \theta$ has a period of 2π. This means that, starting at 0, $y = \sin b\theta$ will repeat its values beginning at $b\theta = 2\pi$, which is to say, when $\theta = \frac{2\pi}{b}$. We say that $y = \sin b\,\theta$ has a *period* of $\frac{2\pi}{b}$, which means that the graph will repeat itself every $\frac{2\pi}{b}$ units.

Graphs of sine curves and cosine curves with a period different from 2π have the same shape as the regular sine and cosine curve but are "stretched" or "shrunken" in appearance.

Example: Sketch the graph of $y = \sin 2\theta$ on the same pair of axes as $y = \sin \theta$.

First of all, note that $y = \sin 2\theta$ has a period of $\frac{2\pi}{2} = \pi$. Thus,

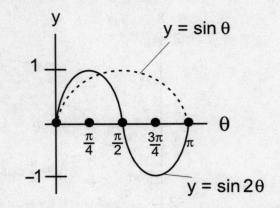

In general, the graph of $y = a \sin b\theta$ or $y = a \cos b\theta$ has amplitude a and period $\frac{2\pi}{b}$.

E. The Inverses of the Trigonometric Functions

1. Introductory Concepts

Recall that we previously saw that a function has an inverse if and only if it is one-to-one. Since the trigonometric functions are periodic, they certainly are not one-to-one. Thus, the inverses of the trigonometric functions are relations, not functions.

In order to understand how to think about the inverse of a trigonometric function, consider the equation $y = \sin x$. While we often talk about y, the sine of x, we may also wish to consider the number x *whose sine is y*. This concept is so important that "the value of x whose sine is y" is given a name and a notation.

2. Notation

The inverse of $y = \sin x$ is written as $x = \arcsin y$ and can be thought of as meaning "x is a value whose sine is y." Another common notation used to indicate that x is the arcsin of y is "$x = \sin^{-1} y$."

Example: Find all of the values for x such that $x = \arcsin \frac{1}{2}$.

The equation tells us that x is the angle whose sine is $\frac{1}{2}$.

Thus, for starters, x may be $\frac{\pi}{6}$, a first quadrant angle, or $\frac{5\pi}{6}$, a second quadrant angle. However, due to the periodicity of the sine function, y can also be $\frac{\pi}{6} \pm 2\pi n$ or $\frac{5\pi}{6} \pm 2\pi n$ for any integer n. Thus, the arcsin of $\frac{1}{2}$ is represented by an infinite number of possible angles.

The remaining inverse trigonometric relations are defined in the same way. For example, $x = \arccos y$ represents the angle whose cosine is y, and $x = \arctan y$ represents the angle whose tangent is y.

3. The Inverse Trigonometric Functions

By suitably restricting the domains of the trigonometric functions, we can obtain functions that are one-to-one. For example, as the graph below shows, the function $y = \sin x$ is one-to-one on the interval $-\frac{\pi}{2} \leq x \leq \frac{\pi}{2}$.

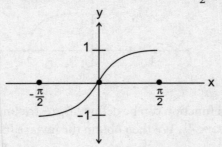

Hence, the sine function, when restricted to this particular interval, has an inverse. In order to distinguish the inverse sine *function* from the inverse sine relation, we use the notation $x = \text{Arcsin } y$ or $x = \text{Sin}^{-1} y$.

Recall from our previous work that the graph of an inverse function is the reflection of the graph of the given function in the line $x = y$. Below, we use this technique to obtain the graph of $y = \text{Arcsin } x$. Note that the domain of this function is $-1 \leq x \leq 1$, and the range is $-\frac{\pi}{2} \leq y \leq \frac{\pi}{2}$.

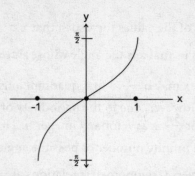

In a similar fashion, we define the Arccos function by restricting the domain of the cosine function to $0 \leq x \leq \pi$. We then obtain the inverse function shown below. The domain is of the Arccos function is $-1 \leq x \leq 1$, and the range is $0 \leq y \leq \pi$.

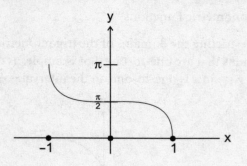

Finally, the Arctan function can be defined by restricting the domain of the tangent function to $-\frac{\pi}{2} < x < \frac{\pi}{2}$. We then obtain the inverse function shown below, which has a domain of all real numbers, and a range of $-\frac{\pi}{2} < x < \frac{\pi}{2}$.

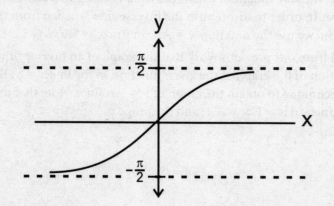

Questions

1. Sketch each of the following angles in standard position, labeling the initial side and the terminal side.

    a. 45°

    b. −60°

    c. 270°

    d. −720°

2. The terminal side of an angle in standard position is in the third quadrant. What are the possible values of the degree measure for this angle if the terminal side has rotated less than a full rotation?

3. For each of the following angles, find a positive angle of less than one revolution that is co-terminal with the given angle.

    a. 500°

    b. −900°

4. Change the following degree measures to radian measures.

    a. 30°

    b. 75°

5. Change the following radian measures to degree measures.

    a. 1

    b. $\dfrac{\pi}{3}$

6. For each of the following angles, find a positive angle of less than one revolution that is co-terminal with the given angle.

    a. 7π

    b. $\dfrac{17\pi}{2}$

In problems 7 and 8, a point on the terminal side of angle θ is given. If angle θ is in standard position, evaluate the six trigonometric functions of θ.

7. $(0, -1)$

8. $\left(\dfrac{1}{2}, \dfrac{\sqrt{3}}{2}\right)$

Fundamental Identities

1. If $\sin \theta = \dfrac{1}{2}$, and $\cos \theta = -\dfrac{\sqrt{3}}{2}$, find the values of the other 4 trigonometric functions.

2. Find all 6 functions of θ if $\cos \theta = \dfrac{3}{5}$, and θ is in the fourth quadrant.

3. If $\sin \theta = -\dfrac{4}{5}$ and θ is in the third quadrant, find the values of the other 5 trigonometric functions of θ.

4. If, for a particular value of θ, all 6 trigonometric functions are positive, then θ must be in which quadrant?

5. If θ is a third quadrant angle, then which trigonometric functions are positive and which are negative?

Function Values

In exercises 1 through 5 below, find the reference angle for the given angle.

1. 170°

135

2. 200°

3. 320°

4. $\dfrac{5\pi}{12}$

5. $\dfrac{5\pi}{6}$

In exercises 6 through 10, use reference angles and periodicity concepts to find the exact values of the functions given.

6. cos 405°

7. sin 420°

8. $\csc\left(\dfrac{9\pi}{2}\right)$

9. $\sec\left(\dfrac{9\pi}{4}\right)$

10. $\tan\left(\dfrac{17\pi}{4}\right)$

Graphs of the Trigonometric Functions

In problems 1 through 5 below, find the amplitude and period of the given sine or cosine function, and draw the graph.

1. $y = 6 \sin 2x$

2. $y = 2 \cos\left(\dfrac{x}{2}\right)$

3. $y = -\sin x$

4. $y = -2 \cos x$

5. $y = -3 \sin (2x)$

Inverses of Trigonometric Functions

In problems 1 through 5, evaluate the given expression.

1. $\text{Arcsin}\left(\dfrac{\sqrt{3}}{2}\right)$

2. $\text{Arccos}\,(0)$

3. $\text{Arctan}\,\sqrt{3}$

4. $\text{Arcsin}\left(\dfrac{-\sqrt{2}}{2}\right)$

5. $\text{Arccos}\,(-2)$

In exercises 6 through 8, evaluate the given expressions.

6. $\cos\,(\text{Arcsin}\,(1))$

7. $\sin\,(\text{Arccos}\,(-1))$

8. $\sin\,(\text{Arctan}\,1)$

Answers

Basic Concepts

1.

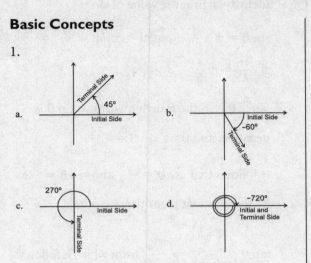

2. Let θ represent the angle. Then, $180° < \theta < 270°$. This can also be written as $-180° < \theta < -90°$.

3. a. $500° = 360° + 140°$. Thus, a $500°$ angle is co-terminal with a $140°$ angle.

   b. $-900° = -1080° + 180°$. Thus, a $-900°$ angle is co-terminal with a $180°$ angle.

4. a. $30° = 30\left(\dfrac{\pi}{180}\right) = \dfrac{\pi}{6}$ radians

   b. $75° = 75\left(\dfrac{\pi}{180}\right) = \dfrac{5\pi}{12}$ radians

5. a. 1 radian $= 1\left(\dfrac{180}{\pi}\right)° = \dfrac{180}{\pi}$ degrees. Since $\pi \approx 3.14$, this is about $57.3°$.

   b. $\dfrac{\pi}{3}$ radians $= \dfrac{\pi}{3}\left(\dfrac{180}{\pi}\right) = \dfrac{180}{3} = 60°$.

6. a. An angle of 6π represents an angle of 3 complete revolutions. Thus, an angle of 7π is co-terminal with an angle of $7\pi - 6\pi = \pi$ radians.

   b. Since $\dfrac{17\pi}{2} = 8\pi + \dfrac{\pi}{2}$, the angle $\dfrac{17\pi}{2}$ is co-terminal with an angle of $\dfrac{\pi}{2}$.

7. Consider the diagram below.

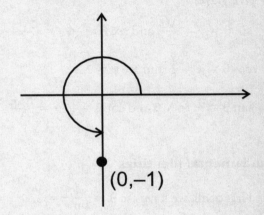

$(0,-1)$

Since $\sin\theta = y$, we have $\sin\theta = -1$. Similarly, $\cos\theta = x = 0$.

Then, $\tan\theta = \dfrac{y}{x} = \dfrac{-1}{0}$, which is undefined.

By the definitions of the reciprocal functions, $\csc\theta = -1$, $\sec\theta$ is undefined, and $\cot\theta = 0$.

8. Consider the diagram below.

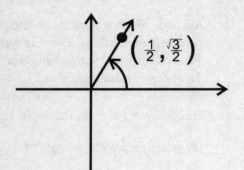

We have:

$$\sin \theta = y = \frac{\sqrt{3}}{2} \text{ and } \csc \theta = \frac{2}{\sqrt{3}} = \frac{2\sqrt{3}}{3}$$

$$\cos \theta = x = \frac{1}{2} \text{ and } \sec \theta = 2$$

$$\tan \theta = \frac{y}{x} = \sqrt{3} \text{ and } \cot \theta = \frac{1}{\sqrt{3}} = \frac{\sqrt{3}}{3}$$

Fundamental Identities

1. First of all, we have $\csc \theta = \dfrac{1}{\sin \theta} = 2$.

Similarly, $\sec \theta = \dfrac{1}{\cos \theta} = \dfrac{-2}{\sqrt{3}} = -\dfrac{2\sqrt{3}}{3}$.

Next, $\tan \theta = \dfrac{\sin \theta}{\cos \theta} = \dfrac{\left(\frac{1}{2}\right)}{\left(\frac{-\sqrt{3}}{2}\right)} = \dfrac{-1}{\sqrt{3}}$

$$= -\frac{\sqrt{3}}{3}.$$

The value of $\cot \theta$ is the reciprocal of $\tan \theta$, so $\cot \theta$ is $-\sqrt{3}$.

2. We can begin by using the Pythagorean identity to find the value of $\sin \theta$.

$$\sin \theta = \pm \sqrt{1 - \cos^2\theta} = \pm\sqrt{1 - \frac{9}{25}} =$$
$$\pm\sqrt{\frac{16}{25}} = \pm\frac{4}{5}$$

Since θ is in the fourth quadrant, $\sin \theta$ is negative, and thus, $\sin \theta = -\dfrac{4}{5}$.

It follows that $\csc \theta = -\dfrac{5}{4}$ and $\sec \theta = \dfrac{5}{3}$.

By the quotient identities, we obtain

$$\tan \theta = \frac{\left(\frac{-4}{5}\right)}{\left(\frac{3}{5}\right)} = -\frac{4}{3}, \text{ from which it follows}$$

that $\cot \theta = \dfrac{-3}{4}$.

3. If $\sin \theta = -\dfrac{4}{5}$, we can obtain the value of $\cos \theta$ by using the Pythagorean identity:

$$\cos \theta = \pm\sqrt{1 - \sin^2 \theta} = \pm\sqrt{1 - \frac{16}{25}} =$$
$$\pm\sqrt{\frac{9}{25}} = \pm\frac{3}{5}$$

In the third quadrant, cosine is negative, so $\cos \theta = -\dfrac{3}{5}$. Then, from the reciprocal identities, $\csc \theta = -\dfrac{5}{4}$ and $\sec \theta = -\dfrac{5}{3}$.

From the quotient identities, we find

$$\tan \theta = \frac{\left(\frac{-4}{5}\right)}{\left(\frac{-3}{5}\right)} = \frac{4}{3}, \text{ and } \cot \theta = \frac{3}{4}.$$

4. From the definition of sine and cosine, we can easily see that the only quadrant in which they are both positive is the first quadrant. Since the other four functions are reciprocals and quotients of sine and cosine, they are positive in the first quadrant as well. Thus, θ is a first quadrant angle.

5. In the third quadrant, both x and y are negative, so $\sin \theta$ and $\cos \theta$ are negative. The values of $\csc \theta$ and $\sec \theta$ are also negative since they are reciprocals of $\sin \theta$ and $\cos \theta$ respectively. However, $\tan \theta$ and $\cot \theta$ are positive since they are the quotient of two negative values.

Function Values

1. The reference angle for $170°$ is $180° - 170° = 10°$.

2. The reference angle for $200°$ is $200° - 180° = 20°$.

3. The reference angle for $320°$ is $360° - 320° = 40°$.

4. The reference angle for $\frac{5\pi}{12}$ is $\frac{5\pi}{12}$ since $\frac{5\pi}{12}$ is a first quadrant angle.

5. The reference angle for $\frac{5\pi}{6}$ is $\pi - \frac{5\pi}{6} = \frac{\pi}{6}$.

6. $\cos 405° = \cos (360° + 45°) = \cos 45°$
$= \frac{\sqrt{2}}{2}$

7. $\sin 420° = \sin (360° + 60°) = \sin 60°$
$= \frac{\sqrt{3}}{2}$

8. $\csc \left(\frac{9\pi}{2} \right) = \csc \left(4\pi + \frac{\pi}{2} \right) = \csc \left(\frac{\pi}{2} \right) = 1$

9. $\sec \left(\frac{9\pi}{4} \right) = \sec \left(2\pi + \frac{\pi}{4} \right) = \sec \left(\frac{\pi}{4} \right)$
$= \frac{1}{\cos \frac{\pi}{4}} = \sqrt{2}$

10. $\tan \left(\frac{17\pi}{4} \right) = \tan \left(4\pi + \frac{\pi}{4} \right) = \tan \left(\frac{\pi}{4} \right) = 1$

Graphs of the Trigonometric Functions

1. For $y = 6 \sin 2x$, the amplitude is 6 and the period is $\frac{2\pi}{2} = \pi$.

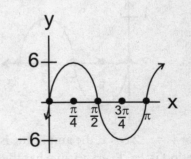

2. For $y = 2 \cos \left(\frac{x}{2} \right)$, the amplitude is 2 and the

    period is $\frac{2\pi}{\frac{1}{2}} = 4\pi$.

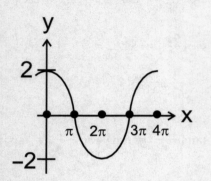

3. For $y = - \sin x$, the amplitude is 1 and the period is 2π. Every y value has the opposite sign of the y values of $y = \sin x$.

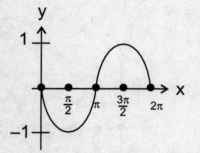

4. For $y = -2 \cos x$, the amplitude is 2 and the period is 2π. Every y value has the opposite sign of the y values of $y = 2 \cos x$.

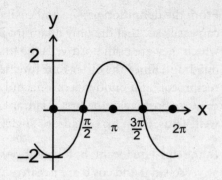

5. For $y = -3 \sin 2x$, the amplitude is 3 and the period is $\frac{2\pi}{2} = \pi$. Every y value has the opposite sign of the y values of $y = 3 \sin 2x$.

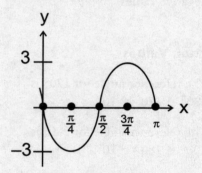

Inverses of Trigonometric Functions

Note: In answering questions 1 through 5, be sure that the angle you give is within the appropriate restricted range.

1. If $\theta = \frac{\pi}{3}$, $\sin \theta = \frac{\sqrt{3}}{2}$. Thus,

    $\text{Arcsin} \left(\frac{\sqrt{3}}{2} \right) = \frac{\pi}{3}$.

2. If $\theta = \frac{\pi}{2}$, $\cos \theta = 0$. Thus, $\text{Arccos} (0) = \frac{\pi}{2}$.

3. If $\theta = \frac{\pi}{3}$, $\tan \theta = \sqrt{3}$. Thus,

   $\text{Arctan} (\sqrt{3}) = \frac{\pi}{3}$.

4. If $\theta = -\frac{\pi}{4}$, $\sin \theta = -\frac{\sqrt{2}}{2}$. Thus,

   $\text{Arcsin} \left(-\frac{\sqrt{2}}{2}\right) = -\frac{\pi}{4}$.

5. Arccos (-2) is undefined, since the values of the cosine function are between -1 and $+1$.

6. This question asks us to determine the cosine of the angle whose sine is 1. The angle with sine of 1 in the region $-\frac{\pi}{2} \leq x \leq \frac{\pi}{2}$ is $\frac{\pi}{2}$. The cosine of $\frac{\pi}{2}$ is 0.

7. This question asks us to determine the sine of the angle whose cosine is -1. The angle with cosine of -1 in the region $0 \leq y \leq \pi$ is π. The sine of π is 0.

8. This question asks us to determine the sine of the angle whose tangent is 1. The angle with tangent of 1 in the region $-\frac{\pi}{2} < x \leq \frac{\pi}{2}$ is $\frac{\pi}{4}$. The sine of $\frac{\pi}{4}$ is $\frac{\sqrt{2}}{2}$.

Chapter 7

Trigonometric Identities and Equations

A. Identities

  1. Definitions

      Equation: An equation is a statement that two expressions A and B are equal. In general, an equation has the form $A = B$. An equation may be true for some, all, or none of the values of its variables. For example, the equation $2x + 1 = 2x + 3$ is true for no values of x, while the equation $4x + 3 = 19$ is true for the value $x = 4$.

      Identity: An equation that is true for all possible values of its variables is called an identity. For example, $(x + 4)^2 = x^2 + 8x + 16$ is an identity, true for all real numbers x.

  2. Manipulating Trigonometric Expressions

      Before we begin to solve trigonometric identities, it is helpful to practice manipulating trigonometric expressions. In the previous chapter, we developed the eight fundamental identities below; keep them in mind while solving the examples that follow.

      The Eight Fundamental Trigonometric Identities:

      $$\csc x = \frac{1}{\sin x}$$

      $$\sec x = \frac{1}{\cos x}$$

      $$\cot x = \frac{1}{\tan x}$$

      $$\tan x = \frac{\sin x}{\cos x}$$

$$\cot x = \frac{\cos x}{\sin x}$$

$$\sin^2 x + \cos^2 x = 1$$
$$1 + \tan^2 x = \sec^2 x$$
$$1 + \cot^2 x = \csc^2 x$$

In the examples below, use the fundamental identities to write the given expressions in terms of one trigonometric function or constant.

Example 1: $\sec \theta \sin \theta$

$$\sec \theta \sin \theta = \left(\frac{1}{\cos \theta}\right) \sin \theta = \frac{\sin \theta}{\cos \theta} = \tan \theta$$

Example 2: $\sec^2 \theta - \sec^2 \theta \sin^2 \theta$

$$\sec^2 \theta - \sec^2 \theta \sin^2 \theta = \sec^2 \theta (1 - \sin^2 \theta) = \sec^2 \theta \cos^2 \theta = \left(\frac{1}{\cos^2 \theta}\right) \cos^2 \theta = 1$$

3. Proving Trigonometric Identities

Concept: The eight fundamental identities above can be used to establish that other trigonometric equations are, in fact, identities. To demonstrate that an equation is an identity, we must use a series of algebraic manipulations to show that the expression on one side of the equals sign can be changed into the expression on the other side of the equals sign.

Equivalently, we can demonstrate that both expressions can be transformed into some third expression. However, we cannot "perform the same operation on both sides of the equation," as is the standard practice when solving algebraic equations.

Example 1: Prove that $5 \sin^2 \theta + 3 \cos^2 \theta - 2 = 2 \sin^2 \theta + 1$ is an identity.

$$5 \sin^2 \theta + 3 \cos^2 \theta - 2 = 2 \sin^2 \theta + 3 \sin^2 \theta + 3 \cos^2 \theta - 2$$
$$= 2 \sin^2 \theta + 3 (\sin^2 \theta + \cos^2 \theta) - 2$$
$$= 2 \sin^2 \theta + 3(1) - 2$$
$$= 2 \sin^2 \theta + 3 - 2$$
$$= 2 \sin^2 \theta + 1$$

Example 2: Prove that $\csc x - \cos x \cot x = \sin x$ is an identity.

$$\csc x - \cos x \cot x = \frac{1}{\sin x} - \frac{\cos^2 x}{\sin x} = \frac{1 - \cos^2 x}{\sin x} = \frac{\sin^2 x}{\sin x} = \sin x$$

B. Solving Trigonometric Equations

1. Concepts

    Essentially the same procedures can be used to solve trigonometric equations
    as we have already used to solve other types of equations. In some cases, when
    solving trigonometric equations, we are interested in finding all solutions
    within a certain range, such as between 0 and 2π. In other cases, we wish to
    find all possible solutions. For example, between 0 and 2π, the equation $\tan \theta$
    $= 1$ has two solutions: $\theta = \dfrac{\pi}{4}$ (which is in the first quadrant), and $\theta = \dfrac{5\pi}{4}$
    (which is in the third quadrant). However, since the tangent function is peri-
    odic with period π, there are other solutions outside of the range between 0
    and 2π. In fact, the set of all solutions is $\theta = \dfrac{\pi}{4} + n\pi, n = 0, \pm 1, \pm 2, \dots$.

2. Solving Linear Equations

    A *linear trigonometric equation* is one in which all trigonometric functions
    involved are raised to only the first power. Linear trigonometric equations
    can be solved using the techniques we have already studied for other linear
    equations.

    Example 1: Solve the following equation for all values of θ.

    $16 \sin \theta - 12 = 4 \sin \theta - 6$

    $16 \sin \theta - 12 = 4 \sin \theta - 6$

    $12 \sin \theta = 6$

    $\sin \theta = \dfrac{1}{2}$

    Now, $\sin \theta = \dfrac{1}{2}$ for $\theta = 30°$ and $\theta = 150°$. Since the sine function is periodic
    with period 2π, the full set of solutions is $\theta = 30° + n(360°)$ and
    $150° + n(360°)$, with $n =$ an integer. Of course, the answer could also be
    expressed in radians.

    Example 2: Solve the following equation for all values of θ in the range
    $0 \le \theta < 2\pi$.

    $\sin \theta = \cos \theta$

    $\sin \theta = \cos \theta$ Divide both sides by $\cos \theta$.

$$\frac{\sin \theta}{\cos \theta} = \frac{\cos \theta}{\cos \theta}$$

$$\tan \theta = 1$$

As we saw above, the solutions to this equation are $\frac{\pi}{4}$ and $\frac{5\pi}{4}$.

3. Solving Quadratic Equations

A quadratic trigonometric equation is one in which at least one of the trigonometric functions involved is raised to the second power. Quadratic trigonometric equations can be solved using the techniques we have already studied for other quadratic equations.

Example: Find all of the solutions of $4 \sin^2 \theta - 8 \sin \theta + 3 = 0$ in the range $0 \le \theta < 2\pi$.

$$4 \sin^2 \theta - 8 \sin \theta + 3 = 0$$

$$(2 \sin \theta - 3)(2 \sin \theta - 1) = 0$$

Thus, either $2 \sin \theta = 3$ or $2 \sin \theta = 1$. This means that either $\sin \theta = \frac{3}{2}$ or $\sin \theta = \frac{1}{2}$. The first of these equations has no solutions, since $\sin \theta$ is never bigger than 1. The second equation is true for $\theta = \frac{\pi}{6}$ and $\frac{5\pi}{6}$. Thus, the equation has 2 solutions, $\theta = \frac{\pi}{6}$ and $\frac{5\pi}{6}$.

C. The Sums and Differences of Angles

1. Basic Formulas

Occasionally, we must deal with trigonometric functions of the sum or difference of two angles, such as $\cos(A - B)$. The easiest way to handle these expressions is to expand them using the sum and difference formulas below:

$$\sin(A + B) = \sin A \cos B + \cos A \sin B$$

$$\sin(A - B) = \sin A \cos B - \cos A \sin B$$

$$\cos(A + B) = \cos A \cos B - \sin A \sin B$$

$$\cos(A - B) = \cos A \cos B + \sin A \sin B$$

$$\tan(A + B) = \frac{(\tan A + \tan B)}{(1 - \tan A \tan B)}$$

$$\tan(A - B) = \frac{(\tan A - \tan B)}{(1 + \tan A \tan B)}$$

2. **Deriving Identities from the Basic Formulas**

    The formulas above can be used to determine other useful identities, as in the following examples.

    Example 1: Use the formulas above to prove that $\cos(90° - \theta) = \sin\theta$.

    $\cos(90° - \theta) = \cos 90° \cos\theta + \sin 90° \sin\theta$.
    Recall that $\cos 90° = 0$ and $\sin 90° = 1$.

    Then,

    $\cos 90° \cos\theta + \sin 90° \sin\theta = (0)\cos\theta + (1)\sin\theta = \sin\theta$.

    Example 2: Use the formulas above to prove that $\sin(-\theta) = -\sin\theta$.

    $\sin(-\theta) = \sin(0 - \theta) = \sin 0° \cos\theta - \cos 0° \sin\theta =$
    $(0)\cos\theta - (1)\sin\theta = -\sin\theta$.

3. **Using the Basic Formulas to Find the Values of Certain Angles**

    The basic formulas can also be used to evaluate the trigonometric functions of certain angles, as the example below shows.

    Example: Compute $\tan 75°$.

    $\tan 75° = \tan(30° + 45°)$

    $$\frac{\tan 30° + \tan 45°}{1 - \tan 30° \tan 45°} = \sqrt{3} + 1\backslash 1 - 1\left(\frac{\sqrt{3}}{3}\right) = \frac{\sqrt{3} + 3}{3 - \sqrt{3}} = \frac{\sqrt{3} + 3}{3 - \sqrt{3}} \times \frac{3 + \sqrt{3}}{3 + \sqrt{3}}$$

    $$\frac{9 + 6\sqrt{3} + 3}{9 - 3} = \frac{12 + 6\sqrt{3}}{6} = 2 + \sqrt{3} \approx 3.732$$

D. **Double and Half Angle Formulas**

1. **The Double Angle Formulas**

    The sum and difference formulas discussed above can be used to develop what are known as the *double angle formulas*.

$\sin 2\theta = 2 \sin \theta \cos \theta$

$\cos 2\theta = \cos^2\theta - \sin^2\theta$

$\tan 2\theta = \dfrac{2 \tan \theta}{1 - \tan^2\theta}$

By using the Pythagorean Identity $\sin^2\theta + \cos^2\theta = 1$, the following two equivalent expressions for $\cos 2\theta$ can be obtained:

$\cos 2\theta = 1 - 2 \sin^2\theta$

$\cos 2\theta = 2 \cos^2\theta - 1$

Example 1: Use an appropriate sum or difference formula to prove $\sin 2\theta = 2 \sin \theta \cos \theta$.

Since, $\sin(A + B) = \sin A \cos B + \cos A \sin B$, we have

$\sin 2\theta = \sin(\theta + \theta) = \sin \theta \cos \theta + \cos \theta \sin \theta = 2 \sin \theta \cos \theta$

Example 2: Given that $\cos 2\theta = \cos^2\theta - \sin^2\theta$, prove that $\cos 2\theta = 1 - 2 \sin^2\theta$.

Since $\sin^2\theta + \cos^2\theta = 1$, we have $\cos^2\theta = 1 - \sin^2\theta$. Thus,

$\cos 2\theta = \cos^2\theta - \sin^2\theta = (1 - \sin^2\theta) - \sin^2\theta = 1 - 2 \sin^2\theta$.

Example 3: If $\sin x = -\dfrac{1}{4}$ and $\pi < x < \dfrac{3\pi}{2}$, find the value of $\cos 2x$ and $\sin 2x$.

Since $\sin^2 x + \cos^2 x = 1$, we have $\cos^2 x = 1 - \sin^2 x$. Thus,

$\cos x = -\sqrt{1 - \left(-\dfrac{1}{4}\right)^2} = -\dfrac{\sqrt{15}}{4}$

(negative since x is in the third quadrant)

Then since $\cos 2x = \cos^2 x - \sin^2 x$, we have

$\cos 2x = \left(\dfrac{-\sqrt{15}}{4}\right)^2 - \left(\dfrac{-1}{4}\right)^2 = \dfrac{15}{16} - \dfrac{1}{16} = \dfrac{14}{16} = \dfrac{7}{8}$

And, since $\sin 2x = 2 \sin x \cos x$, we have

$\sin 2x = 2\left(-\dfrac{1}{4}\right)\left(-\dfrac{\sqrt{15}}{4}\right) = \dfrac{\sqrt{15}}{8}$

2. The Half Angle Formulas

The double angle formulas can now be used to derive the formulas for the sine, cosine, and tangent of one-half of an angle.

$$\sin\left(\frac{1}{2}x\right) = \pm\sqrt{\frac{1-\cos x}{2}}$$

$$\cos\left(\frac{1}{2}x\right) = \pm\sqrt{\frac{1+\cos x}{2}}$$

$$\tan\left(\frac{1}{2}x\right) = \pm\sqrt{\frac{1-\cos x}{1+\cos x}}$$

Note the $\pm$ sign in front of the radicals. It is there because the functions of half angles may be either positive or negative.

Example: Find the value of $\sin\left(\dfrac{5\pi}{8}\right)$.

$$\sin\left(\frac{5\pi}{8}\right) = \pm\sqrt{\frac{1-\cos\left(\frac{5\pi}{4}\right)}{2}} = \pm\sqrt{\frac{1-\left(-\frac{\sqrt{2}}{2}\right)}{2}}$$

$$= \pm\sqrt{\frac{2+\sqrt{2}}{4}} \qquad = \pm\frac{1}{2}\sqrt{2+\sqrt{2}}$$

Then, since $\dfrac{5\pi}{8}$ is in the second quadrant, it follows that the answer is

$$\frac{1}{2}\sqrt{2+\sqrt{2}}.$$

Questions

Identities

In exercises 1 through 3 below, use the fundamental identities to write the given expressions in terms of one trigonometric function or a constant.

1. $\cot x \tan^2 x$

2. $\sin^2 x \cot^2 x + \cos^2 x \tan^2 x$

3. $\sec x - \dfrac{\cos x}{1 + \sin x}$

In exercise 4, prove that the given equation is an identity.

4. $\sin^3 x = \sin x - \sin x \cos^2 x$

Solving Trigonometric Equations

In Problems 1 through 3, solve the given equation for all values of θ such that $0 \le \theta < 2\pi$.

1. $\sin \theta \tan \theta = \sin \theta$

2. $\cos \theta + 1 = \sin^2 \theta$

3. $\cos^2 \theta + 2 \cos \theta = 3$

In problems 4 – 6, find all possible solutions of the given equations.

4. $\cos \theta = \dfrac{\sqrt{3}}{2}$

5. $4 \cos^2 \theta = 3$

6. $\cos^2 \theta = 1$

Sums and Differences of Angles

1. Use the appropriate formula to verify that $\tan (\theta + \pi) = \tan \theta$.

2. Prove that $\cos (-\theta) = \cos \theta$.

3. Evaluate $\cos \left(\dfrac{7\pi}{12} \right)$.

4. Evaluate $\sin \left(\dfrac{7\pi}{12} \right)$.

In exercises 5 and 6, evaluate each of the expressions by reducing it to a function of a single term.

5. $\cos 950° \cos 550° - \sin 950° \sin 550°$

6. $\cos 50° \cos 20° + \sin 50° \sin° 20$

7. Prove that $\cot (90° - \theta) = \tan \theta$.

Double and Half Angle

In problems 1 through 3 below, $\tan x = \dfrac{3}{5}$ for $0 < x < \pi$.

1. Find the value of $\sin 2x$.

2. Find the value of $\cos 2x$.

3. Find the value of $\sin 4x$.

4. Use an appropriate sum or difference formula to prove that $\cos 2\theta = \cos^2 \theta - \sin^2 \theta$.

Answers

Identities

1. $\cot x \tan^2 x = (\cot x \tan x) \tan x = (1)\tan x$
   $= \tan x$

2. $\sin^2 x \cot^2 x + \cos^2 x \tan^2 x =$

   $\sin^2 x \left(\dfrac{\cos^2 x}{\sin^2 x} \right) + \cos^2 x \left(\dfrac{\sin^2 x}{\cos^2 x} \right) =$

   $\cos^2 x + \sin^2 x = 1$

3. $\sec x - \dfrac{\cos x}{1 + \sin x} = \dfrac{1}{\cos x} - \dfrac{\cos x}{1 + \sin x}$.

   $\dfrac{1 - \sin x}{1 - \sin x} =$

   $\dfrac{1}{\cos x} - \dfrac{\cos x(1 - \sin x)}{1 - \sin^2 x} = \dfrac{1}{\cos x} -$

   $\dfrac{\cos x \,(1 - \sin x)}{\cos^2 x} = \dfrac{\cos x}{\cos^2 x} -$

   $\dfrac{\cos x - \cos x \sin x}{\cos^2 x} =$

   $\dfrac{\cos x - \cos x + \cos x \sin x}{\cos^2 x} =$

   $\dfrac{\cos x \sin x}{\cos^2 x} = \dfrac{\sin x}{\cos x} = \tan x$

4. $\sin^3 x = \sin x \sin^2 x$
   $= \sin x \,(1 - \cos^2 x)$
   $= \sin x - \sin x \cos^2 x$

Solving Trigonometric Equations

1. $\sin \theta \tan \theta = \sin \theta$

   $\sin \theta \tan \theta - \sin \theta = 0$

   $\sin \theta \,(\tan \theta - 1) = 0$

   Thus, either $\sin \theta = 0$ or $\tan \theta = 1$.

If $\sin \theta = 0$, $\theta = 0$ or π. If $\tan \theta = 1$,

$\theta = \dfrac{\pi}{4}$ and $\dfrac{5\pi}{4}$. Thus, the solution set is

$\{0, \dfrac{\pi}{4}, \pi, \dfrac{5\pi}{4}\}$.

Note that if you had tried to solve the equation by dividing both sides by $\sin \theta$, you would have lost the solutions 0 and π. The reason for this is that for $\theta = 0$ or π, $\sin \theta = 0$, and division by 0 is not allowed. In general, never divide both sides of an equation by a variable, unless you are sure that the variable is never equal to 0 for any of its possible values.

2. $\cos \theta + 1 = \sin^2 \theta$

   Begin by rewriting $\sin^2 \theta$ as $1 - \cos^2 \theta$. Then, the equation becomes

   $\cos \theta + 1 = 1 - \cos^2 \theta$ or

   $\cos^2 \theta + \cos \theta = 0$ Factor

   $\cos \theta \,(\cos \theta + 1) = 0$ so that

   $\cos \theta = 0$ or $\cos \theta = -1$.

   $\cos \theta = 0$ for $\theta = \dfrac{\pi}{2}$ and $\dfrac{3\pi}{2}$

   $\cos \theta = -1$ for $\theta = \pi$. Thus, the solution

   set is $\{\dfrac{\pi}{2}, \pi, \dfrac{3\pi}{2}\}$.

3. $\cos^2 \theta + 2 \cos \theta = 3$

   First, rewrite the equation as

   $\cos^2 \theta + 2 \cos \theta - 3 = 0$ Now, factor

   $(\cos \theta - 1)(\cos \theta + 3) = 0$ so that

   $\cos \theta = 1$ or $\cos \theta = -3$. Now, $\cos \theta$ is never -3, since it can be no smaller than -1.

$\cos \theta = 1$ for $\theta = 0$. Thus, the only solution in the given region is 0.

4. $\cos \theta = \dfrac{\sqrt{3}}{2}$

First, recall that cosine is positive in the first and fourth quadrants. In the first quadrant, $\cos\left(\dfrac{\pi}{6}\right) = \dfrac{\sqrt{3}}{2}$. In the fourth quadrant, $\cos\left(-\dfrac{\pi}{6}\right) = \dfrac{\sqrt{3}}{2}$. Since the cosine function has a period of 2π, the complete set of solutions is

$\theta = \dfrac{\pi}{6} + 2\pi n$, $-\dfrac{\pi}{6} + 2\pi n$ for $n = 0, \pm 1, \pm 2, \ldots$

5. $4 \cos^2 \theta = 3$. Then, $\cos^2 \theta = \dfrac{3}{4}$. Now $\left(\dfrac{\sqrt{3}}{2}\right)^2 = \dfrac{3}{4}$ and $\left(-\dfrac{\sqrt{3}}{2}\right)^2 = \dfrac{3}{4}$. We must consider two cases here,

$\cos \theta = +\dfrac{\sqrt{3}}{2}$ and $\cos \theta = -\dfrac{\sqrt{3}}{2}$.

As we saw in problem 4, if $\cos \theta = +\dfrac{\sqrt{3}}{2}$, then $\theta = \dfrac{\pi}{6} + 2\pi n$, $-\dfrac{\pi}{6} + 2\pi n$ for $n = 0, \pm 1, \pm 2, \ldots$. Further, for $\cos \theta = -\dfrac{\sqrt{3}}{2}$, we have solutions of $\dfrac{5\pi}{6}$ in the second quadrant and $\dfrac{7\pi}{6}$ in the third quadrant.

Overall, then, for $\cos \theta = -\dfrac{\sqrt{3}}{2}$, we have solutions of $\dfrac{5\pi}{6} + 2\pi n$ and $\dfrac{7\pi}{6} + 2\pi n$.

Thus, it is possible to represent all of the solutions to the equation as

$\theta = \dfrac{\pi}{6} + 2\pi n$, $-\dfrac{\pi}{6} + 2\pi n$,

$\dfrac{5\pi}{6} + 2\pi n$ and $\dfrac{7\pi}{6} + 2\pi n$, for $n = 0, \pm 1, \pm 2, \ldots$

6. $\cos^2 \theta = 1$

$\cos^2 \theta - 1 = 0$

$(\cos \theta - 1)(\cos \theta + 1) = 0$

$\cos \theta = 1$ or $\cos \theta = -1$

Now, $\cos \theta = 1$ at $0, \pm 2\pi, \pm 4\pi$, etcetera. This can be expressed as $\theta = 2\pi n$, $n = 0, \pm 1, \pm 2$, etcetera.

$\cos \theta = -1$ at $\pi, 3\pi, 5\pi$, etcetera. This can be written as $(2n + 1)\pi$ where $n = 0, \pm 1, \pm 2$, etcetera. Overall, then, $\theta = \pi n$ where $n = 0, \pm 1, \pm 2$, etcetera.

Sums and Differences of Angles

1. By the sum of angles formula for tangent, $\tan (\theta + \pi) = \dfrac{\tan \theta + \tan \pi}{1 - \tan \theta \tan \pi}$. Since $\tan \pi = 0$, we have

$\tan (\theta + \pi) = \dfrac{\tan \theta + 0}{1 - \tan \theta\,(0)} = \dfrac{\tan \theta}{1} = \tan \theta$.

2. Begin by writing $\cos (-\theta)$ as $\cos (0 - \theta)$. Then, by the formula $\cos(A - B) = \cos A \cos B + \sin A \sin B$, we have

$\cos (0 - \theta) = \cos 0 \cos \theta + \sin 0 \sin \theta$. Recall that $\cos 0 = 1$ and $\sin 0 = 0$. Thus, $\cos (0 - \theta) = \cos 0 \cos \theta + \sin 0 \sin \theta = (1) \cos \theta + (0) \sin \theta = \cos \theta$.

3. When attempting to use the sum and difference formulas to evaluate trigonometric functions for particular angles, it is often easier to begin by thinking in terms of degrees instead of radians. Thus, $7\frac{\pi}{12} = 105°$, which is the sum of $60°$ and $45°$, and $\cos\frac{7\pi}{12} =$

   $\cos(105°) = \cos(60° + 45°)$. From the formula $\cos(A + B) = \cos A \cos B - \sin A \sin B$, we obtain:

   $\cos(60° + 45°) = \cos 60° \cos 45° - \sin 60° \sin 45°$. Substituting in the values derived in the previous chapter,

   $\cos 60° \cos 45° - \sin 60° \sin 45° =$

   $\left(\frac{1}{2}\right)\left(\frac{\sqrt{2}}{2}\right) - \left(\frac{\sqrt{3}}{2}\right)\left(\frac{\sqrt{2}}{2}\right) =$

   $\frac{\sqrt{2}}{4} - \frac{\sqrt{2}\sqrt{3}}{4} = \left(\frac{\sqrt{2}}{4}\right)(1 - \sqrt{3})$.

4. The value of $\sin\frac{7\pi}{12}$ can be derived in the same fashion as above.

   $\sin\frac{7\pi}{12} = \sin(105°) = \sin(60° + 45°)$.

   From the formula $\sin(A + B) = \sin A \cos B + \cos A \sin B$, we obtain

   $\sin(60° + 45°) = \sin 60° \cos 45° + \cos 60° \sin 45°$. Again, substitute the values for the sin and cos of $45°$.

   $\sin 60° \cos 45° + \cos 60° \sin 45° =$

   $\left(\frac{\sqrt{3}}{2}\right)\left(\frac{\sqrt{2}}{2}\right) + \left(\frac{1}{2}\right)\left(\frac{\sqrt{2}}{2}\right) =$

   $\frac{\sqrt{2}}{4} + \frac{\sqrt{2}\sqrt{3}}{4} = \left(\frac{\sqrt{2}}{4}\right)(1 - \sqrt{3})$.

The solution to this problem can also be obtained by using the Pythagorean identity $\sin^2\theta + \cos^2\theta = 1$. Letting $\theta = 105°$, we obtain $\sin^2(105°) + \cos^2(105°) = 1$. Since we found the value for $\cos 105°$ in problem 3, we can substitute this value in $\sin^2(105°) + \cos^2(105°) = 1$, and solve for $\sin 105°$.

5. $\cos 950° \cos 550° - \sin 950° \sin 550° = \cos(950° + 550°) = \cos 1{,}500° =$

   $\cos 60° = \frac{1}{2}$

6. $\cos 50° \cos 20° + \sin 50° \sin° 20 =$

   $\cos(50° - 20°) = \cos 30° = \frac{\sqrt{3}}{2}$

7. Since $\cot\theta = \frac{\cos\theta}{\sin\theta}$, we have

   $\cot(90° - \theta) = \frac{\cos(90° - \theta)}{\sin(90° - \theta)}$.

   Now, $\cos(90° - \theta) = \cos 90° \cos\theta + \sin 90° \sin\theta = \sin\theta$.

   Further, $\sin(90° - \theta) = \sin 90° \cos\theta - \cos 90° \sin\theta = \cos\theta$.

   Thus, $\cot(90° - \theta) = \frac{\cos(90° - \theta)}{\sin(90° - \theta)} = \frac{\sin\theta}{\cos\theta} = \tan\theta$.

Double and Half Angle

1. Because tan x is positive, x must be in the first quadrant. As the diagram below shows,

    $\sin x = \dfrac{3}{\sqrt{34}}$ and $\cos x = \dfrac{5}{\sqrt{34}}$.

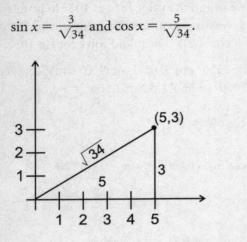

Then, $\sin 2x = 2 \sin x \cos x =$

$2\left(\dfrac{3}{\sqrt{34}}\right)\left(\dfrac{5}{\sqrt{34}}\right) = \dfrac{30}{34} = \dfrac{15}{17}.$

2. We can determine $\cos 2x$ by using the value of $\sin 2x$ determined above and the Pythagorean Identity, or we can use the double angle formula for $\cos 2x$. Let's solve this problem the latter way.

    $\cos 2x = \cos^2 x - \sin^2 x =$

    $\left(\dfrac{5}{\sqrt{34}}\right)^2 - \left(\dfrac{3}{\sqrt{34}}\right)^2 = \dfrac{25}{34} - \dfrac{9}{34} = \dfrac{16}{34} = \dfrac{8}{17}.$

3. $\sin 4x = 2 \sin 2x \cos 2x =$

    $2\left(\dfrac{15}{17}\right)\left(\dfrac{8}{17}\right) = \dfrac{240}{289} \approx .8304$

4. Write $\cos 2\theta$ as $\cos(\theta + \theta)$. Then,
    $\cos(\theta + \theta) = \cos\theta\cos\theta - \sin\theta\sin\theta = \cos^2\theta - \sin^2\theta.$

Chapter 8

Trigonometry—Triangle Solution

A. Area of a Triangle

1. The Geometric Formula

    When you studied the geometry of triangles, you saw that the area of a triangle could be computed by using the formula $A = \frac{1}{2}\,bh$, where b represents one of the three sides (bases) of the triangle, and h is the corresponding height. This formula is of limited value, however, since its use requires the knowledge of the height of the triangle. In the geometry problem in which, for example, you know the lengths of the sides of the triangle as well as the measures of the angles, you still do not, in general, have enough information to find the area.

2. The Trigonometric Formula

    Using trigonometry, the formula for the area of a triangle can be extended to enable us to find the area in a larger set of circumstances. In particular, the formula for the area of a triangle can be written as $A = \frac{1}{2}\,ab \sin C$, where a and b are two of the sides of the triangle, and C is the included angle. In general, the area of a triangle is equal to one-half the product of the lengths of two sides and the sine of their included angle.

    Example:

    Find the area of the triangle for which $a = 7$, $b = 12$, and the measure of angle C is $24°$.

    Area $= \frac{1}{2}ab \sin C = \frac{1}{2}(7)(12)\sin 24°$. From a table or a calculator, determine that $\sin 24° = .4067$. Thus:

    Area $= \frac{1}{2}ab \sin C = \frac{1}{2}(7)(12)\sin 24° = 42(.4067) \approx 17.1$

155

B. General Solution of Triangles

1. Definitions

   Solving a Triangle: Solving a triangle refers to the process of taking the given information about the sides and angles of a triangle and computing the lengths and measures of the missing sides and angles. In this section, we will see how to solve triangles that are not right triangles.

   Law of Sines, Law of Cosines: The law of sines and law of cosines are two trigonometric theorems that, when taken together, enable us to solve *any* triangle, provided that enough information has been given to determine the triangle uniquely.

2. The Use of the Two Laws

   The following table lists the various combinations of sides and angles that we could possibly be given, and indicates which law we can use to solve the triangle.

Symbol	Items Given	Law to be Used to Solve Triangle
SSS	Three sides	The Law of Cosines
SAS	Two sides and included angle	The Law of Cosines
SSA	Two sides and the angle opposite one of the sides	The Law of Sines (ambiguous case)
ASA	Two angles and a side	The Law of Sines

   In the SSA (ambiguous) case, as we will see, the triangle may have no solutions, one solution, or two solutions, depending on the values given. In the AAA case (given three angles and no sides), the triangle cannot be solved, since there are an infinite number of similar triangles for any given three angles.

3. The Law of Sines

   The *Law of Sines* states that for any triangle the lengths of the sides are proportional to the sines of the opposite angles. In other words, in any triangle ABC with corresponding sides a, b, and c, it is true that $\dfrac{a}{\sin A} = \dfrac{b}{\sin B} = \dfrac{c}{\sin C}$.

Solve the triangle with $A = 70°$, $B = 55°$, and $a = 12$.

By the law of sines, $\dfrac{12}{\sin 70°} = \dfrac{b}{\sin 55°}$. Thus,

$$b = \dfrac{12}{\sin 70°} \times \sin 55° \approx \dfrac{12}{.9397} \times .8192 \approx 10.46.$$

Since $A = 70°$ and $B = 55°$, $C = 180° - 70° - 55° = 55°$. Thus, the triangle is isosceles, and $c = b$.

For the given triangle, $c = b = 10.46$ and the measure of angle C is $55°$.

4.   The Law of Cosines

The *Law of Cosines* is simply a generalization of the Pythagorean Theorem, differing only in the extra term at the end. The Law of *Cosines* states that in any triangle ABC, with corresponding sides a, b, and c,

$$a^2 = b^2 + c^2 - 2bc \cos A$$
$$b^2 = a^2 + c^2 - 2ac \cos B$$
$$c^2 = a^2 + b^2 - 2ab \cos C$$

Example:

Find the measures of the three angles in the triangle with sides $a = 5$, $b = 7$, and $c = 10$.

To find angle A, use the formula $a^2 = b^2 + c^2 - 2bc \cos A$. We have

$5^2 = 7^2 + 10^2 - 2(7)(10) \cos A$

$25 = 49 + 100 - 140 \cos A$

$-124 = -140 \cos A$

$\cos A = \dfrac{124}{140} \approx .8857.$

From a table or a calculator, we find that $A = 27.66°$.

To find angle B, use the formula $b^2 = a^2 + c^2 - 2ac \cos B$. We have:

$7^2 = 5^2 + 10^2 - 2(5)(10) \cos B$

$49 = 25 + 100 - 100 \cos B$

$-76 = -100 \cos B$

$\cos B = \dfrac{76}{100} = .7600.$

From a table or a calculator, we find that $B = 40.54°$.

Finally, by subtracting, we obtain $C = 111.80°$.

5. Applications

The Law of Sines and the Law of Cosines can be used to help solve a wide variety of application problems that require solving triangles. In solving all such problems, it is extremely useful to draw a diagram of the situation and to label what is known and unknown.

Example:

Two airplane radar stations are 5,000 meters from each other. At the moment that an airplane passes directly over the line between the two stations, the distances from the plane to the stations are 2,500 meters and 4,000 meters. What is the altitude of the plane?

Consider the following diagram.

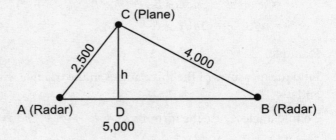

We need to find the value of h. Let's begin by using the Law of Cosines to determine the measure of angle A.

$a^2 = b^2 + c^2 - 2bc \cos A$

$4000^2 = 2500^2 + 5,000^2 - 2\,(2500)(5,000) \cos A$

$16,000,000 = 6,250,000 + 25,000,000 - 25,000,000 \cos A$

$16,000,000 = 31,250,000 - 25,000,000 \cos A$

$-15,250,000 = -25,000,000 \cos A$

$\cos A = .61$

Thus, $A \approx 52.41°$

Now, we can take advantage of the fact that triangle ACD is a right triangle to determine h.

$$\sin 52.41° = \frac{h}{2500}$$

$$h = 2500 \sin 52.41° = 2500 \, (.7924) = 1980.99 \text{ meters}$$

Thus, the altitude of the plane is about 1980.99 meters.

C. Right Triangle Trigonometry

1. Trigonometric Functions as Ratios of Sides

    Previously, the sine, cosine, and tangent of particular angles were expressed as the ratios of the lengths of sides of a right triangle. Recall that in a right triangle,

    $$\sin A = \frac{\text{side opposite } A}{\text{hypotenuse}}$$

    $$\cos A = \frac{\text{side adjacent to } A}{\text{hypotenuse}}$$

    $$\tan A = \frac{\text{side opposite } A}{\text{side adjacent to } A}$$

2. Relating Trigonometric Ratios to the Laws of Sines and Cosines

    The ratios given above can be viewed as special cases of the laws of sines and cosines, when these laws are applied to right triangles.

    For example, consider triangle ABC, with angle C a right angle, and c, therefore, the hypotenuse. By the Law of Sines,

    $\frac{a}{\sin A} = \frac{c}{\sin C}$. Since C measures 90°, $\sin C = 1$, and we obtain

    $\frac{a}{\sin A} = c$. This can be manipulated to tell us

    $\sin A = \frac{a}{c}$, which is consistent with the result above—

    $\sin A = \frac{\text{opposite}}{\text{hypotenuse}}$.

    Similarly, let us use the law of cosines for the same triangle. First of all, $c^2 = a^2 + b^2 - 2ab \cos C$. Since $\cos C = \cos 90° = 0$, we see that $c^2 = a^2 + b^2$, which, of course, is the Pythagorean Theorem.

    Rewrite this result as $a^2 = c^2 - b^2$.

Then, since $a^2 = b^2 + c^2 - 2bc \cos A$, we have $c^2 - b^2 = b^2 + c^2 - 2bc \cos A$.
Canceling the c^2 from both sides, and manipulating, we

obtain $2b^2 = 2bc \cos A$ or $\cos A = \dfrac{b}{c}$. This, of course, is the

above definition, $\cos A = \dfrac{\text{adjacent}}{\text{hypotenuse}}$.

3.   Applications

There are many problems that can be solved by applying the trigonometric functions in a right triangle. Some of them refer to the "angle of elevation" or "the angle of depression." When an object observed is above the horizontal plane, the angle between the line of sight from the eye to the object and the horizontal plane is called the angle of elevation. When the object observed is below the horizontal plane, the angle is called the angle of depression.

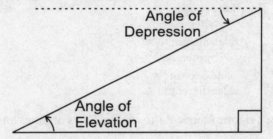

Example:

From a point on the ground 150 feet away from the foot of a lighthouse, the angle of elevation to the top is 67°. How tall is the lighthouse?

The situation is sketched in the following figure.

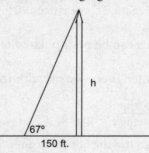

We have $\tan 67° = \dfrac{h}{150}$ or $h = 150 \tan 67° \approx 150\,(2.356) = 353.4$.

The lighthouse is about 353.4 feet tall.

Questions

Area of a Triangle

1. Find the area of the triangle with the following measurements:
   $b = 14, c = 5, A = 30°$.

2. Find the area of the triangle with the following measurements:
   $a = 5, c = 7.2, B = 71°$

3. A garden is in the shape of a parallelogram. The lengths of the two sides are 25 feet and 27 feet, and the acute angle between the two sides measures 38°. What is the area of the garden?

Solving Triangles

In problems 1 through 7 below, determine all of the missing parts of the triangle from the given information

1. $A = 50°, C = 33.5°, b = 76$

2. $A = 40°, a = 20, b = 15$

3. $A = 37°, a = 12, b = 16.1$

4. Mr. Linnell plans to sail from island A to island B, a distance of 75 miles. However, due to a strong wind, he travels 33° off course for a distance of 20 miles. How far away is he now from island B?

Right Triangle Trigonometry

1. A child's kite is caught in the top branches of a tree. If the 120 foot kite string makes an angle of 28° with the ground, what is the approximate height of the tree?

2. A surveyor measures the angle of elevation between the top of a mountain and ground level to be 43°. One half kilometer from the point of the initial measurement and farther from the base of the mountain, the angle of elevation is measured to be 39°. How high is the mountain?

3. A tower casts a shadow 30 meters long. If the angle formed by the shadow and a line segment connecting the tip of the shadow furthest from the tower to a point on the top of the tower is 64°, what is the height of the tower?

4. A tree at the edge of a river is 60 feet high. From the opposite side of the river to the top of the tree, the angle of elevation is 35°. How wide is the river?

5. A telephone pole is braced by a wire from the ground that is attached at a point 19 feet up the pole. Find the length of the wire if it makes an angle of 40° with the horizontal.

Answers

Area of a Triangle

1. Area $= \frac{1}{2}bc \sin A = \frac{1}{2}(14)(5) \sin 30° =$

   $35\left(\frac{1}{2}\right) = 17.5$

2. Area $= \frac{1}{2}ac \sin B = \frac{1}{2}(5)(7.2) \sin 71° \approx$

   $18(.9455) = 17.0$

3. Following is a sketch of the garden.

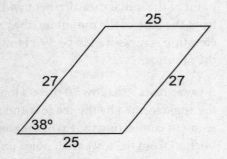

By drawing in the diagonal as shown below, we see that the garden can be viewed as consisting of two congruent triangles.

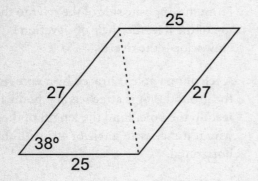

The area of one of the triangles is given by $A = \frac{1}{2}(25)(27) \sin 38° \approx \frac{1}{2}(25)(27)(.6157)$

$= 207.80$ square feet.

The area of the garden would be twice this number, or about 415.6 square feet.

Solving Triangles

1. This is the ASA case, that is, we are given two angles and the included side. From the table above, we see that we can solve this problem by using the Law of Sines. To begin, note that $B = 180° - 50° - 33.5° = 96.5°$. Then,

   $$\frac{a}{\sin A} = \frac{b}{\sin B}$$

   $$\frac{a}{\sin 50°} = \frac{76}{\sin 96.5°}, \text{ or}$$

   $$a = \frac{76}{\sin 96.5°} \times \sin 50$$

   $$a = \frac{76}{.9936} \times .7660 = 58.60.$$

   Similarly, $\frac{b}{\sin B} = \frac{c}{\sin C}$ or

   $$\frac{76}{\sin 96.5°} = \frac{c}{\sin 33.5°}$$

   $$c = \frac{76}{\sin 96.5°} \times \sin 33.5° \approx 42.22$$

2. $A = 40°, a = 20, b = 15$

   This is the SSA case, which can be solved using the law of sines. Recall, however, that this situation is also called "the ambiguous case," since there may be no, one, or two solutions depending on the data given. It is usually easiest to begin by determining which of the three possible situations we are given. Assuming, as in this problem, that we are given angle A

and sides a and b, the following guidelines can be used to tell us how many solutions we have:

a. If the measure of angle $A \geq 90°$, there is one solution if $a > b$ and no solutions if $a \leq b$.

b. If the measure of angle $A < 90°$ and $a \geq b$, there is one solution

c. If the measure of angle $A < 90°$ and $a < b$, there may be no, one, or two solutions. We can determine the outcome by using the Law of Sines. If, upon using the Law, we compute that $\sin B = 1$, there is one solution. There are no solutions if we compute $\sin B > 1$ and two solutions if we compute $\sin B < 1$.

In our problem, we are in case b, and thus we will have one solution.

$$\frac{a}{\sin A} = \frac{b}{\sin B}$$

$$\frac{20}{\sin 40°} = \frac{15}{\sin B}$$

$$\sin B = 15 \times \frac{\sin 40°}{20} \approx .4821$$

Thus, $B = 28.82°$.

C, then, is approximately equal to $180° - 28.82° - 40° = 111.18°$, and

$$\frac{a}{\sin A} = \frac{c}{\sin C}$$

$$\frac{20}{\sin 40°} = \frac{c}{\sin 111.18°}$$

$$c = \frac{20}{\sin 40°} \times \sin 111.18° \approx 29.01.$$

3. $A = 37°$, $a = 12$, $b = 16.1$

Again, we have the ambiguous case. Here, since $A < 90°$ and $a < b$, we may have 0, 1, or 2 solutions. To determine which is the case, we use the Law of Sines.

$$\frac{a}{\sin A} = \frac{b}{\sin B}$$

$$\frac{12}{\sin 37°} = \frac{16.1}{\sin B}$$

$$\sin B = \frac{\sin 37°}{12} \times 16.1 \approx .8074.$$

Since this answer is less than one, there will be two solutions to this problem. Both may be determined by the Law of Sines. Notice that we have computed $\sin B = .8074$. There are two solutions to this equation for $0° < B < 180°$. The first is $B = \sin^{-1}(.8074) = 53.85°$. The second solution is the supplement of $53.85°$, or $180° - 53.85° = 126.15°$. Let's consider the case in which $B = 53.85°$ first.

In this case, we have $A = 37°$, $a = 12$, $b = 16.1$, and $B = 53.85°$. Thus, $C = 180° - 53.85° - 37° = 89.15°$. Then,

$$\frac{a}{\sin A} = \frac{c}{\sin C}$$

$$\frac{12}{\sin 37°} = \frac{c}{\sin 89.15°}. \text{ Thus,}$$

$$c = \frac{12}{\sin 37°} \times \sin 89.15° \approx 19.94, \text{ and one}$$

solution to the problem is:

$A = 37°$, $a = 12$, $b = 16.1$, $B = 53.85°$, $C = 89.15°$, $c = 19.94$.

As for the second solution, we have $A = 37°$, $a = 12$, $b = 16.1$, and $B = 126.15°$.

Thus, $C = 180° - 126.15° - 37° = 16.85°$.

Then,

$$\frac{a}{\sin A} = \frac{c}{\sin C}$$

$$\frac{12}{\sin 37°} = \frac{c}{\sin 16.85°}.\text{ Thus,}$$

$$c = \frac{12}{\sin 37°} \times \sin 16.85° \approx 5.78.\text{ Thus,}$$

the other solution to the problem is:

$A = 37°, a = 12, b = 16.1, B = 126.15°, C = 16.85°, c = 5.78.$

4. The diagram below illustrates the situation in the problem. We are looking for the distance labeled a:

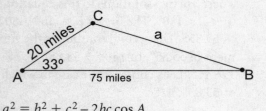

$a^2 = b^2 + c^2 - 2bc \cos A$

$a^2 = 20^2 + 75^2 - 2(20)(75) \cos 33°$

$a^2 = 400 + 5{,}625 - 3{,}000(.8387) = 6{,}025 - 2{,}516.01 = 3{,}508.99$

$a = \sqrt{3508.99} \approx 59.24$

He still has 59.24 miles to go.

Right Triangle Trigonometry

1. As the following figure indicates, let h denote the height of the kite.

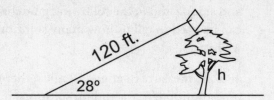

$$\frac{h}{120} = \sin 28° \quad h = 120 \sin 28°$$

$$h \approx 120\,(.4695) = 56.34 \text{ feet}$$

2. Let the distances h and z be as indicated in the diagram below.

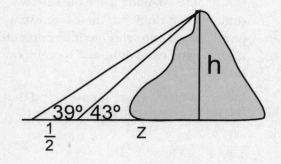

Then, $\dfrac{h}{z} = \tan 43°$ and $\dfrac{h}{\left(z + \frac{1}{2}\right)} = \tan 39°$, so that

$$h = z \tan 43° \text{ and } h = \left(z + \frac{1}{2}\right) \tan 39°.$$

Setting these two results equal,

$$z \tan 43° = \left(z + \frac{1}{2}\right) \tan 39°$$

$$z \tan 43° = z \tan 39° + \frac{1}{2} \tan 39°.$$

$$z\,(\tan 43° - \tan 39°) = \frac{1}{2} \tan 39°.$$

So $z = \dfrac{\frac{1}{2}(\tan 39°)}{\tan 43° - \tan 39°} \approx 32.99\text{km}$

Then, since $h = z \tan 43°$,
$h = (3.299) \tan 43° = (3.299)(.9325)$
≈ 3.08 km

The mountain is 3.08 km high.

3. Consider the figure below.

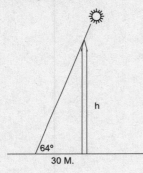

We have $\tan 64° = \dfrac{h}{30}$. Thus,

$h = 30 \tan 64° = 30\,(2.050) \approx 61.51$.

The tower is approximately 61.51 meters high.

4. The situation depicted in the problem is drawn below:

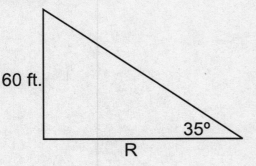

We have $\tan 35° = \dfrac{60}{R}$. Thus,

$R = \dfrac{60}{\tan 35°} = \dfrac{60}{.7002} \approx 85.69$.

The river is approximately 85.69 feet across.

5.

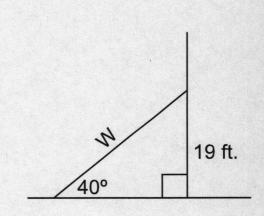

We have $\sin 40° = \dfrac{19}{w}$, or

$w = \dfrac{19}{\sin 40°} = \dfrac{19}{.6428} \approx 29.56$ feet.

The wire is about 29.56 feet long.

Chapter 9

Probability

A. A Review of Permutations, Combinations, and Simple Probability

1. Definitions

   Permutation: A permutation is any arrangement of the elements of a set in definite order. For example, consider the set $A = \{a, b, c\}$. There are six different ways in which the elements of this set can be ordered: *abc, acb, bac, bca, cab,* and *cba*. Thus, there are six permutations of the set A.

   Combination: A combination is any arrangement of the elements of a set without regard to order. For example, consider the set $B = \{a, b, c, d\}$. How many subsets containing 3 elements does this set have? The subsets are $\{a, b, c\}$, $\{a, b, d\}$, $\{a, c, d\}$, and $\{b, c, d\}$. Thus, we say that the number of combinations of 4 objects taken 3 at a time, is 4."

2. Notation

   Factorial Notation: The product $4 \times 3 \times 2 \times 1$ can be written in what is called factorial notation as 4!, which is read "four factorial." Similarly, $6! = 6 \times 5 \times 4 \times 3 \times 2 \times 1$. In general, we have the definition $n! = n \times (n - 1) \times (n - 2) \times \ldots\ldots \times 3 \times 2 \times 1$.

   The Number of Permutations: The number of permutations of n objects taken r at a time is written $_nP_r$, and read "*nPr*."

   The Number of Combinations: The number of combinations of n objects taken r at a time is written $_nC_r$, and read "*nCr*." Thus, for example, the number of combinations of 4 objects taken 3 at a time is written $_4C_3$ and read "4C3." We saw above that $_4C_3 = 4$.

3. Counting the Number of Permutations

   The number of permutations of n elements taken r at a time is given by
   $$_nP_r = n(n - 1)(n - 2) \ldots [n - (r - 1)].$$

Example: Recall the problem above, in which we determined that there were 6 permutations of the set $A = \{a, b, c\}$ by actual counting. To use the formula, instead, simply note that we are looking for the number of permutations of three objects taken three at a time. Thus, we need to compute $_3P_3 = 3(2)(1) = 6$. This example illustrates the following fact about permutations: The number of permutations of a set containing n members is $n!$.

Example: How many permutations are there of six elements from a set taken 3 at a time?

We need to find $_6P_3$. By the formula above, this is equal to $6 \times 5 \times 4 = 120$ permutations.

4. Counting the Number of Combinations

The formula for the number of combinations of n objects taken r at a time is given by $_nC_r = \dfrac{n!}{r!\,(n-r)!}$ *Example*: In how many ways can a special committee of 3 members be chosen from an association of 10 people?

We need to find the number of combinations of 10 objects taken 3 at a time. $_nC_r = \dfrac{10!}{3!7!} = \dfrac{10 \times 9 \times 8}{3 \times 2 \times 1} = 120$

5. Simple Probability

a. The Concept

Probability: Probability can be thought of as a numerical measure of the likelihood, or the chance, that an event will occur. A probability value is always a number between 0 and 1. The nearer a probability value is to 0, the more unlikely the event is to occur; a probability value near 1 indicates that the event is almost certain to occur.

Experiment: An experiment is any process that yields one of a number of well-defined outcomes. Thus, tossing a coin is an experiment with two possible outcomes: heads or tails. Rolling a die is an experiment with 6 possible outcomes; playing a game of hockey is an experiment with three possible outcomes (win, lose, tie).

b. Computing Probabilities

Experiments with Equally Likely Outcomes: In some experiments, all possible outcomes are equally likely. In such an experiment, with n possible outcomes, we assign a probability of $\dfrac{1}{n}$ to each outcome.

Example: In the experiment of tossing a coin, which has two equally likely outcomes, we say that the probability of each outcome is $\frac{1}{2}$. In the experiment of tossing a fair die, for which there are 6 equally likely outcomes, we say that the probability of each outcome is $\frac{1}{6}$.

Example: What is the probability of obtaining an even number when tossing a single die?

There are three ways that an even number can be obtained: tossing a 2, a 4, or a 6. The probability of each one of these three outcomes is $\frac{1}{6}$. The probability, then, of obtaining an even number is just the sum of the probabilities of these three favorable outcomes, which is $\frac{1}{6} + \frac{1}{6} + \frac{1}{6} = \frac{3}{6} = \frac{1}{2}$.

This result leads us to the fundamental formula for computing probabilities for events with equally likely outcomes:

$$\text{The probability of an event occurring} = \frac{\text{(number of favorable outcomes)}}{\text{(total number of possible outcomes)}}$$

In the case of tossing a die and obtaining an even number, as we saw, there are 6 possible outcomes, three of which are favorable, leading to a probability of $\frac{3}{6} = \frac{1}{2}$.

Example:

What is the probability of drawing one card from a standard deck of 52 cards and having it be a jack?

When you select a card from a deck, there are 52 possible outcomes, 4 of which are favorable. Thus, the probability of drawing a jack is $\frac{4}{52} = \frac{1}{13}$.

B. Bernoulli Experiments

1. Definitions

Experiment: A process that yields one of a possible number of outcomes that cannot be predicted with certainty in advance

Trial: When an experiment is performed repeatedly, each repetition is referred to as a trial.

Example: If a coin is tossed 5 times and the outcomes noted, we can say that we have undertaken 5 trials of the coin tossing experiment.

Bernoulli Experiment: A Bernoulli Experiment is the name given to a series of trials of a basic experiment performed under the following conditions:

1. On each trial, we focus our attention on the occurrence or nonoccurrence of a certain event. If the event occurs, it is referred to as a success, if the event does not happen, it is referred to as a failure.

2. The probability of success is the same for all trials. The value of this probability is called p. The probability of failure, then, is $1 - p$, which is usually denoted by q.

3. The outcome of a particular trial is not in any way influenced by the outcome of any other trial (that is to say, the trials are independent).

2. Finding the Probability of r Successes in n Trials

Introductory Example: Suppose we wanted to determine the probability of rolling exactly one 6 in 6 tosses of a die. In terms of the vocabulary above, rolling a 6 is called a success, and rolling something other than a 6 is termed a failure. We would like to know the probability of 1 success and 5 failures.

To simplify the problem, let's begin by finding the probability of success (rolling the 6) on the first toss and then failure (not rolling a 6) on the next 5 tosses. The probability of success is $\frac{1}{6}$, and the probability of failure is $\frac{5}{6}$.

Since the 6 trials are independent, we simply need to multiply the probability of each of the 6 desired events to obtain the overall probability.

Therefore, the probability of getting a 6 on the first toss and not getting a 6 on the next 5 tosses is $\frac{1}{6} \times \frac{5}{6} \times \frac{5}{6} \times \frac{5}{6} \times \frac{5}{6} \times \frac{5}{6} = \left(\frac{1}{6}\right)^1\left(\frac{5}{6}\right)^5$.

Now, return to the original problem. Initially, the 6 was not required to occur first. The 6 could actually occur as the result of any one of the 6 tosses. Thus, we take the probability we found above and multiply it by 6. Therefore, the probability of rolling *exactly* one 6 is $(6)\left(\frac{1}{6}\right)^1\left(\frac{5}{6}\right)^5$.

Generalized Bernoulli Trials: Now, let's generalize the result from above. Suppose we are performing n trials and wish to determine the probability of exactly r successes (and, therefore, $n - r$ failures). Begin by assuming that we wish to get the r successes first. Then, the probability of each success is p; the probability of r successes is the product of r factors of p, that is, p^r. After that, the probability of each failure is q; the probability of $n - r$ failures is q^{n-r}. The overall probability of r successes and $n - r$ failures, with the r successes coming first, is $p^r q^{n-r}$.

Now, in how many different ways can r successes occur? The number of ways of obtaining r successes in n trials in any order is given by $_nC_r$. Therefore, the probability of obtaining exactly r successes in n trials is given by $nC_r\, p^r q^{n-r}$.

C. The Binomial Theorem

1. Background

In performing algebraic manipulations, it often becomes necessary to raise binomials to various positive integer powers. By hand, it is possible to compute the binomial powers for the first several powers.

$$(p + q)^0 = 1$$
$$(p + q)^1 = p + q$$
$$(p + q)^2 = p^2 + 2pq + q^2$$
$$(p + q)^3 = p^3 + 3p^2q + 3pq^2 + q^3$$
$$(p + q)^4 = p^4 + 4p^3q + 6p^2q^2 + 4pq^3 + q^4$$
$$(p + q)^5 = p^5 + 5p^4q + 10p^3q^2 + 10p^2q^3 + 5pq^4 + q^5$$

However, to compute any further than this by hand becomes extremely time consuming. The Binomial Theorem gives us a method of determining the powers of binomials without actually multiplying them together.

2. Pascal's Triangle

The coefficients of the terms in the binomial expansion of $(p + q)^n$ are called binomial coefficients.

It is of interest to note that binomial coefficients can be arranged in a triangular array, called Pascal's Triangle, as follows:

$(p + q)^0$	1
$(p + q)^1$	1 1
$(p + q)^2$	1 2 1
$(p + q)^3$	1 3 3 1
$(p + q)^4$	1 4 6 4 1
$(p + q)^5$	1 5 10 10 5 1
....	. . . .

In this arrangement, the numbers in each row are the coefficients in the expansion of the binomial at the left of the row. Note that each number (except the 1's) in any row is equal to the two numbers in the row above it, one to the left and the other to the right. For example, in the sixth row, the first 5 is equal to the $1 + 4$ above it, and the second 10 is equal to the $6 + 4$ above it.

3. The Binomial Theorem

Statement of the Theorem: If n is any positive integer, then

$$(p + q)^n = {}_nC_0p^n + {}_nC_1p^{n-1}q^1 + {}_nC_2p^{n-2}q^2 + {}_nC_3 p^{n-3}q^3 + \ldots + {}_nC_nq^n$$

Properties of the Binomial Expansion:

1. The expansion has $n + 1$ terms.

2. The first term is p^n and the last term is q^n (since ${}_nC_0 = {}_nC_n = 1$).

3. In each successive term after the first, the exponent of p decreases by 1 and the exponent of q increases by 1. Thus, the sum of the exponents in each term is n.

4. The formula for the generic term involving q^r is ${}_nC_r p^{n-r}q^r$.

Example: Use the Binomial Theorem to evaluate $(p + q)^4$.

For $n = 4$, we obtain:

$$(p + q)^4 = p^4 + {}_4C_1p^3q^1 + {}_4C_2p^2q^2 + {}_4C_3p^1q^3 + q^4$$
$$= p^4 + 4p^3q^1 + 6p^2q^2 + 4p^1q^3 + q^4$$

Note that this result agrees with the result we obtained by actual multiplication above.

Questions

Permutations, Combinations, and Simple Probability

1. In how many different orders can five books be placed on a shelf?

2. In how many different ways can first, second, and third place be decided in a horse race with 13 horses?

3. A science teacher wishes to assign as homework three problems from a set of ten problems. How many different homework assignments are possible?

4. A comic book seller has 40 different comic books that Charles wishes to purchase. However, he only has enough money to buy four of the comic books. How many choices does he have?

5. A bag contains seven blue marbles, three red marbles, and two white marbles. If one marble is chosen at random from the bag, what is the probability that it will be red? What is the probability that it will not be blue?

6. A man has a quarter, two dimes, and two pennies in his pocket. What is the probability that a coin chosen at random will be worth at least 10 cents?

7. From a club of seven members, four members are to be selected at random to attend an out-of-state conference. The club has 4 girls and 3 boys as members. What is the probability that all 4 girls will be selected?

Bernoulli Experiment

1. A coin is flipped 8 times in succession. Find the probability that
   a. exactly 3 of the 8 flips are heads.
   b. either 3 or 4 of the flips are heads.

2. To win a particular carnival game, a person throws three balls and must knock down a stuffed animal on each throw. If the probability of knocking down a stuffed animal on each throw is $\frac{1}{4}$, what is the probability that a person wins the game?

3. A die is tossed 5 times in a row. What is the probability of an even number showing up at least 4 times?

4. In a particular production process, the probability that a defective item is produced is 0.02. What is the probability that of 100 items produced no more than three are defective?

5. A pair of dice is tossed 5 times in a row. What is the probability of a sum of 7 showing up at least three times?

Binomial Theorem

1. Find the 6th term in the expansion of $(x + y)^{10}$.

2. Find the 6th term in the expansion of $(a^2 + 2x)^{12}$.

3. For the expansion in problem 2, find the term involving x^4.

4. Use the Binomial Theorem to write the expansion of $(a + b)^6$.

5. Find the term involving y^5 in the expansion of $(x + y)^{15}$.

Answers

Permutations, Combinations, and Simple Probability

1. We are looking for the number of permutations of 5 objects taken 5 at a time. As we saw above, the answer is given by $5! = 5 \times 4 \times 3 \times 2 \times 1 = 120$.

2. We are looking for $_{13}P_3$. Thus, there are $13 \times 12 \times 11 = 1{,}716$ ways in which the first three positions in the race could be determined.

3. We need to count the number of combinations of ten objects taken three at a time. This number is given by

    $$_nC_r = \frac{n!}{r!(n-r)!}, \text{ with } n = 10 \text{ and } r = 3.$$

    Thus, we need to evaluate

    $$\frac{n!}{r!(n-r)!} = \frac{10!}{3!7!} = \frac{10 \times 9 \times 8}{3 \times 2 \times 1} =$$

    $10 \times 3 \times 4 = 120$.

4. We need to count the number of combinations of 40 objects taken four at a time. This number is given by

    $$_nC_r = \frac{n!}{r!(n-r)!} \text{ with } n = 40 \text{ and } r = 4.$$

    Thus, we need to evaluate

    $$\frac{n!}{r!(n-r)!} = \frac{40!}{4!36!} = \frac{40 \times 39 \times 38 \times 37}{4 \times 3 \times 2 \times 1} =$$

    $10 \times 13 \times 19 \times 37 = 91{,}390$.

5. There are twelve marbles in the bag. Since three of them are red, the probability of picking a red marble is $\frac{3}{12} = \frac{1}{4}$. There are five marbles in the bag that are not blue, so the probability of picking a marble that is not blue is $\frac{5}{12}$.

6. There are 5 coins in his pocket, and 3 of them are worth at least 10 cents. Thus, the probability that a coin chosen at random will be worth at least 10 cents is $\frac{3}{5}$.

7. The total number of ways that the traveling group could possibly be selected is $_7C_4$, which is equal to $\frac{7!}{4!3!} = \frac{7 \times 6 \times 5}{3 \times 2 \times 1} = 35$. Of these, only one group has all four girls, so the desired probability is $\frac{1}{35} \approx 0.029$.

Bernoulli Experiment

1. In this problem, we are flipping a coin. Success equals getting heads, and failure equals getting tails. The probability of success is $\frac{1}{2}$, and the probability of failure is also $\frac{1}{2}$.

    a. The coin is flipped 8 times, and we are interested in 3 successes. This probability is given by:

    $$_8C_3\left(\frac{1}{2}\right)^3\left(\frac{1}{2}\right)^5 = \frac{8!}{5!3!}\left(\frac{1}{2}\right)^8 =$$

    $$\frac{8 \times 7 \times 6}{3 \times 2 \times 1}\left(\frac{1}{2}\right)^8 = 56\left(\frac{1}{2}\right)^8 = \frac{56}{256} \approx 0.219$$

b. The probability that either 3 or 4 of the flips are heads is the probability of getting 3 heads plus the probability of getting 4 heads. We already know what the probability for 3 heads is, so we simply need to find the probability for 4 heads.

The probability for 4 heads is:

$$_8C_4 \left(\frac{1}{2}\right)^8 = \frac{8!}{(4!)(4!)} \left(\frac{1}{2}\right)^8 =$$

$$\frac{8 \times 7 \times 6 \times 5}{4 \times 3 \times 2 \times 1} \left(\frac{1}{2}\right)^8 = \frac{70}{256} \approx 0.273$$

The probability, thus, of obtaining 3 or 4 heads is approximately $0.219 + 0.273 = 0.492$.

2. In this problem, knocking over an animal is a success, and the probability of a success is $\frac{1}{4}$. We would like to determine the probability of three successes on three throws. This probability is given by

$$_3C_3 \left(\frac{1}{4}\right)^3 \left(\frac{3}{4}\right)^0 = 1 \left(\frac{1}{4}\right)^3 = \frac{1}{64} \approx 0.016.$$

3. We are tossing a die 5 times. Obtaining an even number is a success, and the probability of a success is $\frac{1}{2}$. Obtaining an odd number is a failure, and the probability of a failure is also $\frac{1}{2}$. We want the probability of obtaining 4 or 5 evens.

The probability of 4 evens is

$$_5C_4 \left(\frac{1}{2}\right)^4 \left(\frac{1}{2}\right)^1 = 5 \left(\frac{1}{2}\right)^5 = \frac{5}{32} \approx 0.156$$

The probability of 5 evens is

$$_5C_5 \left(\frac{1}{2}\right)^5 = \frac{1}{32} \approx 0.031$$

The overall probability is approximately $0.031 + 0.156 = 0.187$

4. If we called a success the production of a defective item, we would like the number of successes to be 0, 1, 2, or 3. The probability of success is 0.02, and the probability of failure is 0.98.

The probability of no defective items is
$$_{100}C_0 \, (.02)^0 \, (.98)^{100} = (.98)^{100}$$

The probability of one defective item is
$$_{100}C_1 \, (.02)^1 \, (.98)^{99} = 100(.02)^1(.98)^{99}$$

The probability of two defective items is
$$_{100}C_2 \, (.02)^2 \, (.98)^{98} = 4950(.02)^2(.98)^{98}$$

The probability of three defective items is
$$_{100}C_3 \, (.02)^3 \, (.98)^{97} = 161,700 \, (.02)^3 \, (.98)^{97}.$$

Thus, the desired probability is given by
$(.98)^{100} + 100 \, (.02)^1 \, (.98)^{99} + 4950 \, (.02)^2 \, (.98)^{98} + 161,700 \, (.02)^3 \, (.98)^{97}$

It would require a scientific calculator to evaluate this expression.

5. When a pair of dice is tossed, there are 36 different outcomes, of which six have a sum of 7 (1 and 6, 2 and 5, 3 and 4, 4 and 3, 5 and 2, 6 and 1). Thus, the probability of getting a sum of 7 is $\frac{1}{6}$. A pair of dice is tossed

five times in a row. A success is getting a sum of 7, and the probability of success is $\frac{1}{6}$. A failure is getting a sum other than 7, and the probability of failure is $\frac{5}{6}$. We need the sum of the probabilities of getting a sum of 7 three times, four times, and five times.

The probability of getting a 7 three times is $_5C_3 \left(\frac{1}{6}\right)^3 \left(\frac{5}{6}\right)^2 \approx 10(.0032) = .0322.$

The probability of getting a 7 four times is $_5C_4 \left(\frac{1}{6}\right)^4 \left(\frac{5}{6}\right)^1 \approx 5(.0006) = .0032.$

The probability of getting a 7 five times is $_5C_5 \left(\frac{1}{6}\right)^5 \left(\frac{5}{6}\right)^0 \approx 1(.0001) = .0001.$

Therefore, the desired probability is approximately $.0322 + .0032 + .0001 = .0355.$

Binomial Theorem

1. The sixth term is $_{10}C_5 \, x^{10-5}y^5 =$

$\frac{10!}{5!5!} x^5 y^5 = \frac{10 \times 9 \times 8 \times 7 \times 6}{5 \times 4 \times 3 \times 2 \times 1} x^5 y^5 =$

$252 \, x^5 y^5.$

2. For the sixth term in the expansion of $(a^2 + 2x)^{12}$, the exponent of the $2x$ term is 5, and the exponent of the a^2 term is $12 - 5 = 7$. The coefficient is

$_{12}C_5 = \frac{12!}{7!5!} = \frac{12 \times 11 \times 10 \times 9 \times 8}{5 \times 4 \times 3 \times 2 \times 1} = 792.$

Thus, the required term is

$792(a^2)^7 \, (2x)^5 = 792 \, (a^{14})(32x) =$

$25,344 \, a^{14} x^5.$

3. The term involving x^4 in the binomial expansion of $(a^2 + 2x)^{12}$ must have an exponent of 4 in the term involving $2x$. Thus, the term involving a^2 must have an exponent of $12 - 4 = 8$. The coefficient of the term is:

$_{12}C_4 = \frac{12!}{(8!)(4!)} = \frac{12 \times 11 \times 10 \times 9}{4 \times 3 \times 2 \times 1} = 495$

Thus, the required term is

$495(a^2)^8 \, (2x)^4 = 495 \, (a^{16})(16x^4) =$

$7920 \, a^{16}x^4$

4. $(a + b)^6 = a^6 + {}_6C_1 \, a^5 \, b + {}_6C_2 \, a^4 \, b^2 +$

$_6C_3 \, a^3 \, b^3 + {}_6C_4 \, a^2b^4 + {}_6C_5 \, a^1b^5 + b^6 =$

$a^6 + 6a^5b + 15a^4 \, b^2 + 20a^3b^3 +$

$15a^2b^4 + 6a^1b^5 + b^6$

5. The term involving y^5 in the expansion of $(x + y)^{15}$ must have x raised to the exponent 10.

The coefficient is

$_{15}C_5 = \frac{15!}{10!5!} = \frac{15 \times 14 \times 13 \times 12 \times 11}{5 \times 4 \times 3 \times 2 \times 1}$

$= 3003$

Thus, the desired term is $3003x^{10}y^5.$

Chapter 10

Statistics

A. A Review of Measures of Central Tendency

1. Definitions:

> *Data:* Data is numerical information that is obtained through the process of measurement.

> *Measures of Central Tendency:* It is often necessary to represent an entire set of data by means of a single number. A number that in some way describes or represents the center of a set of data is called a measure of central tendency, or a measure of central location.

> Mathematicians have created a large number of measures of central tendency to enable us to obtain an appropriate measure of the center in different situations. In this section, we will review the three most common measures of central tendency.

2. The Mean (Arithmetic Mean, Average)

> *Definition:* The mean is by far the best known measure of central tendency. The mean of a set of data is simply the sum of the data divided by the number of data values.

> Example:

> During the twelve months of 1996, an executive charged 4, 1, 5, 6, 3, 5, 1, 0, 5, 6, 4, and 3 business luncheons at the East 60's Club. What was the mean number of luncheons charged by the executive each month?

> The mean number of luncheons charged was

> $$\frac{4 + 1 + 5 + 6 + 3 + 5 + 1 + 0 + 5 + 6 + 4 + 3}{12} = \frac{43}{12} = 3.58$$

> Note that, of course, he didn't actually charge 3.58 luncheons during any given month. This figure is just a representative number for a typical month.

> Example: Brian got marks of 92, 89, and 86 on his first three math tests. What grade must he get on his final test to have an overall average of 90?

Let G = the grade on the final test. Then,

$$\frac{(92 + 89 + 86 + G)}{4} = 90 \text{ Multiply by 4}$$

$(92 + 89 + 86 + G) = 360$

$267 + G = 360$

$G = 93.$ Brian must get a 93 on the final test.

Properties of the Mean: It is not an accident that the mean is the most popular measure of central tendency. In addition to being easy to compute and familiar to most people, it has the following desirable properties:

1. It can be calculated from any set of numerical data, therefore it always exists.

2. Any set of numerical data has only one mean, so the mean is unique.

3. As we will see, the mean lends itself to further statistical treatment.

4. It is a very useful measure when undertaking statistical inference.

5. It takes into account every item of data.

On occasion, property 5 above can lead to a bit of trouble, however. Since the mean takes into account every item of data, it can be greatly influenced by a very small or very large piece of data, such as one obtained from an inaccurate measurement or a computational error.

Example:

a. In order to determine the expected mileage for a particular car, an automobile manufacturer conducts a carefully controlled factory test on five of these cars. The results, in miles per gallon, are 24.3, 24.6, 23.8, 24.0, and 24.3. What is the mean mileage?

$$\frac{24.3 + 24.6 + 23.8 + 24.0 + 24.3}{5} = 24.2 \text{ miles per gallon}$$

b. Suppose the car with the 23.8 miles per gallon had a faulty fuel injection system and obtained a mileage of 11.8 miles per gallon instead. What would the mean mileage have been?

$$\frac{24.3 + 24.6 + 11.8 + 24.0 + 24.3}{5} = 21.8 \text{ miles per gallon}$$

The one faulty measurement has lowered the average by almost $2\frac{1}{2}$ miles per gallon. The possibility of being misled by a very small or very large value can be eliminated by using a different measure of central tendency called the median.

3. The Median

    Definition: The median of a set of data is the value of the item in the middle, when the data is arranged in increasing or decreasing order of magnitude. If there are an even number of items, the median is the mean of the two items in the middle.

    Example:

    a. Find the median miles per gallon in both case a. and b. of the example above.

    When the measurements are 24.3, 24.6, 23.8, 24.0, and 24.3, the median is 24.3. With the faulty measurement of 11.8, the median would still be 24.3.

    b. If a sixth car had been included and had obtained a mileage of 24.1 miles per gallon in the initial measurements of 24.3, 24.6, 23.8, 24.0, and 24.3 above, what would the median have been?

    In this case, when we put the numbers in order, we obtain two numbers in the middle: 24.1 and 24.3. In this case, the median is the mean of these two numbers, which is 24.2.

4. The Mode

    Definition: The mode is another measure of central tendency. It is simply the data value that occurs most often. The mode had two major advantages: It requires no calculations to compute it, and it is the only measure of central tendency that can be used with qualitative data.

    Example:

    Recall the miles per gallon problem above. What is the mode of the original set of data 24.3, 24.6, 23.8, 24.0, and 24.3?

    The mode is 24.3, which occurs twice.

    Example: In a recent survey, 15 people were asked for their favorite automobile color. The results were: red, blue, white, white, black, red, red, blue, grey, blue, black, green, white, black, red. What was the modal choice?

Red, which was chosen by 4 people, is the modal choice.

There can be more than one mode. If the mode is not unique, then each of the items tied for most times is a mode. For example, in the problem above, if 4 people had chosen red and 4 people had chosen white, the two modes would be red and white.

B. Σ—Notation

1. Definition

In statistics, it is frequently necessary to calculate the means of many different sets of data. As such, it is useful to have a convenient formula that is always applicable. To develop such a formula, we use what is called *summation notation*.

Summation notation uses the Greek letter sigma, which looks like Σ, to stand for "sum" or "add up all of the values that follow." The symbol Σ is generally used with an indexing variable to indicate exactly what is to be summed. For example, the symbol $\sum_{i=1}^{5} i$ instructs us to add up all of the integers, designated by the letter i, as i goes from 1 to 5. Therefore $\sum_{i=1}^{5} i = 1 + 2 + 3 + 4 + 5 = 15$.

The expression "$i = 1$" below the Σ tells us to start summing with $i = 1$, and the 5 on top tells us to stop when $i = 5$.

Example:

Evaluate $\sum_{i=2}^{4} i^2$

$\sum_{i=2}^{4} i^2$ is equal to $2^2 + 3^2 + 4^2 = 4 + 9 + 16 = 29$

2. Formula for the Mean

Sample size: The sample size of a set of data is the number of data elements in it. The sample size of a set of data is usually represented by the letter n.

xn Notation: Consider a set of data of sample size n. Choosing to work with the letter x (any other letter could be used as well), we refer to the n data elements as $x_1, x_2, x_3, \ldots\ldots x_n$.

Mean Formula: Using the notation above, the mean of a set of data of sample size n can be written as $\dfrac{x_1 + x_2 + x_3 + \ldots\ldots + x_n}{n}$

It is standard to use the notation $\bar{x}$ (read "x-bar") to stand for the mean. Thus, the formula above can be written as

$$\bar{x} = \frac{x_1 + x_2 + x_3 + \ldots\ldots + x_n}{n}$$

Using Σ-notation, the formula above can be written as

$$\bar{x} = \frac{1}{n} \sum_{i=1}^{n} x_i$$

which is usually simplified as $\bar{x} = \dfrac{\Sigma x_i}{n}$

C. Measures of Variability

1. The Concept

Although it is very common to use measures of central tendency to describe a set of data, there are circumstances in which central tendency by itself is not enough. For example, consider two high school classes that both take the same math test. Let us assume that both classes have the same average grade of 75. Does this mean that we can assume that the students in the two classes are about equal in terms of math skills?

Suppose each class had 4 students. Further, suppose that those in the first class all got exactly 75 on their tests, but in the second class, the grades were 100, 100, 50, and 50. Clearly, the two classes do not contain students with approximately the same ability. The first class seems to have 4 "C"-level students, while the second class has 2 "A" students and 2 "F" students.

The mean is just a single number that represents the middle value. But the mean gives us no idea of the extent to which the numbers in a set of data are scattered or dispersed from the middle number. We use *measures of variability*, or *measures of dispersion* to assess this.

2. The Range

The range is the simplest measure of variability. It is simply the difference between the largest and the smallest numbers in a set. While it is easy to calculate and understand, it is not a particularly useful measure of variability since it only uses two data values and tells us nothing about the numbers in between.

Example:

Recall the gasoline mileage problem presented earlier in this chapter.

a. In order to determine the expected mileage for a particular car, an automobile manufacturer conducts a carefully controlled factory test on five of these cars. The results, in miles per gallon, are 24.3, 24.6, 23.8, 24.0, and 24.3. What is the range of this data?

$24.6 - 23.8 = 0.8$ miles per gallon

b. Suppose the car with the 23.8 miles per gallon had a faulty fuel injection system and obtained a mileage of 11.8 miles per gallon instead. What would the range of the data have been?

$24.6 - 11.8 = 12.8$ miles per gallon

Note how much the one faulty measurement changed the range of the data. For this reason, the range is not used very often.

3. The Mean Absolute Deviation

The Deviation from the Mean: Consider a set of data $x_1, x_2, \ldots, x_n$, which has a mean of $\bar{x}$. For each data element x_i, the deviation from the mean is the difference between the data value and the mean, $x_i - \bar{x}$.

One way to develop a measure of dispersion that takes every piece of data into account would be to compute the mean of a set of data and then find the "deviation from the mean" of every data value. Intuitively, if we add these up, we should get a number representing total deviation from the mean, which seems like a reasonable measure of dispersion. Unfortunately, adding these deviations together always yields the number 0.

Example: Find the sum of the deviations from the mean for the data 46, 54, 42, 46, and 32.

The mean for this data is 44. The following table enables us to determine the sum of the deviations from the mean.

Data Value	Deviation from Mean
46	2
54	10
42	−2
46	2
32	−12

Sum = 0

The Total Absolute Deviation: One way to avoid getting a sum of 0 would be to take the absolute value of each deviation before adding. We then obtain what is called the total absolute deviation.

Data Value	Deviation from Mean	Absolute Value
46	2	2
54	10	10
42	−2	2
46	2	2
32	−12	12

Total Absolute Deviation = 28

Mean Absolute Deviation: A measure of dispersion based on this concept is called the mean absolute deviation. We simply take the total absolute deviation and divide by n. In the example above, this would give us $\frac{28}{5} = 5.6$. This number tells us, in a sense, that on the average, each data value differs from the mean by about 5.6.

The general formula for the mean absolute deviation is:

$$\frac{1}{n} \sum_{i=1}^{n} \left| x_i - \overline{x} \right|$$

While the notion of the mean absolute deviation makes intuitive sense, the fact that it involves absolute values leads to serious theoretical difficulties in problems involving inference. Thus, it is not used very often. Instead of using absolute values, we must develop another way of avoiding a sum of 0.

4. The Variance

    Definition: The formula for variance is similar to that of the mean absolute deviation, except that instead of summing the absolute values of the deviations from the mean, we sum the squares of the deviations. Squaring guarantees that we will obtain a positive sum when adding.

    Formula: The formula for the variance is $\dfrac{\sum_{i=1}^{n}(x - \overline{x})^2}{n}$.

    To find the variance, therefore, we find the deviations from the mean, square them, add them, and divide by the number of terms.

    Example: Find the variance for the data in the example above.

Data Value	Deviation from Mean	Square of Deviation
46	2	4
54	10	100
42	-2	4
46	2	4
32	-12	144

Sum $= 256$

The variance is thus $\dfrac{256}{5} = 51.2$.

Disadvantages of the Variance: The variance has one primary disadvantage when used as a measure of dispersion: It is difficult to interpret its meaning, because, due to the squaring, we end up looking at a number that is relatively large compared to the data we are studying. However, we can "undo" the distortion that the squaring has introduced by taking the square root of the variance. When we do this, we obtain what is called the standard deviation—the most useful measure of variability.

5. The Standard Deviation

Definition: As described above, the standard deviation is simply the square root of the variance and is therefore computed $\sqrt{\dfrac{\sum\limits_{i=1}^{n}(x_i - \overline{x})^2}{n}}$.

Example: Find the standard deviation of the data in the exercise above.

Since we know the variance (51.2), the standard deviation is simply $\sqrt{51.2} \approx 7.16$.

Statisticians typically use the letter s or the lower case Greek letter sigma (σ) to stand for standard deviation.

Alternative Formulas for the Standard Deviation: Computing the standard deviation can be laborious and is best accomplished by using a table as shown in the problems below. There are two variations of the standard deviation formula that are also useful at times.

The first formula is equivalent to the standard deviation formula given above, and is sometimes easier to use. It can be shown that

$$\sqrt{\frac{\sum\limits^{i=1}(x - \overline{x})^2}{n}} = \sqrt{\frac{\sum x_i^2}{n} - \overline{x}^2}.$$

Another variation of the formula is useful when, in a given set of data values, the same values appear more than once. If the data is first grouped according to its frequency (for example, the value x_1 occurs f_1 times, x_2 occurs f_2 times, x_3 occurs f_3 times, etcetera), then the following expression may be used to compute the standard deviation.

For a set with n data points, k of which are different, we have standard deviation $= \sqrt{\dfrac{1}{n} \sum\limits_{i=1}^{k} f_i(x_i - \overline{x})^2}.$

D. Normal (Bell) Curves

Now that we know how to compute the standard deviation, let us interpret its meaning.

1. The Normal Distribution

The Normal (Bell) Curve: In the sciences, many different types of collections of data, which have been obtained by measuring physical quantities, display a surprising regularity. When the data is graphed, the pattern of the graph can often be closely approximated by a particular mathematical curve, know as a normal curve. A normal curve looks like a bell-shaped curve that extends infinitely in both directions. Data that results in a graph like that below is said to be normally distributed.

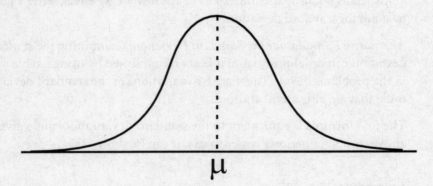

The peak of the curve corresponds to the mean of the group of data. (It is also the median and the mode of the data.) Intuitively, the fact that the curve peaks in the middle represents the fact that most of the data measured is close to the mean. As we move further away from the mean, either to the left or to the right, the curve descends, indicating that there are increasingly fewer values the farther we move away from the mean.

2. Mean, Standard Deviation, and the Bell Curve

We have already seen that the mean of a set of normally distributed data is represented by the peak of the bell curve. The mean and the standard deviation of a set of normally distributed data have the following properties.

1. It can be shown that about 68 percent of the data falls within one standard deviation of the mean. That is to say, if we use the Greek letter μ (mu) to represent the mean of a set of data and the Greek letter σ (lower

case sigma) to represent the standard deviation of a group of data, then the values of about 68 percent of the data lie between $\mu - \sigma$ and $\mu + \sigma$.

2. Further, about 95 percent of the data falls within two standard deviations of the mean or somewhere between the values of $\mu - 2\sigma$ and $\mu + 2\sigma$.

3. Finally, about 99 percent of the data falls within three standard deviations of the mean or somewhere between the values of $\mu - 3\sigma$ and $\mu + 3\sigma$.

Example:

Suppose that you have a set of data that has a mean of 120 and a standard deviation of 10. As long as this data is "normally distributed," we can conclude that approximately 68 percent of the data values lie within one standard deviation of the mean. This means, in this case, that 68 percent of the data values lie between $120 - 10 = 110$ and $120 + 10 = 130$. Similarly, about 95 percent of the data values will lie within 2 standard deviations from the mean; that is, in this case, between 100 and 140. Finally, about 99 percent (which is to say, virtually all) of the data will lie within three standard deviations from the mean. In this case, this means that almost all of the data values will fall between 90 and 150.

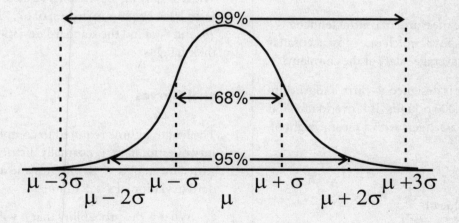

Questions

Measures of Central Tendency

1. Stanley bowls scores of 198, 188, and 215 in his first three games. What score must he bowl in his final game to obtain an average of 200?

2. At TMBG Incorporated, the owner earns an annual salary of $275,000. The two managers each earn $55,000, one supervisor earns $45,000, and the four office workers earn $30,000 each. What is the mean salary for the employees at TMBG Incorporated?

3. What is the median salary for the people at TMBG Incorporated?

4. What is the modal salary for the people at TMBG Incorporated?

5. Of the three measures of central tendency computed above, which one most accurately reflects the average salary at the company?

6. An elevator is designed to carry a maximum weight of 3,000 pounds. Is it overloaded if it carries 17 passengers with a mean weight of 140 pounds?

Σ – Notation

1. Find the value of $\sum_{i=1}^{7} x_i$.

2. What is the value of $\sum_{i=1}^{100} (-1)^i$?

3. Write the expression $1^2 + 2^2 + 3^2 + 4^2 + 5^2$ in sigma notation.

4. Write the expression $-9 + 16 - 25 + 36 - 49 + 64$ in sigma notation.

Measures of Variability

1. The annual incomes of 5 families living on Larchmont Rd. are $32,000, $35,000, $37,500, $39,000, and $320,000. What is the range of the annual incomes?

2. The number of people who went to the Motor Vehicle Bureau to register automobiles on Monday through Friday of a particular week was 390, 400, 380, 420, and 410. Compute the range, variance, and standard deviation for this data.

3. The five starting players on a basketball team have heights, in inches, of 67, 72, 76, 76, and 84. Find the standard deviation of their heights.

Normal Curves

1. The length of time required to complete a jury questionnaire is normally distributed with a mean of $\mu = 40$ minutes and a standard deviation of $s = 5$ minutes.

   a. What is the probability that it will take a prospective juror between 35 and 45 minutes to complete the questionnaire?

   b. What is the probability that it will take a prospective juror between 30 and 50 minutes to complete the questionnaire?

2. The scores on a standardized admissions test are normally distributed with a mean of 500 and a standard deviation of 100.

   a. What is the probability that a randomly selected student will score between 400 and 600 on the test?

   b. What is the probability that a randomly selected student will score 500 or greater on the test?

3. The annual amount of snowfall in Buffalo, New York, is 32 inches, with a standard deviation of 4 inches. Assuming the amount of snowfall is normally distributed:

   a. What is the probability that in any one year the amount of snowfall will be between 20 and 44 inches?

   b. What is the probability that in any one year the amount of snowfall will be between 32 and 36 inches?

4. It is estimated that 68 percent of people will be able to assemble a particular outdoor gas grill in 2.5 to 3.5 hours. Assuming gas grill assembly times to be normally distributed with a mean of 3 hours:

   a. What is the probability that a person will be able to assemble the grill in 2 to 4 hours?

   b. What is the probability that a person will be able to assemble the grill in 3 to 4 hours?

Answers

Measures of Central Tendency

1. Let S = his score for the last game. Then:

$$\frac{198 + 188 + 215 + S}{4} = 200$$

$$\frac{601 + S}{4} = 200$$

$$601 + S = 800$$

$$S = 199$$

Stanley must bowl 199 in his final game.

2. The salaries (in thousands) are $275, $55, $55, $45, $30, $30, $30, and $30. The mean salary for the employees at TMBG Incorporated, in thousands, is

$$\frac{275 + 55 + 55 + 45 + 30 + 30 + 30 + 30}{8} =$$

$$\frac{550}{8} = 68.75$$

The mean salary is $68,750.

3. The median salary for the people at TMBG Incorporated is the mean of the two salaries in the middle, $45 and $30. Thus, the median salary is $37,500.

4. The modal salary for the people at TMBG Incorporated is $30,000—the most frequently occurring rate of pay.

5. The mean is strongly affected by the owner's salary and seems too high to give a good feel for the typical salary. The mode is too low; half of the people at the company make well more than $30,000. The median seems to be the best. It tells us that half the people earn more and half the people earn less than $37,500.

6. Since the mean is the total of the data divided by the number of pieces of data, that is

$$\text{mean} = \frac{\text{total}}{\text{number}}, \text{ we have}$$

$$(\text{mean})(\text{number}) = \text{total}.$$

Thus, the weight of the people on the elevator totals $(17)(140) = 2,380$. It is not overloaded.

Σ–Notation

1. $\displaystyle\sum_{i=1}^{7} x_i = 1 + 2 + 3 + 4 + 5 + 6 + 7 = 28$

2. $\displaystyle\sum_{i=1}^{100} (-1)^i = (-1)^1 + (-1)^2 + (-1)^3$

$$+ (-1)^4 + \ldots\ldots + (-1)^{100} =$$

$$-1 + 1 - 1 + 1 \ldots\ldots = 0.$$

3. $1^2 + 2^2 + 3^2 + 4^2 + 5^2 = \displaystyle\sum_{i=1}^{5} i^2$

4. $-9 + 16 - 25 + 36 - 49 + 64 =$

$$\sum_{i=3}^{8} (-1)^i (i^2)$$

Measures of Variability

1. The range is $320,000 - 32,000 = \$288,000$. It can be seen that the range is not a particularly good measure of variability, since 4 of the 5 values are within $7,000 of each other.

2. The range is $420 - 380 = 40$.

To compute the variance and standard deviation, we first need to find the mean.

$$\bar{x} = \frac{1}{n} \sum_{i=1}^{n} x_i$$

$$= \frac{390 + 400 + 380 + 420 + 410}{5}$$

$$= \frac{2{,}000}{5} = 400$$

x_i	$x_i - \bar{x}$	$(x_i - \bar{x})^2$
390	-10	100
400	0	0
380	-20	400
420	20	400
410	10	100

Thus, $\sum (x_i - \bar{x})^2 = 1000$, and the variance is $\frac{1000}{5} = 200$. The standard deviation, which is the square root of this number, is $\sqrt{200} \approx 14.1$.

3. $\bar{x} = \frac{\sum x_i}{n} = \frac{67 + 72 + 76 + 76 + 84}{5} = 75$

x_i	$x_i - \bar{x}$	$(x_i - \bar{x})^2$
67	-8	64
72	-3	9
76	1	1
76	1	1
84	9	81

$$\sum (x_i - \bar{x})^2 = 64 + 9 + 1 + 1 + 81 = 156$$

$$\frac{\sum (x_i - \bar{x})^2}{n} = \frac{156}{5} = 31.2$$

(This is the variance.)

$$\sqrt{31.2} \approx 5.59$$

The standard deviation is approximately 5.59.

Normal Curves

1. a. About 68 percent

   b. About 95 percent

2. a. 68 percent

   b. 50 percent

3. a. Since the two given numbers are three standard deviations from the mean on either side, each year it is virtually certain that the amount of snowfall will be within the given range.

   b. The probability that an amount of snowfall will be within one standard deviation of the mean on either side is about 68 percent. Thus, the probability that the amount of snowfall will be within one standard deviation above the mean is about

   $$\frac{68\%}{2} = 34\%.$$

4. a. Because the mean of 3 hours is midway between 2.5 hours and 3.5 hours, the probability of 68% of having the assembly time between 2.5 hours and 3.5 hours means that the standard deviation is $3.5 - 3.0$, or 0.5 hours.

Approximately 95 percent will be able to assemble the grill in the given time. The times given are two standard deviations from the mean on either side.

b. The probability that the assembly time will be above the mean and within two standard deviations of the mean is $\frac{95\%}{2} = 47.5\%$.

Part IV

Practice Tests and Answers

Reference Formulas for Mathematics

Pythagorean and Quotient Identities

$$\sin^2 A + \cos^2 A = 1 \qquad \tan A = \frac{\sin A}{\cos A}$$

$$\tan^2 A + 1 = \sec^2 A$$

$$\cot^2 A + 1 = \csc^2 A \qquad \cot A = \frac{\cos A}{\sin A}$$

Functions of the Sum of Two Angles

$$\sin (A + B) = \sin A \cos B + \cos A \sin B$$

$$\cos (A + B) = \cos A \cos B - \sin A \sin B$$

$$\tan (A + B) = \frac{\tan A + \tan B}{1 - \tan A \tan B}$$

Functions of the Difference of Two Angles

$$\sin (A - B) = \sin A \cos B - \cos A \sin B$$

$$\cos (A - B) = \cos A \cos B + \sin A \sin B$$

$$\tan (A - B) = \frac{\tan A - \tan B}{1 + \tan A \tan B}$$

Law of Sines

$$\frac{a}{\sin A} = \frac{b}{\sin B} = \frac{c}{\sin C}$$

Law of Cosines

$$a^2 = b^2 + c^2 - 2bc \cos A$$

Functions of the Double Angle

$$\sin 2A = 2 \sin A \cos A$$

$$\cos 2A = \cos^2 A - \sin^2 A$$

$$\cos 2A = 2 \cos^2 A - 1$$

$$\cos 2A = 1 - 2 \sin^2 A$$

$$\tan 2A = \frac{2 \tan A}{1 - \tan^2 A}$$

Functions of the Half Angle

$$\sin \tfrac{1}{2}A = \pm \sqrt{\frac{1 - \cos A}{2}}$$

$$\cos \tfrac{1}{2}A = \pm \sqrt{\frac{1 + \cos A}{2}}$$

$$\tan \tfrac{1}{2}A = \pm \sqrt{\frac{1 - \cos A}{1 + \cos A}}$$

Area of Triangle

$$K = \tfrac{1}{2}ab \sin C$$

Standard Deviation

$$\text{S.D.} = \sqrt{\frac{1}{n} \sum_{i=1}^{n} (\bar{x} - x_i)^2}$$

Table A: Common Logarithms of Numbers*

N	0	1	2	3	4	5	6	7	8	9
10	0000	0043	0086	0128	0170	0212	0253	0294	0334	0374
11	0414	0453	0492	0531	0569	0607	0645	0682	0719	0755
12	0792	0828	0864	0899	0934	0969	1004	1038	1072	1106
13	1139	1173	1206	1239	1271	1303	1335	1367	1399	1430
14	1461	1492	1523	1553	1584	1614	1644	1673	1703	1732
15	1761	1790	1818	1847	1875	1903	1931	1959	1987	2014
16	2041	2068	2095	2122	2148	2175	2201	2227	2253	2279
17	2304	2330	2355	2380	2405	2430	2455	2480	2504	2529
18	2553	2577	2601	2625	2648	2672	2695	2718	2742	2765
19	2788	2810	2833	2856	2878	2900	2923	2945	2967	2989
20	3010	3032	3054	3075	3096	3118	3139	3160	3181	3201
21	3222	3243	3263	3284	3304	3324	3345	3365	3385	3404
22	3424	3444	3464	3483	3502	3522	3541	3560	3579	3598
23	3617	3636	3655	3674	3692	3711	3729	3747	3766	3784
24	3802	3820	3838	3856	3874	3892	3909	3927	3945	3962
25	3979	3997	4014	4031	4048	4065	4082	4099	4116	4133
26	4150	4166	4183	4200	4216	4232	4249	4265	4281	4298
27	4314	4330	4346	4362	4378	4393	4409	4425	4440	4456
28	4472	4487	4502	4518	4533	4548	4564	4579	4594	4609
29	4624	4639	4654	4669	4683	4698	4713	4728	4742	4757
30	4771	4786	4800	4814	4829	4843	4857	4871	4886	4900
31	4914	4928	4942	4955	4969	4983	4997	5011	5024	5038
32	5051	5065	5079	5092	5105	5119	5132	5145	5159	5172
33	5185	5198	5211	5224	5237	5250	5263	5276	5289	5302
34	5315	5328	5340	5353	5366	5378	5391	5403	5416	5428
35	5441	5453	5465	5478	5490	5502	5514	5527	5539	5551
36	5563	5575	5587	5599	5611	5623	5635	5647	5658	5670
37	5682	5694	5705	5717	5729	5740	5752	5763	5775	5786
38	5798	5809	5821	5832	5843	5855	5866	5877	5888	5899
39	5911	5922	5933	5944	5955	5966	5977	5988	5999	6010
40	6021	6031	6042	6053	6064	6075	6085	6096	6107	6117
41	6128	6138	6149	6160	6170	6180	6191	6201	6212	6222
42	6232	6243	6253	6263	6274	6284	6294	6304	6314	6325
43	6335	6345	6355	6365	6375	6385	6395	6405	6415	6425
44	6435	6444	6454	6464	6474	6484	6493	6503	6513	6522
45	6532	6542	6551	6561	6571	6580	6590	6599	6609	6618
46	6628	6637	6646	6656	6665	6675	6684	6693	6702	6712
47	6721	6730	6739	6749	6758	6767	6776	6785	6794	6803
48	6812	6821	6830	6839	6848	6857	6866	6875	6884	6893
49	6902	6911	6920	6928	6937	6946	6955	6964	6972	6981
50	6990	6998	7007	7016	7024	7033	7042	7050	7059	7067
51	7076	7084	7093	7101	7110	7118	7126	7135	7143	7152
52	7160	7168	7177	7185	7193	7202	7210	7218	7226	7235
53	7243	7251	7259	7267	7275	7284	7292	7300	7308	7316
54	7324	7332	7340	7348	7356	7364	7372	7380	7388	7396
N	0	1	2	3	4	5	6	7	8	9

* This table gives the mantissas of numbers with the decimal point omitted in each case. Characteristics are determined from the numbers by inspection.

Table A: Common Logarithms of Numbers*

N	0	1	2	3	4	5	6	7	8	9
55	7404	7412	7419	7427	7435	7443	7451	7459	7466	7474
56	7482	7490	7497	7505	7513	7520	7528	7536	7543	7551
57	7559	7566	7574	7582	7589	7597	7604	7612	7619	7627
58	7634	7642	7649	7657	7664	7672	7679	7686	7694	7701
59	7709	7716	7723	7731	7738	7745	7752	7760	7767	7774
60	7782	7789	7796	7803	7810	7818	7825	7832	7839	7846
61	7853	7860	7868	7875	7882	7889	7896	7903	7910	7917
62	7924	7931	7938	7945	7952	7959	7966	7973	7980	7987
63	7993	8000	8007	8014	8021	8028	8035	8041	8048	8055
64	8062	8069	8075	8082	8089	8096	8102	8109	8116	8122
65	8129	8136	8142	8149	8156	8162	8169	8176	8182	8189
66	8195	8202	8209	8215	8222	8228	8235	8241	8248	8254
67	8261	8267	8274	8280	8287	8293	8299	8306	8312	8319
68	8325	8331	8338	8344	8351	8357	8363	8370	8376	8382
69	8388	8395	8401	8407	8414	8420	8426	8432	8439	8445
70	8451	8457	8463	8470	8476	8482	8488	8494	8500	8506
71	8513	8519	8525	8531	8537	8543	8549	8555	8561	8567
72	8573	8579	8585	8591	8597	8603	8609	8615	8621	8627
73	8633	8639	8645	8651	8657	8663	8669	8675	8681	8686
74	8692	8698	8704	8710	8716	8722	8727	8733	8739	8745
75	8751	8756	8762	8768	8774	8779	8785	8791	8797	8802
76	8808	8814	8820	8825	8831	8837	8842	8848	8854	8859
77	8865	8871	8876	8882	8887	8893	8899	8904	8910	8915
78	8921	8927	8932	8938	8943	8949	8954	8960	8965	8971
79	8976	8982	8987	8993	8998	9004	9009	9015	9020	9025
80	9031	9036	9042	9047	9053	9058	9063	9069	9074	9079
81	9085	9090	9096	9101	9106	9112	9117	9122	9128	9133
82	9138	9143	9149	9154	9159	9165	9170	9175	9180	9186
83	9191	9196	9201	9206	9212	9217	9222	9227	9232	9238
84	9243	9248	9253	9258	9263	9269	9274	9279	9284	9289
85	9294	9299	9304	9309	9315	9320	9325	9330	9335	9340
86	9345	9350	9355	9360	9365	9370	9375	9380	9385	9390
87	9395	9400	9405	9410	9415	9420	9425	9430	9435	9440
88	9445	9450	9455	9460	9465	9469	9474	9479	9484	9489
89	9494	9499	9504	9509	9513	9518	9523	9528	9533	9538
90	9542	9547	9552	9557	9562	9566	9571	9576	9581	9586
91	9590	9595	9600	9605	9609	9614	9619	9624	9628	9633
92	9638	9643	9647	9652	9657	9661	9666	9671	9675	9680
93	9685	9689	9694	9699	9703	9708	9713	9717	9722	9727
94	9731	9736	9741	9745	9750	9754	9759	9763	9768	9773
95	9777	9782	9786	9791	9795	9800	9805	9809	9814	9818
96	9823	9827	9832	9836	9841	9845	9850	9854	9859	9863
97	9868	9872	9877	9881	9886	9890	9894	9899	9903	9908
98	9912	9917	9921	9926	9930	9934	9939	9943	9948	9952
99	9956	9961	9965	9969	9974	9978	9983	9987	9991	9996
N	0	1	2	3	4	5	6	7	8	9

* This table gives the mantissas of numbers with the decimal point omitted in each case. Characteristics are determined from the numbers by inspection.

Table B: Values of Trigonometric Functions

Angle	Sin	Cos	Tan	Cot		
0° 00′	.0000	1.0000	.0000	—	90°	00′
10	.0029	1.0000	.0029	343.77		50
20	.0058	1.0000	.0058	171.89		40
30	.0087	1.0000	.0087	114.59		30
40	.0116	.9999	.0116	85.940		20
50	.0145	.9999	.0145	68.750		10
1° 00′	.0175	.9998	.0175	57.290	89°	00′
10	.0204	.9998	.0204	49.104		50
20	.0233	.9997	.0233	42.964		40
30	.0262	.9997	.0262	38.188		30
40	.0291	.9996	.0291	34.368		20
50	.0320	.9995	.0320	31.242		10
2° 00′	.0349	.9994	.0349	28.636	88°	00′
10	.0378	.9993	.0378	26.432		50
20	.0407	.9992	.0407	24.542		40
30	.0436	.9990	.0437	22.904		30
40	.0465	.9989	.0466	21.470		20
50	.0494	.9988	.0495	20.206		10
3° 00′	.0523	.9986	.0524	19.081	87°	00′
10	.0552	.9985	.0553	18.075		50
20	.0581	.9983	.0582	17.169		40
30	.0610	.9981	.0612	16.350		30
40	.0640	.9980	.0641	15.605		20
50	.0669	.9978	.0670	14.924		10
4° 00′	.0698	.9976	.0699	14.301	86°	00′
10	.0727	.9974	.0729	13.727		50
20	.0756	.9971	.0758	13.197		40
30	.0785	.9969	.0787	12.706		30
40	.0814	.9967	.0816	12.251		20
50	.0843	.9964	.0846	11.826		10
5° 00′	.0872	.9962	.0875	11.430	85°	00′
10	.0901	.9959	.0904	11.059		50
20	.0929	.9957	.0934	10.712		40
30	.0958	.9954	.0963	10.385		30
40	.0987	.9951	.0992	10.078		20
50	.1016	.9948	.1022	9.7882		10
6° 00′	.1045	.9945	.1051	9.5144	84°	00′
10	.1074	.9942	.1080	9.2553		50
20	.1103	.9939	.1110	9.0098		40
30	.1132	.9936	.1139	8.7769		30
40	.1161	.9932	.1169	8.5555		20
50	.1190	.9929	.1198	8.3450		10
7° 00′	.1219	.9925	.1228	8.1443	83°	00′
10	.1248	.9922	.1257	7.9530		50
20	.1276	.9918	.1287	7.7704		40
30	.1305	.9914	.1317	7.5958		30
40	.1334	.9911	.1346	7.4287		20
50	.1363	.9907	.1376	7.2687		10
8° 00′	.1392	.9903	.1405	7.1154	82°	00′
10	.1421	.9899	.1435	6.9682		50
20	.1449	.9894	.1465	6.8269		40
30	.1478	.9890	.1495	6.6912		30
40	.1507	.9886	.1524	6.5606		20
50	.1536	.9881	.1554	6.4348		10
9° 00′	.1564	.9877	.1584	6.3138	81°	00′
10	.1593	.9872	.1614	6.1970		50
20	.1622	.9868	.1644	6.0844		40
30	.1650	.9863	.1673	5.9758		30
40	.1679	.9858	.1703	5.8708		20
50	.1708	.9853	.1733	5.7694		10
10° 00′	.1736	.9848	.1763	5.6713	80°	00′
10	.1765	.9843	.1793	5.5764		50
20	.1794	.9838	.1823	5.4845		40
30	.1822	.9833	.1853	5.3955		30
40	.1851	.9827	.1883	5.3093		20
50	.1880	.9822	.1914	5.2257		10
11° 00′	.1908	.9816	.1944	5.1446	79°	00′
10	.1937	.9811	.1974	5.0658		50
20	.1965	.9805	.2004	4.9894		40
30	.1994	.9799	.2035	4.9152		30
40	.2022	.9793	.2065	4.8430		20
50	.2051	.9787	.2095	4.7729		10
12° 00′	.2079	.9781	.2126	4.7046	78°	00′
	Cos	Sin	Cot	Tan	Angle	

Angle	Sin	Cos	Tan	Cot		
12° 00′	.2079	.9781	.2126	4.7046	78°	00′
10	.2108	.9775	.2156	4.6382		50
20	.2136	.9769	.2186	4.5736		40
30	.2164	.9763	.2217	4.5107		30
40	.2193	.9757	.2247	4.4494		20
50	.2221	.9750	.2278	4.3897		10
13° 00′	.2250	.9744	.2309	4.3315	77°	00′
10	.2278	.9737	.2339	4.2747		50
20	.2306	.9730	.2370	4.2193		40
30	.2334	.9724	.2401	4.1653		30
40	.2363	.9717	.2432	4.1126		20
50	.2391	.9710	.2462	4.0611		10
14° 00′	.2419	.9703	.2493	4.0108	76°	00′
10	.2447	.9696	.2524	3.9617		50
20	.2476	.9689	.2555	3.9136		40
30	.2504	.9681	.2586	3.8667		30
40	.2532	.9674	.2617	3.8208		20
50	.2560	.9667	.2648	3.7760		10
15° 00′	.2588	.9659	.2679	3.7321	75°	00′
10	.2616	.9652	.2711	3.6891		50
20	.2644	.9644	.2742	3.6470		40
30	.2672	.9636	.2773	3.6059		30
40	.2700	.9628	.2805	3.5656		20
50	.2728	.9621	.2836	3.5261		10
16° 00′	.2756	.9613	.2867	3.4874	74°	00′
10	.2784	.9605	.2899	3.4495		50
20	.2812	.9596	.2931	3.4124		40
30	.2840	.9588	.2962	3.3759		30
40	.2868	.9580	.2994	3.3402		20
50	.2896	.9572	.3026	3.3052		10
17° 00′	.2924	.9563	.3057	3.2709	73°	00′
10	.2952	.9555	.3089	3.2371		50
20	.2979	.9546	.3121	3.2041		40
30	.3007	.9537	.3153	3.1716		30
40	.3035	.9528	.3185	3.1397		20
50	.3062	.9520	.3217	3.1084		10
18° 00′	.3090	.9511	.3249	3.0777	72°	00′
10	.3118	.9502	.3281	3.0475		50
20	.3145	.9492	.3314	3.0178		40
30	.3173	.9483	.3346	2.9887		30
40	.3201	.9474	.3378	2.9600		20
50	.3228	.9465	.3411	2.9319		10
19° 00′	.3256	.9455	.3443	2.9042	71°	00′
10	.3283	.9446	.3476	2.8770		50
20	.3311	.9436	.3508	2.8502		40
30	.3338	.9426	.3541	2.8239		30
40	.3365	.9417	.3574	2.7980		20
50	.3393	.9407	.3607	2.7725		10
20° 00′	.3420	.9397	.3640	2.7475	70°	00′
10	.3448	.9387	.3673	2.7228		50
20	.3475	.9377	.3706	2.6985		40
30	.3502	.9367	.3739	2.6746		30
40	.3529	.9356	.3772	2.6511		20
50	.3557	.9346	.3805	2.6279		10
21° 00′	.3584	.9336	.3839	2.6051	69°	00′
10	.3611	.9325	.3872	2.5826		50
20	.3638	.9315	.3906	2.5605		40
30	.3665	.9304	.3939	2.5386		30
40	.3692	.9293	.3973	2.5172		20
50	.3719	.9283	.4006	2.4960		10
22° 00′	.3746	.9272	.4040	2.4751	68°	00′
10	.3773	.9261	.4074	2.4545		50
20	.3800	.9250	.4108	2.4342		40
30	.3827	.9239	.4142	2.4142		30
40	.3854	.9228	.4176	2.3945		20
50	.3881	.9216	.4210	2.3750		10
23° 00′	.3907	.9205	.4245	2.3559	67°	00′
10	.3934	.9194	.4279	2.3369		50
20	.3961	.9182	.4314	2.3183		40
30	.3987	.9171	.4348	2.2998		30
40	.4014	.9159	.4383	2.2817		20
50	.4041	.9147	.4417	2.2637		10
24° 00′	.4067	.9135	.4452	2.2460	66°	00′
	Cos	Sin	Cot	Tan	Angle	

Table B: Values of Trigonometric Functions

Angle	Sin	Cos	Tan	Cot	Angle
24° 00′	.4067	.9135	.4452	2.2460	66° 00′
10	.4094	.9124	.4487	2.2286	50
20	.4120	.9112	.4522	2.2113	40
30	.4147	.9100	.4557	2.1943	30
40	.4173	.9088	.4592	2.1775	20
50	.4200	.9075	.4628	2.1609	10
25° 00′	.4226	.9063	.4663	2.1445	65° 00′
10	.4253	.9051	.4699	2.1283	50
20	.4279	.9038	.4734	2.1123	40
30	.4305	.9026	.4770	2.0965	30
40	.4331	.9013	.4806	2.0809	20
50	.4358	.9001	.4841	2.0655	10
26° 00′	.4384	.8988	.4877	2.0503	64° 00′
10	.4410	.8975	.4913	2.0353	50
20	.4436	.8962	.4950	2.0204	40
30	.4462	.8949	.4986	2.0057	30
40	.4488	.8936	.5022	1.9912	20
50	.4514	.8923	.5059	1.9768	10
27° 00′	.4540	.8910	.5095	1.9626	63° 00′
10	.4566	.8897	.5132	1.9486	50
20	.4592	.8884	.5169	1.9347	40
30	.4617	.8870	.5206	1.9210	30
40	.4643	.8857	.5243	1.9074	20
50	.4669	.8843	.5280	1.8940	10
28° 00′	.4695	.8829	.5317	1.8807	62° 00′
10	.4720	.8816	.5354	1.8676	50
20	.4746	.8802	.5392	1.8546	40
30	.4772	.8788	.5430	1.8418	30
40	.4797	.8774	.5467	1.8291	20
50	.4823	.8760	.5505	1.8165	10
29° 00′	.4848	.8746	.5543	1.8040	61° 00′
10	.4874	.8732	.5581	1.7917	50
20	.4899	.8718	.5619	1.7796	40
30	.4924	.8704	.5658	1.7675	30
40	.4950	.8689	.5696	1.7556	20
50	.4975	.8675	.5735	1.7437	10
30° 00′	.5000	.8660	.5774	1.7321	60° 00′
10	.5025	.8646	.5812	1.7205	50
20	.5050	.8631	.5851	1.7090	40
30	.5075	.8616	.5890	1.6977	30
40	.5100	.8601	.5930	1.6864	20
50	.5125	.8587	.5969	1.6753	10
31° 00′	.5150	.8572	.6009	1.6643	59° 00′
10	.5175	.8557	.6048	1.6534	50
20	.5200	.8542	.6088	1.6426	40
30	.5225	.8526	.6128	1.6319	30
40	.5250	.8511	.6168	1.6212	20
50	.5275	.8496	.6208	1.6107	10
32° 00′	.5299	.8480	.6249	1.6003	58° 00′
10	.5324	.8465	.6289	1.5900	50
20	.5348	.8450	.6330	1.5798	40
30	.5373	.8434	.6371	1.5697	30
40	.5398	.8418	.6412	1.5597	20
50	.5422	.8403	.6453	1.5497	10
33° 00′	.5446	.8387	.6494	1.5399	57° 00′
10	.5471	.8371	.6536	1.5301	50
20	.5495	.8355	.6577	1.5204	40
30	.5519	.8339	.6619	1.5108	30
40	.5544	.8323	.6661	1.5013	20
50	.5568	.8307	.6703	1.4919	10
34° 00′	.5592	.8290	.6745	1.4826	56° 00′
10	.5616	.8274	.6787	1.4733	50
20	.5640	.8258	.6830	1.4641	40
30	.5664	.8241	.6873	1.4550	30
40	.5688	.8225	.6916	1.4460	20
50	.5712	.8208	.6959	1.4370	10
35° 00′	.5736	.8192	.7002	1.4281	55° 00′
10	.5760	.8175	.7046	1.4193	50
20	.5783	.8158	.7089	1.4106	40
30	.5807	.8141	.7133	1.4019	30
40	.5831	.8124	.7177	1.3934	20
50	.5854	.8107	.7221	1.3848	10
36° 00′	.5878	.8090	.7265	1.3764	54° 00′
	Cos	Sin	Cot	Tan	Angle

Angle	Sin	Cos	Tan	Cot	Angle
36° 00′	.5878	.8090	.7265	1.3764	54° 00′
10	.5901	.8073	.7310	1.3680	50
20	.5925	.8056	.7355	1.3597	40
30	.5948	.8039	.7400	1.3514	30
40	.5972	.8021	.7445	1.3432	20
50	.5995	.8004	.7490	1.3351	10
37° 00′	.6018	.7986	.7536	1.3270	53° 00′
10	.6041	.7969	.7581	1.3190	50
20	.6065	.7951	.7627	1.3111	40
30	.6088	.7934	.7673	1.3032	30
40	.6111	.7916	.7720	1.2954	20
50	.6134	.7898	.7766	1.2876	10
38° 00′	.6157	.7880	.7813	1.2799	52° 00′
10	.6180	.7862	.7860	1.2723	50
20	.6202	.7844	.7907	1.2647	40
30	.6225	.7826	.7954	1.2572	30
40	.6248	.7808	.8002	1.2497	20
50	.6271	.7790	.8050	1.2423	10
39° 00′	.6293	.7771	.8098	1.2349	51° 00′
10	.6316	.7753	.8146	1.2276	50
20	.6338	.7735	.8195	1.2203	40
30	.6361	.7716	.8243	1.2131	30
40	.6383	.7698	.8292	1.2059	20
50	.6406	.7679	.8342	1.1988	10
40° 00′	.6428	.7660	.8391	1.1918	50° 00′
10	.6450	.7642	.8441	1.1847	50
20	.6472	.7623	.8491	1.1778	40
30	.6494	.7604	.8541	1.1708	30
40	.6517	.7585	.8591	1.1640	20
50	.6539	.7566	.8642	1.1571	10
41° 00′	.6561	.7547	.8693	1.1504	49° 00′
10	.6583	.7528	.8744	1.1436	50
20	.6604	.7509	.8796	1.1369	40
30	.6626	.7490	.8847	1.1303	30
40	.6648	.7470	.8899	1.1237	20
50	.6670	.7451	.8952	1.1171	10
42° 00′	.6691	.7431	.9004	1.1106	48° 00′
10	.6713	.7412	.9057	1.1041	50
20	.6734	.7392	.9110	1.0977	40
30	.6756	.7373	.9163	1.0913	30
40	.6777	.7353	.9217	1.0850	20
50	.6799	.7333	.9271	1.0786	10
43° 00′	.6820	.7314	.9325	1.0724	47° 00′
10	.6841	.7294	.9380	1.0661	50
20	.6862	.7274	.9435	1.0599	40
30	.6884	.7254	.9490	1.0538	30
40	.6905	.7234	.9545	1.0477	20
50	.6926	.7214	.9601	1.0416	10
44° 00′	.6947	.7193	.9657	1.0355	46° 00′
10	.6967	.7173	.9713	1.0295	50
20	.6988	.7153	.9770	1.0235	40
30	.7009	.7133	.9827	1.0176	30
40	.7030	.7112	.9884	1.0117	20
50	.7050	.7092	.9942	1.0058	10
45° 00′	.7071	.7071	1.0000	1.0000	45° 00′
	Cos	Sin	Cot	Tan	Angle

Table C: Logarithms of Trigonometric Functions*

Angle	L Sin	L Cos	L Tan	L Cot	Angle
0° 00'	—	10.0000	—		90° 00'
10	7.4637	10.0000	7.4637	12.5363	50
20	7.7648	10.0000	7.7648	12.2352	40
30	7.9408	10.0000	7.9409	12.0591	30
40	8.0658	10.0000	8.0658	11.9342	20
50	8.1627	10.0000	8.1627	11.8373	10
1° 00'	8.2419	9.9999	8.2419	11.7581	89° 00'
10	8.3088	9.9999	8.3089	11.6911	50
20	8.3668	9.9999	8.3669	11.6331	40
30	8.4179	9.9999	8.4181	11.5819	30
40	8.4637	9.9998	8.4638	11.5362	20
50	8.5050	9.9998	8.5053	11.4947	10
2° 00'	8.5428	9.9997	8.5431	11.4569	88° 00'
10	8.5776	9.9997	8.5779	11.4221	50
20	8.6097	9.9996	8.6101	11.3899	40
30	8.6397	9.9996	8.6401	11.3599	30
40	8.6677	9.9995	8.6682	11.3318	20
50	8.6940	9.9995	8.6945	11.3055	10
3° 00'	8.7188	9.9994	8.7194	11.2806	87° 00'
10	8.7423	9.9993	8.7429	11.2571	50
20	8.7645	9.9993	8.7652	11.2348	40
30	8.7857	9.9992	8.7865	11.2135	30
40	8.8059	9.9991	8.8067	11.1933	20
50	8.8251	9.9990	8.8261	11.1739	10
4° 00'	8.8436	9.9989	8.8446	11.1554	86° 00'
10	8.8613	9.9989	8.8624	11.1376	50
20	8.8783	9.9988	8.8795	11.1205	40
30	8.8946	9.9987	8.8960	11.1040	30
40	8.9104	9.9986	8.9118	11.0882	20
50	8.9256	9.9985	8.9272	11.0728	10
5° 00'	8.9403	9.9983	8.9420	11.0580	85° 00'
10	8.9545	9.9982	8.9563	11.0437	50
20	8.9682	9.9981	8.9701	11.0299	40
30	8.9816	9.9980	8.9836	11.0164	30
40	8.9945	9.9979	8.9966	11.0034	20
50	9.0070	9.9977	9.0093	10.9907	10
6° 00'	9.0192	9.9976	9.0216	10.9784	84° 00'
10	9.0311	9.9975	9.0336	10.9664	50
20	9.0426	9.9973	9.0453	10.9547	40
30	9.0539	9.9972	9.0567	10.9433	30
40	9.0648	9.9971	9.0678	10.9322	20
50	9.0755	9.9969	9.0786	10.9214	10
7° 00'	9.0859	9.9968	9.0891	10.9109	83° 00'
10	9.0961	9.9966	9.0995	10.9005	50
20	9.1060	9.9964	9.1096	10.8904	40
30	9.1157	9.9963	9.1194	10.8806	30
40	9.1252	9.9961	9.1291	10.8709	20
50	9.1345	9.9959	9.1385	10.8615	10
8° 00'	9.1436	9.9958	9.1478	10.8522	82° 00'
10	9.1525	9.9956	9.1569	10.8431	50
20	9.1612	9.9954	9.1658	10.8342	40
30	9.1697	9.9952	9.1745	10.8255	30
40	9.1781	9.9950	9.1831	10.8169	20
50	9.1863	9.9948	9.1915	10.8085	10
9° 00'	9.1943	9.9946	9.1997	10.8003	81° 00'
10	9.2022	9.9944	9.2078	10.7922	50
20	9.2100	9.9942	9.2158	10.7842	40
30	9.2176	9.9940	9.2236	10.7764	30
40	9.2251	9.9938	9.2313	10.7687	20
50	9.2324	9.9936	9.2389	10.7611	10
10° 00'	9.2397	9.9934	9.2463	10.7537	80° 00'
10	9.2468	9.9931	9.2536	10.7464	50
20	9.2538	9.9929	9.2609	10.7391	40
30	9.2606	9.9927	9.2680	10.7320	30
40	9.2674	9.9924	9.2750	10.7250	20
50	9.2740	9.9922	9.2819	10.7181	10
11° 00'	9.2806	9.9919	9.2887	10.7113	79° 00'
10	9.2870	9.9917	9.2953	10.7047	50
20	9.2934	9.9914	9.3020	10.6980	40
30	9.2997	9.9912	9.3085	10.6915	30
40	9.3058	9.9909	9.3149	10.6851	20
50	9.3119	9.9907	9.3212	10.6788	10
12° 00'	9.3179	9.9904	9.3275	10.6725	78° 00'
	L Cos	L Sin	L Cot	L Tan	Angle

Angle	L Sin	L Cos	L Tan	L Cot	Angle
12° 00'	9.3179	9.9904	9.3275	10.6725	78° 00'
10	9.3238	9.9901	9.3336	10.6664	50
20	9.3296	9.9899	9.3397	10.6603	40
30	9.3353	9.9896	9.3458	10.6542	30
40	9.3410	9.9893	9.3517	10.6483	20
50	9.3466	9.9890	9.3576	10.6424	10
13° 00'	9.3521	9.9887	9.3634	10.6366	77° 00'
10	9.3575	9.9884	9.3691	10.6309	50
20	9.3629	9.9881	9.3748	10.6252	40
30	9.3682	9.9878	9.3804	10.6196	30
40	9.3734	9.9875	9.3859	10.6141	20
50	9.3786	9.9872	9.3914	10.6086	10
14° 00'	9.3837	9.9869	9.3968	10.6032	76° 00'
10	9.3887	9.9866	9.4021	10.5979	50
20	9.3937	9.9863	9.4074	10.5926	40
30	9.3986	9.9859	9.4127	10.5873	30
40	9.4035	9.9856	9.4178	10.5822	20
50	9.4083	9.9853	9.4230	10.5770	10
15° 00'	9.4130	9.9849	9.4281	10.5719	75° 00'
10	9.4177	9.9846	9.4331	10.5669	50
20	9.4223	9.9843	9.4381	10.5619	40
30	9.4269	9.9839	9.4430	10.5570	30
40	9.4314	9.9836	9.4479	10.5521	20
50	9.4359	9.9832	9.4527	10.5473	10
16° 00'	9.4403	9.9828	9.4575	10.5425	74° 00'
10	9.4447	9.9825	9.4622	10.5378	50
20	9.4491	9.9821	9.4669	10.5331	40
30	9.4533	9.9817	9.4716	10.5284	30
40	9.4576	9.9814	9.4762	10.5238	20
50	9.4618	9.9810	9.4808	10.5192	10
17° 00'	9.4659	9.9806	9.4853	10.5147	73° 00'
10	9.4700	9.9802	9.4898	10.5102	50
20	9.4741	9.9798	9.4943	10.5057	40
30	9.4781	9.9794	9.4987	10.5013	30
40	9.4821	9.9790	9.5031	10.4969	20
50	9.4861	9.9786	9.5075	10.4925	10
18° 00'	9.4900	9.9782	9.5118	10.4882	72° 00'
10	9.4939	9.9778	9.5161	10.4839	50
20	9.4977	9.9774	9.5203	10.4797	40
30	9.5015	9.9770	9.5245	10.4755	30
40	9.5052	9.9765	9.5287	10.4713	20
50	9.5090	9.9761	9.5329	10.4671	10
19° 00'	9.5126	9.9757	9.5370	10.4630	71° 00'
10	9.5163	9.9752	9.5411	10.4589	50
20	9.5199	9.9748	9.5451	10.4549	40
30	9.5235	9.9743	9.5491	10.4509	30
40	9.5270	9.9739	9.5531	10.4469	20
50	9.5306	9.9734	9.5571	10.4429	10
20° 00'	9.5341	9.9730	9.5611	10.4389	70° 00'
10	9.5375	9.9725	9.5650	10.4350	50
20	9.5409	9.9721	9.5689	10.4311	40
30	9.5443	9.9716	9.5727	10.4273	30
40	9.5477	9.9711	9.5766	10.4234	20
50	9.5510	9.9706	9.5804	10.4196	10
21° 00'	9.5543	9.9702	9.5842	10.4158	69° 00'
10	9.5576	9.9697	9.5879	10.4121	50
20	9.5609	9.9692	9.5917	10.4083	40
30	9.5641	9.9687	9.5954	10.4046	30
40	9.5673	9.9682	9.5991	10.4009	20
50	9.5704	9.9677	9.6028	10.3972	10
22° 00'	9.5736	9.9672	9.6064	10.3936	68° 00'
10	9.5767	9.9667	9.6100	10.3900	50
20	9.5798	9.9661	9.6136	10.3864	40
30	9.5828	9.9656	9.6172	10.3828	30
40	9.5859	9.9651	9.6208	10.3792	20
50	9.5889	9.9646	9.6243	10.3757	10
23° 00'	9.5919	9.9640	9.6279	10.3721	67° 00'
10	9.5948	9.9635	9.6314	10.3686	50
20	9.5978	9.9629	9.6348	10.3652	40
30	9.6007	9.9624	9.6383	10.3617	30
40	9.6036	9.9618	9.6417	10.3583	20
50	9.6065	9.9613	9.6452	10.3548	10
24° 00'	9.6093	9.9607	9.6486	10.3514	66° 00'
	L Cos	L Sin	L Cot	L Tan	Angle

* These tables give the logarithms increased by 10. Hence in each case 10 should be subtracted.

Table C: Logarithms of Trigonometric Functions*

Angle	L Sin	L Cos	L Tan	L Cot	
24° 00′	9.6093	9.9607	9.6486	10.3514	66° 00′
10	9.6121	9.9602	9.6520	10.3480	50
20	9.6149	9.9596	9.6553	10.3447	40
30	9.6177	9.9590	9.6587	10.3413	30
40	9.6205	9.9584	9.6620	10.3380	20
50	9.6232	9.9579	9.6654	10.3346	10
25° 00′	9.6259	9.9573	9.6687	10.3313	65° 00′
10	9.6286	9.9567	9.6720	10.3280	50
20	9.6313	9.9561	9.6752	10.3248	40
30	9.6340	9.9555	9.6785	10.3215	30
40	9.6366	9.9549	9.6817	10.3183	20
50	9.6392	9.9543	9.6850	10.3150	10
26° 00′	9.6418	9.9537	9.6882	10.3118	64° 00′
10	9.6444	9.9530	9.6914	10.3086	50
20	9.6470	9.9524	9.6946	10.3054	40
30	9.6495	9.9518	9.6977	10.3023	30
40	9.6521	9.9512	9.7009	10.2991	20
50	9.6546	9.9505	9.7040	10.2960	10
27° 00′	9.6570	9.9499	9.7072	10.2928	63° 00′
10	9.6595	9.9492	9.7103	10.2897	50
20	9.6620	9.9486	9.7134	10.2866	40
30	9.6644	9.9479	9.7165	10.2835	30
40	9.6668	9.9473	9.7196	10.2804	20
50	9.6692	9.9466	9.7226	10.2774	10
28° 00′	9.6716	9.9459	9.7257	10.2743	62° 00′
10	9.6740	9.9453	9.7287	10.2713	50
20	9.6763	9.9446	9.7317	10.2683	40
30	9.6787	9.9439	9.7348	10.2652	30
40	9.6810	9.9432	9.7378	10.2622	20
50	9.6833	9.9425	9.7408	10.2592	10
29° 00′	9.6856	9.9418	9.7438	10.2562	61° 00′
10	9.6878	9.9411	9.7467	10.2533	50
20	9.6901	9.9404	9.7497	10.2503	40
30	9.6923	9.9397	9.7526	10.2474	30
40	9.6946	9.9390	9.7556	10.2444	20
50	9.6968	9.9383	9.7585	10.2415	10
30° 00′	9.6990	9.9375	9.7614	10.2386	60° 00′
10	9.7012	9.9368	9.7644	10.2356	50
20	9.7033	9.9361	9.7673	10.2327	40
30	9.7055	9.9353	9.7701	10.2299	30
40	9.7076	9.9346	9.7730	10.2270	20
50	9.7097	9.9338	9.7759	10.2241	10
31° 00′	9.7118	9.9331	9.7788	10.2212	59° 00′
10	9.7139	9.9323	9.7816	10.2184	50
20	9.7160	9.9315	9.7845	10.2155	40
30	9.7181	9.9308	9.7873	10.2127	30
40	9.7201	9.9300	9.7902	10.2098	20
50	9.7222	9.9292	9.7930	10.2070	10
32° 00′	9.7242	9.9284	9.7958	10.2042	58° 00′
10	9.7262	9.9276	9.7986	10.2014	50
20	9.7282	9.9268	9.8014	10.1986	40
30	9.7302	9.9260	9.8042	10.1958	30
40	9.7322	9.9252	9.8070	10.1930	20
50	9.7342	9.9244	9.8097	10.1903	10
33° 00′	9.7361	9.9236	9.8125	10.1875	57° 00′
10	9.7380	9.9228	9.8153	10.1847	50
20	9.7400	9.9219	9.8180	10.1820	40
30	9.7419	9.9211	9.8208	10.1792	30
40	9.7438	9.9203	9.8235	10.1765	20
50	9.7457	9.9194	9.8263	10.1737	10
34° 00′	9.7476	9.9186	9.8290	10.1710	56° 00′
10	9.7494	9.9177	9.8317	10.1683	50
20	9.7513	9.9169	9.8344	10.1656	40
30	9.7531	9.9160.	9.8371	10.1629	30
40	9.7550	9.9151	9.8398	10.1602	20
50	9.7568	9.9142	9.8425	10.1575	10
35° 00′	9.7586	9.9134	9.8452	10.1548	55° 00′
10	9.7604	9.9125	9.8479	10.1521	50
20	9.7622	9.9116	9.8506	10.1494	40
30	9.7640	9.9107	9.8533	10.1467	30
40	9.7657	9.9098	9.8559	10.1441	20
50	9.7675	9.9089	9.8586	10.1414	10
36° 00′	9.7692	9.9080	9.8613	10.1387	54° 00′
	L Cos	L Sin	L Cot	L Tan	Angle

Angle	L Sin	L Cos	L Tan	L Cot	
36° 00′	9.7692	9.9080	9.8613	10.1387	54° 00′
10	9.7710	9.9070	9.8639	10.1361	50
20	9.7727	9.9061	9.8666	10.1334	40
30	9.7744	9.9052	9.8692	10.1308	30
40	9.7761	9.9042	9.8718	10.1282	20
50	9.7778	9.9033	9.8745	10.1255	10
37° 00′	9.7795	9.9023	9.8771	10.1229	53° 00′
10	9.7811	9.9014	9.8797	10.1203	50
20	9.7828	9.9004	9.8824	10.1176	40
30	9.7844	9.8995	9.8850	10.1150	30
40	9.7861	9.8985	9.8876	10.1124	20
50	9.7877	9.8975	9.8902	10.1098	10
38° 00′	9.7893	9.8965	9.8928	10.1072	52° 00′
10	9.7910	9.8955	9.8954	10.1046	50
20	9.7926	9.8945	9.8980	10.1020	40
30	9.7941	9.8935	9.9006	10.0994	30
40	9.7957	9.8925	9.9032	10.0968	20
50	9.7973	9.8915	9.9058	10.0942	10
39° 00′	9.7989	9.8905	9.9084	10.0916	51° 00′
10	9.8004	9.8895	9.9110	10.0890	50
20	9.8020	9.8884	9.9135	10.0865	40
30	9.8035	9.8874	9.9161	10.0839	30
40	9.8050	9.8864	9.9187	10.0813	20
50	9.8066	9.8853.	9.9212	10.0788	10
40° 00′	9.8081	9.8843	9.9238	10.0762	50° 00′
10	9.8096	9.8832	9.9264	10.0736	50
20	9.8111	9.8821	9.9289	10.0711	40
30	9.8125	9.8810	9.9315	10.0685	30
40	9.8140	9.8800	9.9341	10.0659	20
50	9.8155	9.8789	9.9366	10.0634	10
41° 00′	9.8169	9.8778	9.9392	10.0608	49° 00′
10	9.8184	9.8767	9.9417	10.0583	50
20	9.8198	9.8756	9.9443	10.0557	40
30	9.8213	9.8745	9.9468	10.0532	30
40	9.8227	9.8733	9.9494	10.0506	20
50	9.8241	9.8722	9.9519	10.0481	10
42° 00′	9.8255	9.8711	9.9544	10.0456	48° 00′
10	9.8269	9.8699	9.9570	10.0430	50
20	9.8283	9.8688	9.9595	10.0405	40
30	9.8297	9.8676	9.9621	10.0379	30
40	9.8311	9.8665	9.9646	10.0354	20
50	9.8324	9.8653	9.9671	10.0329	10
43° 00′	9.8338	9.8641	9.9697	10.0303	47° 00′
10	9.8351	9.8629	9.9722	10.0278	50
20	9.8365	9.8618	9.9747	10.0253	40
30	9.8378	9.8606	9.9772	10.0228	30
40	9.8391	9.8594	9.9798	10.0202	20
50	9.8405	9.8582	9.9823	10.0177	10
44° 00′	9.8418	9.8569	9.9848	10.0152	46° 00′
10	9.8431	9.8557	9.9874	10.0126	50
20	9.8444	9.8545	9.9899	10.0101	40
30	9.8457	9.8532	9.9924	10.0076	30
40	9.8469	9.8520	9.9949	10.0051	20
50	9.8482	9.8507	9.9975	10.0025	10
45° 00′	9.8495	9.8495	10.0000	10.0000	45° 00′
	L Cos	L Sin	L Cot	L Tan	Angle

* These tables give the logarithms increased by 10. Hence in each case 10 should be subtracted.

Practice Test 2

Part I

Answer 30 questions from this part. Each correct answer will receive 2 credits. No partial credit will be allowed. Write your answers in the spaces provided on the separate answer sheet. Where applicable, answers may be left in terms of π or in radical form.   [60]

1 Express $\frac{5\pi}{9}$ radians in degree measure.

2 A translation maps (2,1) onto (–3,2). Find the image of (4,–1) under the same translation.

3 Express $3\sqrt{-16} - 2\sqrt{-9}$ in terms of i.

4 In $\triangle ABC$, $a = 6$, $b = 8$, and $\sin C = \frac{1}{4}$. Find the area of $\triangle ABC$.

5 Write the coordinates of P', the image of $P(5,-1)$ after a clockwise rotation of $180°$ about the origin.

6 Solve for x: $4^4 = 2^{3x-1}$

7 In the accompanying diagram, $\overline{TS}$ is tangent to circle O at S and $\overline{TUV}$ is a secant. If $TU = 3$ and $UV = 9$, find the length of $\overline{TS}$.

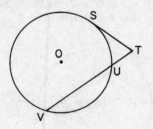

8 Find the value of $\cos\left(\text{Arc } \sin \frac{4}{5}\right)$.

9 Solve for y: $\dfrac{5}{3y} - \dfrac{6}{4y} = \dfrac{1}{6}$

10 Evaluate: $3\sum_{k=2}^{4} (k - 2)^2$

11 In $\triangle ABC$, $\sin A = \frac{1}{2}$, $\sin C = \frac{1}{3}$, and $a = 12$. Find the length of side c.

12 Factor completely: $x^3 - x^2 - 6x$

13 The probability that Team A will beat Team B in a sporting event is $\frac{2}{3}$. What is the probability that Team B will win all three games of a three-game series?

14 If $\sin \theta = 0.3347$, find the measure of positive acute angle θ to the *nearest minute*.

Directions (15–35): For *each* question chosen, write on the separate answer sheet the *numeral* preceding the word or expression that best completes the statement or answers the question.

15 If $f(x) = kx^2$ and $f(2) = 12$, then k equals
(1) 1   (3) 3
(2) 2   (4) 4

16 Which letter has horizontal line symmetry but not vertical line symmetry?
(1) H   (3) S
(2) K   (4) T

17 Which is an equation of the graph shown below?

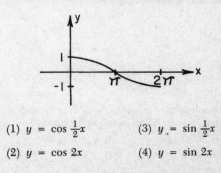

(1) $y = \cos \frac{1}{2}x$ (3) $y = \sin \frac{1}{2}x$
(2) $y = \cos 2x$ (4) $y = \sin 2x$

205

18 The expression $\dfrac{6}{3 - \sqrt{3}}$ is equivalent to

  (1) $2(3 + \sqrt{3})$ (3) $3 + \sqrt{3}$

  (2) $18 - 6\sqrt{3}$ (4) $3 - \sqrt{3}$

19 Which expression is equivalent to $\sin(-120°)$?

  (1) $\sin 60°$ (3) $\cos 30°$

  (2) $-\sin 60°$ (4) $-\sin 30°$

20 The expression $\frac{1}{2} \log a - 2 \log b$ is equivalent to

  (1) $\log \dfrac{\sqrt{a}}{b^2}$ (3) $\log \dfrac{a^2}{\sqrt{b}}$

  (2) $\log \sqrt{ab}$ (4) $\log (\sqrt{a} - b^2)$

21 Which is the solution set for $|x - 1| < 5$?

  (1) $\{x \,|\, -6 < x < 4\}$
  (2) $\{x \,|\, -4 < x < 6\}$
  (3) $\{x \,|\, x < -4 \text{ or } x > 6\}$
  (4) $\{x \,|\, x < -6 \text{ or } x > 4\}$

22 The value of $\left(\frac{8}{27}\right)^{-\frac{2}{3}}$ is

  (1) $\frac{4}{9}$ (3) $-\frac{2}{3}$

  (2) $-\frac{4}{9}$ (4) $\frac{9}{4}$

23 The expression $(2 + 3i)^2$ is equal to

  (1) -5 (3) $-5 + 12i$

  (2) 13 (4) $13 + 12i$

24 The fraction $\dfrac{1 + \dfrac{1}{x}}{1 - \dfrac{1}{x^2}}$ is equivalent to

  (1) x (3) $\dfrac{x}{x + 1}$

  (2) $-x$ (4) $\dfrac{x}{x - 1}$

25 If the graph of the equation $y = 3^x$ is reflected in the x-axis, the equation of the reflection is

  (1) $y = 3^{-x}$ (3) $y = \log_x 3$

  (2) $y = -(3^x)$ (4) $y = x^3$

26 If $x = 5^a$, then the value of $5x$ is

  (1) $x + 1$ (3) $a + 5$

  (2) 6^a (4) 5^{a+1}

27 The expression $\sin 2A + \cos A$ is equivalent to

  (1) $\cos A(2 \sin A + 1)$ (3) $2(\sin A + \cos A)$

  (2) $\cos A(\cos A + 1)$ (4) $\cos A(\sin A + 1)$

28 The third term of the expansion of $(x - 2y)^6$ is

  (1) $60x^4y^2$ (3) $160x^3y^3$

  (2) $-60x^4y^2$ (4) $-160x^3y^3$

29 The graph of which equation is symmetric with respect to the origin?

  (1) $y = -3$ (3) $y = \sin x$

  (2) $x = 2$ (4) $y = \cos x$

30 In a normal distribution, $\bar{x} + 2\sigma = 80$ and $\bar{x} - 2\sigma = 40$ when $\bar{x}$ represents the mean and σ represents the standard deviation. The standard deviation is

  (1) 10 (3) 30

  (2) 20 (4) 60

31 In the diagram below, chords $\overline{AB}$ and $\overline{CD}$ intersect at E. If $m\angle AEC = 4x$, $m\widehat{AC} = 120$, and $m\widehat{DB} = 2x$, what is the value of x?

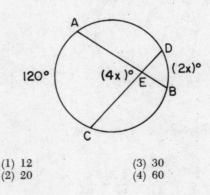

  (1) 12 (3) 30

  (2) 20 (4) 60

32 What is the solution set of the equation $x^2 + 9 = 0$?

  (1) $\{3i\}$ (3) $\{\ \}$

  (2) $\{-3i\}$ (4) $\{3i, -3i\}$

33 In right triangle ABC, m$\angle C$ = 90. Which equation is true for this triangle?

(1) $a = b \sin A$ (3) $a = c \cos A$
(2) $a = c \tan A$ (4) $a = c \sin A$

34 If m$\angle A$ = 30, $a = \sqrt{5}$, and $b = 6$, the number of triangles that can be constructed is
(1) 1
(2) 2
(3) 0
(4) an infinite number

35 What is the minimum value of f(θ) in the equation f(θ) = 3 sin 4θ?
(1) -1 (3) -3
(2) -2 (4) -4

Answers to the following questions are to be written on paper provided by the school.

Part II

Answer four questions from this part. Show all work unless otherwise directed.   [40]

36 Triangle *ABC* has coordinates *A*(–1,3), *B*(3,7), and *C*(0,6).

a On graph paper, draw and label △*ABC*.   [1]

b Graph and state the coordinates of △*A'B'C'*, the image of △*ABC* after a reflection in the line *y* = *x*.   [3]

c Graph and state the coordinates of △*A''B''C''*, the image of △*A'B'C'* following *r*_{y-axis} (△*A'B'C'*).   [3]

d Graph and state the coordinates of △*A'''B'''C'''*, the image of △*A''B''C''* after a translation that maps *P*(0,0) onto *P*(0,–5).   [3]

37 In the accompanying diagram of circle *O*, *AE* and *FD* are chords, *AOBG* is a diameter and is extended to *C*, *CDE* is a secant, *AE* ∥ *FD*, and m$\widehat{AE}$:m$\widehat{ED}$:m$\widehat{DG}$ = 5:3:1.

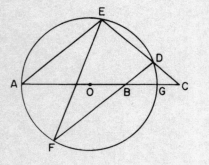

Find:

a m$\widehat{DG}$ [2]

b m∠*AEF*   [2]

c m∠*DBG*   [2]

d m∠*DCA*   [2]

e m∠*CDF*   [2]

38 In the accompanying diagram of right triangle *ACD*, *B* lies on *AC*, *BD* is drawn such that m∠*CDB* = 27, m∠*BDA* = 30, and *BC* = 9. Find *AB* to the *nearest tenth*.   [10]

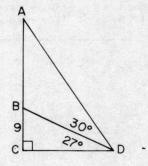

39 In the accompanying diagram, circle *O* is partitioned into six regions by diameters *AOB*, *COD*, *EOF*, *CD* ⊥ *AB*, and m∠*FOB* = 45.

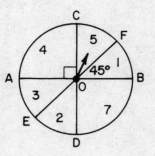

a If the spinner is spun once, determine

(1) *P*(3)   [1]

(2) *P*(EVEN)   [1]

(3) *P*(7)   [1]

b Determine the probability of obtaining

(1) *exactly two* EVEN's on three spins   [2]

(2) *no more than one* 3 on three spins   [3]

(3) *exactly one* 7 on four spins   [2]

☞ **GO RIGHT ON TO THE NEXT PAGE.**

40 The table below represents the weights of 10 girls from the seventh grade class. Find the standard deviation of these weights to the *nearest tenth*. [10]

Measure of Weight (x_i)	Frequency (f_i)
56	1
75	2
82	2
100	3
110	1
120	1

41 *a* If $x = \log_2 9$, find, to the *nearest tenth*, the value of x. [5]

b Prove the identity:
$$\sin 2x = \tan x(2 - 2\sin^2 x)$$ [5]

42 *a* Express the roots of the equation $x^2 + 1 = 4(x - 1)$ in $a + bi$ form. [5]

b Find, to the *nearest degree*, all values of θ in the interval $0° \le \theta \le 360°$ that satisfy the equation $3\sin^2 \theta + 5\sin \theta = 2$. [5]

Practice Test 2

Answers

1. The correct answer is $100°$.

    Use the fact that $180° = \pi$ radians.

    $$\frac{5\pi}{9} = \frac{5(180°)}{9} = 100°$$

2. The correct answer is $(-1,0)$.

    The x-value changes by $-3 - 2 = -5$ and the y-value changes by $2 - 1 = 1$. The image of $(4,-1)$ is $(4 - 5, -1 + 1) = (-1,0)$

3. The correct answer is $6i$.

    $3\sqrt{-16} - 2\sqrt{-9} = 3(4i) - 2(3i) = 12i - 6i$
    $= 6i$

4. The correct answer is 6.

    $\frac{1}{2}(6)(8)(\frac{1}{4}) = 3(2) = 6$

5. The correct answer is $(-5,1)$.

    A clockwise rotation of $180°$ will move the point two quadrants. It is in Quad IV and will move to Quad II and become $(-5,1)$.

6. The correct answer is 3.

    Rewrite 4 as 2^2 so that bases will be the same, then set exponents equal.

    $(2^2)^4 = 2^{3x-1}$

    $2^8 = 2^{3x-1}$

    $8 = 3x - 1$

    $9 = 3x$

    $3 = x$

7. The correct answer is 6.

    $(\overline{TS})^2 = (\overline{TU})(\overline{TV})$

    $= (3)(3 + 9)$

    $= 36$

    so $\overline{TS} = 6$

8. The correct answer is $\frac{3}{5}$.

    Using a right triangle, the angle whose arcsin $= \frac{4}{5}$ has hypotenuse of 5 and opposite side of 4. In order to find the cosine of that angle we need the adjacent side. Using the Pythagorean Theorem:

    $4^2 + x^2 = 5^2$

    $16 + x^2 = 25$

    $x^2 = 9$

    $x = 3$

    The opposite side is 3, so the cosine is $\frac{3}{5}$.

9. The correct answer is 1.

    Multiply by the LCD of $3y$ and $4y$, which is $12y$.

    $\frac{5}{3y} \cdot 12y - \frac{6}{4y} \cdot 12y = \frac{1}{6} \cdot 12y$

    $20 - 18 = 2y$

    $2 = 2y$

    $1 = y$

10. The correct answer is 15.

    Replace k with 2, 3 and 4 then add

    $3[(2-2)^2 + (3-2)^2 + (4-2)^2]$

    $3[0^2 + 1^2 + 2^2]$

    $3[0+1+4]$

    $3[5] = 15$

11. The correct answer is 8.

    Use the Law of Sines

    $\dfrac{c}{\frac{1}{3}} = \dfrac{12}{\frac{1}{2}}$ Cross multiply.

    $\dfrac{1}{2}c = \dfrac{1}{3} \cdot 12$

    $\dfrac{1}{2}c = 4$ Multiply by 2.

    $c = 8$

12. The correct answer is $x(x-3)(x+2)$

    $x(x^2 - x - 6)$Common factor.

    $x(x-3)(x+2)$Factor the trinomial.

13. The correct answer is $\dfrac{1}{27}$.

    The probability that Team B wins is $\dfrac{1}{3}$. The probability they win all three games is:

    $\left(\dfrac{1}{3}\right)\left(\dfrac{1}{3}\right)\left(\dfrac{1}{3}\right) = \dfrac{1}{27}$

14. The correct answer is $19°33'$.

    Since $\sin \theta = .3347$, use a calcuator to find θ = 19.55429. To find the minutes, subtract 19 and multiply by 60 to get 33.257768.

Thus $\theta = 19°\ 33'$.

15. The correct answer is (3).

    $f(2) = k(2)^2 = 4k$. If $4k = 12$ then $k = 3$.

16. The correct answer is (2).

    A vertical line through **K** does not yield two identical parts.

17. The correct answer is (1).

    The graph has the shape of one half of the graph of cos x. Thus, the period would be 4π and the equation is $y = \cos \dfrac{1}{2}x$.

18. The correct answer is (3).

    Rationalize the denominator by multiplying numerator and denominator by $3 + \sqrt{3}$

    $\dfrac{6}{3 - \sqrt{3}} \cdot \dfrac{3 + \sqrt{3}}{3 + \sqrt{3}}$

    $\dfrac{6(3 + \sqrt{3})}{(3 - \sqrt{3})(3 + \sqrt{3})} = \dfrac{18 + 6\sqrt{3}}{9 - 3}$

    $= \dfrac{18 + 6\sqrt{3}}{6} = \dfrac{18}{6} + \dfrac{6\sqrt{3}}{6} = 3 + \sqrt{3}$

19. The correct answer is (2).

    They both have the value of $\dfrac{-\sqrt{3}}{2}$.

20. The correct answer is (1).

    $\dfrac{1}{2}\log a - 2\log b = \log a^{\frac{1}{2}} - \log b^2$

    $= \log \sqrt{a} - \log b^2$

    $= \log \dfrac{\sqrt{a}}{b^2}$

21. The correct answer is (2).

    In order for $|x - 1| < 5 \qquad -5 < x - 1 < 5$
    add 1

    $-4 < x < 6$

22. The correct answer is (4).

    $$\left(\frac{8}{27}\right)^{-\frac{2}{3}} = \left(\sqrt[3]{\frac{8}{27}}\right)^{-2}$$

    $$= \left(\frac{2}{3}\right)^{-2}$$

    $$= \left(\frac{3}{2}\right)^{2}$$

    $$= \frac{9}{4}$$

23. The correct answer is (3).

    $$(2 + 3i)^2 = 4 + 12i + 9i^2$$

    $$= 4 + 12i + 9(-1)$$

    $$= 4 + 12i - 9$$

    $$= -5 + 12i$$

24. The correct answer is (4).

    Multiply by the LCD which is x^2.

    $$\frac{1 \cdot x^2 + \frac{1}{x} \cdot x^2}{1 \cdot x^2 - \frac{1}{x^2} \cdot x^2}$$

    $$= \frac{x^2 + x}{x^2 - 1} \qquad \text{Factor.}$$

    $$= \frac{x\cancel{(x+1)}}{\cancel{(x+1)}(x - 1)} \qquad \text{Cancel common factors.}$$

    $$= \frac{x}{x - 1}$$

25. The correct answer is (2).

    Reflection in the x-axis changes the sign of the y-values.

26. The correct answer is (4).

    The value of $5x$ is $5(5^a) = 5^1 \cdot 5^a = 5^{a + 1}$

27. The correct answer is (1).

    $$\sin 2A + \cos A = 2 \sin A \cos A + \cos A$$

    $$= \cos A (2 \sin A + 1)$$

28. The correct answer is (1).

    $${}_6C_2 x^4(- 2y)^2$$

    $$15x^4(4y^2)$$

    $$60x^4y^2$$

29. The correct answer is (3).

    The graph of $\sin x$ is symmetric with respect to the origin.

30. The correct answer is (1).

    Subtract the corresponding sides of the equation $\bar{x} - 2\sigma = 80$ from the sides of the equation $\bar{x} + 2\sigma = 80$.

    $$(\bar{x} + 2\sigma) - (\bar{x} - 2\sigma) = 80 - 40$$
    $$\bar{x} + 2\sigma - \bar{x} - 2\sigma = 40$$
    $$4\sigma = 40$$
    $$\sigma = 10$$

31. The correct answer is (2).

    $$4x = \frac{1}{2}(120 + 2x)$$

    $$4x = 60 + x$$

    $$3x = 60$$

    $$x = 20$$

213

The measure of an angle formed by two chords that intersect within a circle is equal to one-half the sum of the measures of the arcs intercepted by the angle and its vertical angle.

32. The correct answer is (4).

    $x^2 + 9 = 0$

    $x^2 = -9$

    $x = \pm\sqrt{-9}$

    $x = \pm 3i$

33. The correct answer is (4).

    Since $\sin A = \dfrac{\text{opposite}}{\text{hypotenuse}} = \dfrac{a}{c}$.

    Multiplying by c yields $c \sin A = a$.

34. The correct answer is (3).

    Using Law of Sines

    $\dfrac{\sin 30}{\sqrt{5}} = \dfrac{\sin B}{6}$ \qquad Cross-multiply.

    $6 \sin 30 = \sqrt{5} \sin B$

    $6\left(\dfrac{1}{2}\right) = \sqrt{5} \sin B$

    $3 = \sqrt{5} \sin B$, so $\sin B = \dfrac{3}{\sqrt{5}} > 1$

    It is impossible to have an angle whose sine is greater than 1.

35. The correct answer is (3).

    The minimum value of $\sin 4\theta$ is -1, thus the minimum value of $3 \sin 4\theta$ is -3.

36. a.

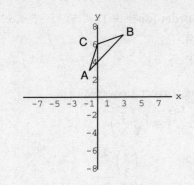

   b. The correct answer is $A'(3, -1)$, $B'(7, 3)$, $C'(6, 0)$.

   To reflect in the line $y = x$, switch the x and y coordinates so $A'(3, -1), B'(7, 3)$, and $C'(6, 0)$.

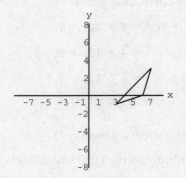

   c. The correct answer is $A''(-3, -1)$, $B''(-7, 3)$, $C''(-6, 0)$, the negative of the x-coordinates.

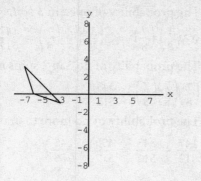

d.   Use $T(0, -5)$ to write the new coordinates as $A'''(-3, -6)$, $B'''(-7, -2)$, $C'''(-6, -5)$.

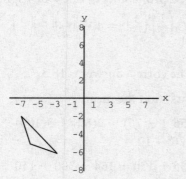

37.   a. The correct answer is 20.

Let $x = m\widehat{DG}$

Then $x + 3x + 5x = 180$

$$9x = 180$$

$$x = 20$$

b.   The correct answer is 30.

$m\angle EFD = \frac{1}{2}(60) = 30$ Inscribed angle is $\frac{1}{2}$

its intercepted arc.

Then $m\angle AEF = m\angle EFD = 30$

c.   The correct answer is 40.

$m\angle EAG = \frac{1}{2}(m\widehat{ED} + m\widehat{DG}) =$

$\frac{1}{2}(60 + 20) = 40°$

Then $m\angle EAG = m\angle DBG = 40$.
Congruent corresponding angles.

d.   The correct answer is 40.

$m\angle DCA = \frac{1}{2}(m\widehat{AE} - m\widehat{DG}) =$

$\frac{1}{2}(100 - 20) = 40°$

e.   The correct answer is 100.

$m\angle ECA = \frac{1}{2}(m\widehat{AE} - m\widehat{DB}) =$

$\frac{1}{2}(100 - 20) = 40°$

Consider ΔDBC. Then $m\angle CDF =$
$180° - m\angle DBC - m\angle DCB =$
$180° - m\angle DBG - m\angle DCA =$
$180° - 40° - 40° = 100°$

38.   The correct answer is 18.2.

Use the law of sines to find CD since
$m\angle CBD = 63°$

$$\frac{CD}{\sin 63°} = \frac{9}{\sin 27°}$$

$$CD = \frac{9 \sin 63°}{\sin 27°} = 17.663$$

Use the law of sines again to find AC since
$m\angle A = 33$.

$$\frac{AC}{\sin 57°} = \frac{17.663}{\sin 33°}$$

$$AC = \frac{17.663 \sin 57°}{\sin 33°} = 27.199$$

$AB + BC = AC$ so

Therefore,

$$AB + 9 = 27.199$$

$$AB = 18.199 \approx 18.2$$

39. a. (1) The correct answer is $\frac{1}{8}$.

   The region containing 3 has area $\frac{1}{8}$ of the entire circle.

   (2) The correct answer is $\frac{3}{8}$.

   Even would be 4 or 2.

   $P(4) = \frac{1}{4}$ since the region containing 4 is $\frac{1}{4}$ of the circle.

   $P(2) = \frac{1}{8}$ since the region containing 2 is $\frac{1}{8}$ of the circle.

   $P(\text{EVEN}) = \frac{1}{4} + \frac{1}{8} = \frac{2}{8} + \frac{1}{8} = \frac{3}{8}$.

   (3) The correct answer is $\frac{1}{4}$.

   The region containing 7 has area $\frac{1}{4}$ of the circle.

   b. (1) The correct answer is $\frac{135}{512}$. On each spin

   $P(\text{EVEN}) = \frac{3}{8}$ so $P(\text{ODD}) = \frac{5}{8}$.

   The probability of exactly 2 evens in 3 spins is $_3C_2\left(\frac{3}{8}\right)^2\left(\frac{5}{8}\right)^1 = 3\left(\frac{3}{8}\right)\left(\frac{3}{8}\right)\left(\frac{5}{8}\right) = \frac{135}{512}$.

   (2) The correct answer is $\frac{245}{256}$.

   On each spin, the probability of a 3 is $\frac{1}{8}$, so $P(\text{not 3}) = \frac{7}{8}$.

The probability of one 3 in 3 spins is

$$_3C_1\left(\frac{1}{8}\right)^1\left(\frac{7}{8}\right)^2 = 3\left(\frac{1}{8}\right)\left(\frac{7}{8}\right)\left(\frac{7}{8}\right) = \frac{147}{512}.$$

The probability of no 3 in 3 spins is

$$\left(\frac{7}{8}\right)\left(\frac{7}{8}\right)\left(\frac{7}{8}\right) = \frac{343}{512}.$$

The probability of no more than one 3 is

$$\frac{147}{512} + \frac{343}{512} = \frac{490}{512} = \frac{245}{256}.$$

   (3) The correct answer is $\frac{27}{64}$.

   $P(7) = \frac{1}{4}$ so $P(\text{not 7}) = \frac{3}{4}$

   The probability of one 7 in 4 spins is

$$_4C_1\left(\frac{1}{4}\right)^1\left(\frac{3}{4}\right)^3 = 4\left(\frac{1}{4}\right)\left(\frac{3}{4}\right)\left(\frac{3}{4}\right)\left(\frac{3}{4}\right) = \frac{108}{256} = \frac{27}{64}.$$

40. The correct answer is 18.3.

   First find the mean

   $[56 + 2(75) + 2(82) + 3(100) + 110 + 120] \div 10 =$

   $[56 + 150 + 164 + 300 + 110 + 120] \div 10$
   $= 900 \div 10 = 90$

   Find each $(\text{result} - \text{mean})^2$.

   $(56 - 90)^2 + 2(75 - 90)^2 + 2(82 - 90)^2 + 3(100 - 90)^2 + (110 - 90)^2 + (120 - 90)^2$

   $(-34)^2 + 2(-15)^2 + 2(-8)^2 + 3(10)^2 + (20)^2 + (30)^2$

   $1{,}156 + 2(225) + 2(64) + 3(100) + 400 + 900$

   $1{,}156 + 450 + 128 + 300 + 400 + 900 = 3{,}334$

   Divide by 10 to get a variance of 333.4.

Take square root of 333.4 to get standard deviation.

$$\sqrt{333.4} = 18.3$$

41. a. The correct answer is 3.2.

If $x = \log_2 9$ then $2^x = 9$. Take log of both sides.

$$\log 2^x = \log 9$$

$$x \log 2 = \log 9$$

$$x = \frac{\log 9}{\log 2} = 3.2$$

b. The correct answer is the following proof.

$$\tan x(2 - 2\sin^2 x) = 2\tan x - 2\sin^2 x \tan x$$

$$= \frac{2\sin x}{\cos x} - 2\sin^2 x \cdot \frac{\sin x}{\cos x}$$

$$= \frac{2\sin x}{\cos x} - \frac{2\sin^3 x}{\cos x}$$

$$= \frac{2\sin x - 2\sin^3 x}{\cos x}$$

$$= \frac{2\sin x(1 - \sin^2 x)}{\cos x}$$

$$= \frac{2\sin x(\cos^2 x)}{\cos x}$$

$$= 2\sin x \cos x$$

$$= \sin 2x$$

42. a. The correct answer is $2 \pm i$.

$$x^2 + 1 = 4(x - 1)$$

$$x^2 + 1 = 4x - 4$$

$$x^2 - 4x + 5 = 0 \quad \text{Use quadratic formula}$$
$$\text{with } a = 1, b = -4, c = 5$$

$$x = \frac{4 \pm \sqrt{4^2 - 4(1)(5)}}{2(1)} = \frac{4 \pm \sqrt{16 - 20}}{2}$$

$$= \frac{4 \pm \sqrt{-4}}{2} = \frac{4 \pm 2i}{2} = \frac{4}{2} \pm \frac{2i}{2} = 2 \pm i$$

b. The correct answer is 19°, 161°

$$3\sin^2\theta + 5\sin\theta = 2$$

$$3\sin^2\theta + 5\sin\theta - 2 = 0$$

$$(3\sin\theta - 1)(\sin\theta + 2) = 0$$

$$3\sin\theta - 1 = 0 \qquad \sin\theta + 2 = 0$$

$$3\sin\theta = 1 \qquad \sin\theta = -2 \quad \text{no solution}$$

$$\sin\theta = \frac{1}{3}$$

$$= 19°, 161°$$

Practice Test 3

Part I

Answer 30 questions from this part. Each correct answer will receive 2 credits. No partial credit will be allowed. Write your answers in the spaces provided on the separate answer sheet. Where applicable, answers may be left in terms of π or in radical form.   [60]

1 If $f(x) = \sqrt{25 - x^2}$, find the value of f(3).

2 An angle that measures $\frac{5\pi}{6}$ radians is drawn in standard position. In which quadrant does the terminal side of the angle lie?

3 In the accompanying diagram, isosceles triangle ABC is inscribed in circle O and m∠BAC = 40. Find m$\overset{\frown}{AC}$.

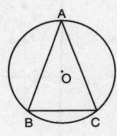

4 Solve for x: $\log_x 125 = 3$

5 Point (−3,4) is rotated 180° about the origin in a counterclockwise direction. What are the coordinates of its image?

6 For which positive value of x is the function $f(x) = \dfrac{5x}{x^2 - 4x - 45}$ undefined?

7 Solve for x: $8^x = 2^{(x+6)}$

8 If $h(x) = 2x - 1$ and $g(x) = 3x + 1$, what is $(h \circ g)(2)$?

9 Subtract $(3 - 2i)$ from $(-2 + 3i)$, and express in $a + bi$ form.

10 In △ABC, $a = 8$, $b = 7$, and m∠C = 30. What is the area of △ABC?

11 Evaluate: $\displaystyle\sum_{r=1}^{3} r^{(r-1)}$

12 Chords $\overline{XY}$ and $\overline{ZW}$ intersect in a circle at P. If $XP = 7$, $PY = 12$, and $WP = 14$, find PZ.

13 Find the number of degrees in the measure of the *smallest* positive angle that satisfies the equation $2 \cos x + 1 = 0$.

14 Find the complete solution set of $|2x - 4| = 8$.

15 In the accompanying diagram, $\overline{AFB}$, $\overline{AEC}$, and $\overline{BGC}$ are tangent to circle O at F, E, and G, respectively. If $AB = 32$, $AE = 20$, and $EC = 24$, find BC.

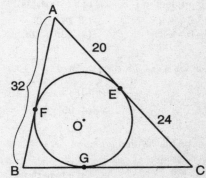

Directions (16–35): For *each* question chosen, write on the separate answer sheet the *numeral* preceding the word or expression that best completes the statement or answers the question.

16 The expression $\dfrac{\sqrt{-36}}{-\sqrt{36}}$ is equivalent to

(1) $6i$ (3) $-i$
(2) i (4) $-6i$

17 If $\sin \theta < 0$ and $\tan \theta = -\frac{4}{5}$, in which quadrant does θ terminate?

(1) I   (3) III
(2) II   (4) IV

18 The expression $\dfrac{\dfrac{a-1}{a}}{\dfrac{a^2-1}{a^2}}$ is equivalent to

(1) $\dfrac{a}{a+1}$ (3) $\dfrac{a}{a-1}$
(2) $\dfrac{a+1}{a}$ (4) $\dfrac{a-1}{a}$

19 The roots of the equation $x^2 + 7x - 8 = 0$ are

(1) real, rational, and equal
(2) real, rational, and unequal
(3) real, irrational, and unequal
(4) imaginary

20 The product of $(-2 + 6i)$ and $(3 + 4i)$ is

(1) $-6 + 24i$ (3) $18 + 10i$
(2) $-6 - 24i$ (4) $-30 + 10i$

21 If $\sin 2A = \cos 3A$, then $m\angle A$ is

(1) $1\frac{1}{2}$ (3) 18
(2) 5   (4) 36

22 The graph of the equation $x = \dfrac{2}{y}$ is best described as

(1) a circle   (3) a hyperbola
(2) an ellipse   (4) a parabola

23 The accompanying diagram represents the graph of f(x).

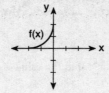

Which graph below represents $f^{-1}(x)$?

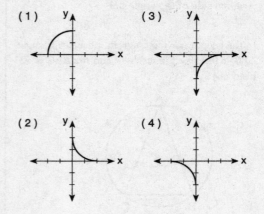

(1)   (3)

(2)   (4)

24 What is the domain of $f(x) = \sqrt{x-4}$ over the set of real numbers?

(1) $\{x \,|\, x \le 4\}$ (3) $\{x \,|\, x > 4\}$
(2) $\{x \,|\, x \ge 4\}$ (4) $\{x \,|\, x = 4\}$

25 What is the solution set of the equation $\sqrt{5-x} + 3 = x$?

(1) $\{1\}$ (3) $\{\ \}$
(2) $\{4,1\}$ (4) $\{4\}$

26 If $\log 28 = \log 4 + \log x$, what is the value of x?

(1) 7   (3) 24
(2) 14   (4) 32

27 If $a = 4$, $b = 6$, and $\sin A = \frac{3}{5}$ in $\triangle ABC$, then $\sin B$ equals

(1) $\frac{3}{20}$ (3) $\frac{8}{10}$

(2) $\frac{6}{10}$ (4) $\frac{9}{10}$

28 What is the image of $(5,-2)$ under the transformation $r_{y=x}$?

(1) $(-5,2)$ (3) $(2,5)$

(2) $(5,2)$ (4) $(-2,5)$

29 Each day the probability of rain on a tropical island is $\frac{7}{8}$. Which expression represents the probability that it will rain on the island exactly n days in the next 3 days?

(1) $_3C_n \left(\frac{7}{8}\right)^n \left(\frac{1}{8}\right)^{3-n}$ (3) $_nC_3 \left(\frac{7}{8}\right)^3 \left(\frac{1}{8}\right)^n$

(2) $_3C_3 \left(\frac{7}{8}\right)^3 \left(\frac{1}{8}\right)^n$ (4) $_8C_7 (3)^n (3)^{8-n}$

30 Which graph represents the solution of the inequality $x^2 + 4x - 21 < 0$?

(1)

(2)

(3)

(4)

31 On a standardized test, the mean is 68 and the standard deviation is 4.5. What is the best approximation of the percentage of scores that will fall in the range 59–77?

(1) 34%   (3) 95%

(2) 68%   (4) 99%

32 In $\triangle ABC$, $a = 6$, $b = 4$, and $c = 9$. The value of $\cos C$ is

(1) $\frac{61}{72}$ (3) $\frac{2}{3}$

(2) $-\frac{29}{48}$ (4) $\frac{4}{9}$

33 If $m\angle A = 125$, $AB = 10$, and $BC = 12$, what is the number of distinct triangles that can be constructed?

(1) 1   (3) 3

(2) 2   (4) 0

34 The graph of which function has an amplitude of 2 and a period of 4π?

(1) $y = 2 \sin \frac{1}{2}x$ (3) $y = 4 \sin \frac{1}{2}x$

(2) $y = 2 \sin 4x$ (4) $y = 4 \sin 2x$

35 What is the sum of the roots of the equation $2x^2 + 6x - 7 = 0$?

(1) $-\frac{7}{2}$ (3) 3

(2) -3 (4) $\frac{7}{2}$

Answers to the following questions are to be written on paper provided by the school.

Part II

Answer four questions from this part. Clearly indicate the necessary steps, including appropriate formula substitutions, diagrams, graphs, charts, etc. Calculations that may be obtained by mental arithmetic or the calculator do not need to be shown. [40]

36 In the accompanying diagram of circle O with inscribed isosceles triangle ABC, $\overline{AB} \cong \overline{AC}$, m$\overparen{CB}$ = 60, $\overline{FC}$ is a tangent, and secant $\overline{FBA}$ intersects diameter $\overline{CD}$ at E.

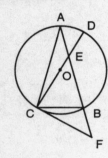

Find:

a m$\angle ABC$ [2]
b m$\overparen{AD}$ [2]
c m$\angle DEB$ [2]
d m$\angle AFC$ [2]
e m$\angle BCF$ [2]

37 a On graph paper, sketch the graph of the equation $y = 2 \cos x$ in the interval $-\pi \le x \le \pi$. [4]

b On the same set of axes, reflect the graph drawn in part a in the x-axis and label it b. [2]

c Write an equation of the graph drawn in part b. [2]

d Using the equation from part c, find the value of y when $x = \frac{\pi}{6}$. [2]

38 Find, to the *nearest degree*, all values of x in the interval $0° \le x < 360°$ that satisfy the equation $3 \cos 2x + \cos x + 2 = 0$. [10]

39 In a contest, the probability of the Alphas beating the Betas is $\frac{3}{5}$. The teams compete four times a season and each contest has a winner. Find the probability that

a the Betas win all four contests [2]

b each team wins two contests during the season [2]

c the Alphas win *at least* two contests during the season [3]

d the Betas win *at most* one contest during the season [3]

40 Answer both a and b.

a For all values of x for which the expressions are defined, prove that the following is an identity:

$$\tan x + \cot x = 2 \csc 2x \quad [6]$$

b Given: $\log 2 = x$ and $\log 3 = y$.

(1) Express $\log \frac{\sqrt{2}}{9}$ in terms of x and y. [2]

(2) Express $\log \sqrt[3]{6}$ in terms of x and y. [2]

☞ GO RIGHT ON TO THE NEXT PAGE.

41 Answer both *a* and *b*.

    a Expand and express in simplest form:

$$\left(x - \frac{1}{x} \right)^4 \qquad [7]$$

    b Solve for *x* to the *nearest tenth*:

$$5^{3x} = 1,000 \qquad [3]$$

42 The lengths of the sides of $\triangle ABC$ are 9.5, 12.8, and 13.7.

    a Find, to the *nearest hundredth of a degree* or the *nearest ten minutes*, the measure of the *smallest* angle in the triangle.   [6]

    b Find, to the *nearest tenth*, the area of $\triangle ABC$. [4]

Practice Test 3

Answers

1. The correct answer is $f(3) = 4$.
   $$f(3) = \sqrt{25 - (3)^2} = \sqrt{25 - 9} = \sqrt{16} = 4$$

2. The correct answer is Quadrant II.
   $\dfrac{5\pi}{6}$ is less than π but larger than $\dfrac{\pi}{2}$.

3. The correct answer is 140.

   Since $\triangle ABC$ is isosceles $m\angle B = m\angle C$. Since the sum of all angles of $\triangle BAC$ is 180 and $m\angle BAC = 40$, then $m\angle B + m\angle C = 140$ and $m\angle B = 70$. Since $\angle B$ is an inscribed angle, the arc it intercepts, AC has twice its angle measure.

4. The correct answer is $x = 5$.

   $\log x\ 125 = 3$ translates to $x^3 = 125$.
   Thus $x = 5$.

5. The correct answer is $(3, -4)$.

   A 180° rotation will move it to Quadrant IV.

6. The correct answer is $x = 9$.

   The function will be undefined when
   $x^2 - 4x - 45 = 0$

   $x^2 - 4x - 45 = 0$ Factor.

   $(x - 9)(x + 5) = 0$ Set each factor equal to 0.

   $x - 9 = 0$ $x + 5 = 0$

   $x = 9$ $x = -5$

   The positive value is 9.

7. The correct answer is $x = 3$.

   Rewrite 8 as 2^3 so that the bases are the same.

$(2^3)^x = 2^{(x+6)}$

$2^{3x} = 2^{(x+6)}$ Since the bases are the same, set exponents equal.

$3x = x + 6$ Subtract x from both sides.

$3x - x = x + 6 - x$

$2x = 6$ Divide by 2.

$x = 3$

8. The correct answer is 13.

   $h \circ g$ means to apply g first then h.
   $(h \circ g)(2) = h(g(2))$
   $g(2) = 3(2) + 1 = 6 + 1 = 7$
   $h(g(2)) = h(7) = 2(7) - 1 = 14 - 1 = 13$

9. The correct answer is $-5 + 5i$.

   $(-2 + 3i) - (3 - 2i)$
   $= -2 + 3i - 3 + 2i$
   $= -2 - 3 + 3i + 2i$
   $= -5 + 5i$

10. The correct answer is 14.

    $\text{Area} = \dfrac{1}{2}\,ab \sin C$

    $= \dfrac{1}{2}\,(8)(7) \sin 30°$

    $= 4(7)(\dfrac{1}{2})$

    $= 2(7) = 14$

11. The correct answer is 12.

    Replace r with 1, 2, and 3 and add.

$1^{(1-1)} + 2^{(2-1)} + 3^{(3-1)}$

$1^0 + 2^1 + 3^2$

$1 + 2 + 9 = 12$

12. The correct answer is 6.

They will form similar triangles and since $PW = 2PX$, then $PY = 2PZ$. Since $PY = 12$, $PZ = 6$

13. The correct answer is 120.

$2 \cos x + 1 = 0$

$2 \cos x = -1$

$\cos x = -\dfrac{1}{2}$ when $x = 120°$.

14. The correct answer is 6 and -2.

$2x - 4 = 8$ or $2x - 4 = -8$

       Add 4 to both sides

$2x-4+4=8+4$ $2x-4+4= -8+4$

$2x = 12$ $2x = -4$ Divide by 2.

$x = 6$ $x = -2$

15. The correct answer is 36.

$AF = AE = 20$. The two tangent segments drawn to a circle from the external point are congruent.

Since $AB = AF + FB$

      $32 = 20 + FB$

      $12 = FB$

Then $BG = BF = 12$. Also $CG = CE = 24$. Finally, $BC = BG + GC = 12 + 24 = 36$.

16. The correct answer is (3).

$\sqrt{-36} = 6i$ so $\dfrac{\sqrt{-36}}{-\sqrt{36}} = \dfrac{6i}{-6} = -i$

17. The correct answer is (4).

If sin is negative and tan is negative, θ terminates in Quad IV.

18. The correct answer is (1).

Invert the denominator and multiply:

$\dfrac{a-1}{a} \cdot \dfrac{a^2}{a^2 - 1}$ Factor.

$\dfrac{\cancel{(a-1)}}{a} \cdot \dfrac{\overset{a}{\cancel{a^2}}}{\cancel{(a-1)}(a+1)}$ Cancel factors.

$\dfrac{a}{a+1}$

19. The correct answer is (2).

The discriminant is
$7^2 - 4(1)(-8) = 49 + 32 = 81 = 9^2$

Thus there are 2 unequal rational roots.

20. The correct answer is (4).

$(-2 + 6i)(3 + 4i)$ Distribute

$(-2)(3) + (-2)(4i) + (6i)(3) + (6i)(4i)$

$-6 + (-8i) + 18i + 24i^2$

$-6 + 10i - 24$

$-30 + 10i$

21. The correct answer is (3).

If $\sin 2A = \cos 3A$ then $2A + 3A = 90$. So $5A = 90$ and $A = 18$.

22. The correct answer is (3).

The equation is equivalent to $xy = 2$. The hyperbola has its two branches in the first and third quadrants.

23. The correct answer is (3), because it is the reflection over the line $y = x$.

24. The correct answer is (2).

    $x - 4 \geq 0$ in order to obtain real results, thus $x \geq 4$.

25. The correct answer is (4).

$\sqrt{5 - x} + 3 = x$	Isolate the radical.
$\sqrt{5 - x} = x - 3$	Square both sides.
$(\sqrt{5 - x})^2 = (x - 3)^2$	
$5 - x = x^2 - 6x + 9$	Set one side equal to zero.
$0 = x^2 - 5x + 4$	Factor the right side.
$0 = (x - 4)(x - 1)$	Set each factor equal to zero.

    $x - 4 = 0 \qquad\qquad x - 1 = 0$

    $x = 4 \qquad\qquad\quad x = 1$

    Check for extraneous solutions

    $x = 4 \ \sqrt{5 - 4} + 3 = \sqrt{1} + 3 = 1 + 3 = 4$

    $\qquad\qquad\qquad\qquad\qquad\qquad$ checks

    $x = 1 \ \sqrt{5 - 1} + 3 = \sqrt{4} + 3 = 2 + 3 \pm 1$

    $\qquad\qquad\qquad\qquad\qquad$ does not check

26. The correct answer is (1).

    $4x$ must equal 28 so $x = 7$

27. The correct answer is (4).

    Use the law of sines, $\sin \dfrac{A}{a} = \dfrac{\sin B}{b}$

    $\dfrac{\frac{3}{5}}{4} = \dfrac{\sin B}{6} \qquad$ Cross multiply.

    $6\left(\dfrac{3}{5}\right) = 4 \sin B$

    $\dfrac{18}{5} = 4 \sin B \qquad$ Multiply both sides by $\dfrac{1}{4}$.

    $\dfrac{1}{\cancel{4}_2} \cdot \dfrac{\cancel{18}^{9}}{5} = \dfrac{1}{4} \cdot 4 \sin B$

    $\dfrac{9}{10} = \sin B$

28. The correct answer is (4).

    Reflect over $y = x$ so you interchange the x and y values.

29. The correct answer is (1).

    The probability of rain is $\left(\dfrac{7}{8}\right)$ and this will happen n times, the probability of no rain is $\left(\dfrac{1}{8}\right)$ and this will happen $3 - n$ times. The number of ways the days might be chosen is $_3C_n$.

30. The correct answer is (1).

    $x^2 + 4x - 21 = 0$ is where the expression will change signs. Factor and set each factor equal to zero.

    $(x + 7)(x - 3) = 0$

    $x + 7 = 0 \qquad\qquad x - 3 = 0$

    $x = -7 \qquad\qquad\quad x = 3$

    Test each region determined by these numbers.

    $x < -7 \qquad\qquad\qquad$ Test $x = -8$

    $(-8 + 7)(-8 - 3) = (-1)(-11) = 11$

    does not check

    $-7 < x < 3 \qquad\qquad$ Test $x = 0$

    $(0 + 7)(0 - 3) = 7(-3) = -21 < 0$

    $3 < x \qquad\qquad\qquad\quad$ Test $x = 4$

    $(4 + 7)(4 - 3) = 11(1) = 11$ does not check.

227

31. The correct answer is (3).

    $68 - 59 = 9$; $77 - 68 = 9$ is 2 standard deviations. Using the $68 - 95 - 99.7$ rule, 95 percent will fall in the 2 standard deviation range.

32. The correct answer is (2).

    Using the law of cosines, $c^2 = a^2 + b^2 - 2ab \cos C$.

    $9^2 = 6^2 + 4^2 - 2(6)(4) \cos C$

    $81 = 36 + 16 - 48 \cos C$

    $81 = 52 - 48 \cos C$

    $29 = -48 \cos C$

    $\dfrac{-29}{48} = \cos C$

33. The correct answer is (1).

    $m\angle A$ is greater than 90.

34. The correct answer is (1).

    For an amplitude of 2, the sine needs a coefficient of 2, and for a period of 4π which is twice the normal 2π, x needs a coefficient of $\dfrac{1}{2}$.

35. The correct answer is (2).

    To find the roots use the formula

    $r_1 + r_2 = \dfrac{-b}{a}$

    $r_1 + r_2 = \dfrac{-6}{2} = -3$

36. a. The correct answer is 75.

    Since $m\overparen{CB} = 60$, $m\angle CAB = 30$. The measure of an inscribed angle is equal to one-half of the measure of its intercepted arc.

Since $\triangle ABC$ is isosceles,
$m\angle ABC = m\angle BCA = 75$.
($180° - 30° = 150°$ and $150° \div 2 = 75°$)

b. The correct answer is 30.

$m\angle DCF = 90$. Every line tangent to a circle is perpendicular to the radius.

Consider $\triangle CBF$.

$m\angle CBF = 105$ since it is supplementary to $\angle ABC$ and $180° - 75° = 105°$.

$m\angle AFC = \dfrac{1}{2}(m\overparen{AC} - m\overparen{BC})$. This is an angle with vertex external to the circle whose degree measure equals one-half of the difference of the degree measures of the two intercepted arcs.

Then $m\angle AFC = \dfrac{1}{2}(m\overparen{AC} - m\overparen{BC})$

$= \dfrac{1}{2}(150 - 60) = 45$

So $m\angle BCF = 180 - 105 - 45 = 30$

since $m\angle DCF = m\angle DCB + m\angle BCF$

$90 = m\angle DCB + 30$

$60 = m\angle DCB$

$m\angle ACB = m\angle ACD + m\angle DCB$

$75 = m\angle ACD + 60$

$15 = m\angle ACD$

Finally, since $\overparen{AD}$ is the intercepted arc for inscribed angle ACB, $m\overparen{AD} = 2(15) = 30$.

c. The correct answer is 135.

Consider $\triangle ECB$.

$m\angle DCB = 60$ \qquad See part (b).

$m\angle ABC = 75$ See part (a).

$m\angle DEB = 60 + 75 = 135$. An exterior angle of a triangle equals the sum of the two nonadjacent interior angles.

d.   The correct answer is 45. See part (b).

e.   The correct answer is 30. See part (b).

37. a.

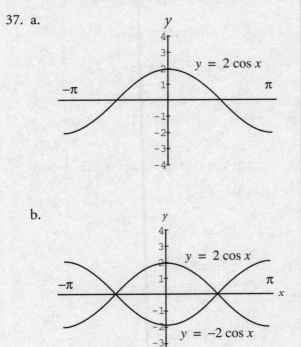

b.

c.   The correct answer is $y = -2 \cos x$.

d.   The correct answer is $-\sqrt{3}$.

$$y = -2\cos\left(\frac{\pi}{6}\right) = -2\left(\frac{\sqrt{3}}{2}\right) = -\sqrt{3}$$

38. The correct answer is 71, 120, 240, 289.

$3\cos 2x + \cos x + 2 = 0$

$3(2\cos^2 x - 1) + \cos x + 2 = 0$

$6\cos^2 x - 3 + \cos x + 2 = 0$

$6\cos^2 x + \cos x - 1 = 0$

Factor and set each factor equal to zero.

$(2\cos x + 1)(3\cos x - 1) = 0$

$2\cos x + 1 = 0$	$3\cos x - 1 = 0$
$2\cos x = -1$	$3\cos x = 1$
$\cos x = -\dfrac{1}{2}$	$\cos x = \dfrac{1}{3}$
$x = 120°, 240°$	$x = 71°, 289°$

39. a.   The correct answer is $\dfrac{16}{625}$.

$$\left(\frac{2}{5}\right)\left(\frac{2}{5}\right)\left(\frac{2}{5}\right)\left(\frac{2}{5}\right) = \frac{16}{625}$$

The probability the Beta's win each contest is $\dfrac{2}{5}$.

b. The correct answer is $\dfrac{216}{625}$.

$$\left(\frac{3}{5}\right)\left(\frac{3}{5}\right)\left(\frac{3}{5}\right)\left(\frac{3}{5}\right) = \frac{36}{625}$$

There are $_4C_2$ or six ways this can happen BBAA, BABA, BAAB ABBA, ABAB, AABB.

Thus the probability is $6 \times \dfrac{36}{625} = \dfrac{216}{625}$.

c. The correct answer is $\dfrac{513}{625}$.

The answer for (b) gives the probability they win exactly 2. We must also include if they win all 4; $\left(\dfrac{3}{5}\right)\left(\dfrac{3}{5}\right)\left(\dfrac{3}{5}\right)\left(\dfrac{3}{5}\right) = \dfrac{81}{625}$.

This can happen only one way. Also they might win 3 games.

This can happen $_4C_3$ or, 4 ways, AAAB,

AABA, ABAA, and BAAA. Thus the probability of winning three games is

$$_4C_3\left(\frac{2}{5}\right)^3\left(\frac{3}{5}\right) = 4\left(\frac{2}{5}\right)\left(\frac{2}{5}\right)\left(\frac{2}{5}\right)\left(\frac{3}{5}\right)$$

$$= 4\left(\frac{54}{625}\right) = \frac{216}{625}.$$

The total probability is

$$\frac{216}{625} + \frac{81}{625} + \frac{216}{625} = \frac{513}{625}.$$

d. The correct answer is $\frac{297}{625}$.

This happens if they win no games, which has a probability of $\left(\frac{3}{5}\right)\left(\frac{3}{5}\right)\left(\frac{3}{5}\right)\left(\frac{3}{5}\right) = \frac{81}{625}$, or if they win one game, which has a prob-ability of $_4C_1\left(\frac{3}{5}\right)^1\left(\frac{2}{5}\right)^3$

$$= 4\left(\frac{3}{5}\right)\left(\frac{2}{5}\right)\left(\frac{2}{5}\right)\left(\frac{2}{5}\right)$$

$$= 4\left(\frac{54}{625}\right) = \frac{216}{625}.$$

Thus the total probability is

$$\frac{81}{625} + \frac{216}{625} = \frac{297}{625}.$$

40. a.

$$\tan x + \cot x = \frac{\sin x}{\cos x} + \frac{\cos x}{\sin x}$$

$$= \frac{\sin^2 x}{\sin x \cos x} + \frac{\cos^2 x}{\sin x \cos x}$$

$$= \frac{\sin^2 x + \cos^2 x}{\sin x \cos x}$$

$$= \frac{1}{\sin x \cos x}$$

$$= \frac{2}{2 \sin x \cos x}$$

$$= \frac{2}{\sin 2x}$$

$$= 2 \csc 2x$$

b. (1) The correct answer is $\frac{x}{2} - 2y$.

$$\log\frac{\sqrt{2}}{9} = \log\sqrt{2} - \log 9$$

$$= \log 2^{\frac{1}{2}} - \log 3^2$$

$$= \frac{1}{2}\log 2 - 2\log 3$$

$$= \frac{x}{2} - 2y$$

(2) The correct answer is $\frac{1}{3}(x + y)$.

$$\log\sqrt[3]{6} = \log 6^{\frac{1}{3}}$$

$$= \frac{1}{3}\log 6$$

$$= \frac{1}{3}\log 2(3)$$

$$= \frac{1}{3}(\log 2 + \log 3)$$

$$= \frac{1}{3}(x + y)$$

41. a. The correct answer is

$$x^4 - 4x^2 + 6 - \frac{4}{x^2} + \frac{1}{x^4}.$$

$$\left(x - \frac{1}{x}\right)^2 = \left(\frac{x^2 - 1}{x}\right) = \frac{(x^2 - 1)^4}{x^4}.$$

$$(x^2 - 1)^4 = {}_4C_0(x^2)^4 - {}_4C_1(x^2)^{4-1}(1)^1 + {}_4C_2(x^2)^{4-2}(1)^2 - {}_4C_3(x^2)(1)^3 + {}_4C_4(1)^4.$$

Thus,

$$\left(x - \frac{1}{x}\right)^4 = \frac{x^8 - 4x^6 + 6x^4 - 4x^2 + 1}{x^4}$$

$$= \frac{x^8}{x^4} - \frac{4x^6}{x^4} + \frac{6x^4}{x^4} - \frac{4x^2}{x^4} + \frac{1}{x^4}$$

$$= x^4 - 4x^2 + 6 - \frac{4}{x^2} + \frac{1}{x^4}$$

b. The correct answer is $x = 1.4$

$5^{3x} = 1{,}000$ Take log of both sides.

$\log 5^{3x} = \log 1{,}000$

$3x \log 5 = 3$

$3x = \dfrac{3}{\log 5}$

$x = \dfrac{1}{\log 5} = 1.4$

42. a.   The correct answer is $41.84°$ *or* $41°50'$.

Use the law of cosines and note that the smallest angle is opposite the smallest side.

$(9.5)^2 = 12.8^2 + 13.7^2 - 2(12.8)(13.7) \cos \theta$

$90.25 = 163.84 + 187.69 - 350.72 \cos \theta$

$90.25 = 351.53 - 350.72 \cos \theta$

$-261.28 = -350.72 \cos \theta$

$\dfrac{261.28}{350.72} = \cos \theta$

$\theta = 41.84°$

b. The correct answer is 58.5.

$\dfrac{1}{2}(12.8)(13.7) \sin 41.84°$

$= 87.68 \sin 41.84°$

$= 58.5$

Practice Test 4

Part I

Answer 30 questions from this part. Each correct answer will receive 2 credits. No partial credit will be allowed. Write your answers in the spaces provided on the separate answer sheet. Where applicable, answers may be left in terms of π or in radical form.　　[60]

1　In the accompanying diagram, $\overline{AB}$ and $\overline{AC}$ are tangents to circle O, and chord $\overline{BC}$ is drawn. If $m\angle ABC = 72$, what is $m\angle A$?

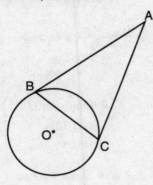

2　Express the product in simplest form:

$$\frac{a^2 - 9}{a^2 - 3a} \cdot \frac{a^2 + a}{a + 3}$$

3　Express 225° in radian measure.

4　Solve for x:　$\sqrt{2x - 2} - 2 = 0$

5　If the transformation $T_{(x,y)}$ maps point $A(1,-3)$ onto point $A'(-4,8)$, what is the value of x?

6　A set of boys' heights is distributed normally with a mean of 58 inches and a standard deviation of 2 inches. Expressed in inches, between which two heights should 95% of the heights fall?

7　If $\sin A > 0$ and $\sec A < 0$, in which quadrant does the terminal side of $\angle A$ lie?

8　In which quadrant does the sum of $3 + 2i$ and $-4 - 5i$ lie?

9　Solve for x:　$2^{x+2} = 4^{x-1}$

10　In $\triangle CAT$, $a = 4$, $c = 5$, and $\cos T = \frac{1}{8}$. What is the length of t?

11　Evaluate:　$\displaystyle\sum_{k=3}^{7} (3k + 2)$

12　Express $\dfrac{5}{2 - i}$ in simplest $a + bi$ form.

13　Solve for y:　$y^{-\frac{1}{2}} = \frac{1}{3}$

14　In $\triangle ABC$, $a = 6$, $b = 7$, and $m\angle B = 30$. Find $\sin A$.

15　Solve for all values of x:　$|3x - 2| = 16$

Directions (16–35): For *each* question chosen, write on the separate answer sheet the *numeral* preceding the word or expression that best completes the statement or answers the question.

16　In the accompanying figure of circle O, $m\angle ABC = 38$.

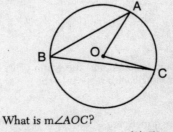

What is $m\angle AOC$?

(1) 19　　　　　　(3) 76
(2) 38　　　　　　(4) 152

17 In a circle, diameter $\overline{AB}$ is perpendicular to chord $\overline{CD}$ at L. Which statement will always be true about this circle?

(1) $CL = LD$ (3) $(CL) \times (LD) = AB$

(2) $AL > LB$ (4) $BL > LA$

18 After which transformation of $\triangle ABC$ could the image $\triangle A'B'C'$ *not* have the same area?

(1) translation   (3) point reflection

(2) rotation   (4) dilation

19 The expression $\sin 50° \cos 40° + \cos 50° \sin 40°$ is equivalent to

(1) $\sin 10°$ (3) $\sin 90°$

(2) $\cos 10°$ (4) $\cos 90°$

20 If $\log_b x = y$, then $\log_b x^2$ is

(1) $y + 2$ (3) $y - 2$

(2) $2y$ (4) y

21 Which graph represents an inverse variation between all values of x and y?

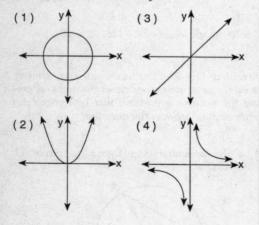

(1)   (3)

(2)   (4)

22 The graph of any function and the graph of its inverse are symmetric with respect to the

(1) x-axis

(2) y-axis

(3) graph of the equation $y = -x$

(4) graph of the equation $y = x$

23 If $m\angle B = 60$, $a = 6$, and $c = 10$, what is the area of $\triangle ABC$?

(1) 15   (3) $15\sqrt{3}$

(2) 30   (4) $30\sqrt{3}$

24 What is the period of the equation $y = -6 \sin 2x$?

(1) $-\frac{2}{6}$ (3) 2π

(2) -6π (4) π

25 The expression $\dfrac{1 + \cos 2x}{\sin 2x}$ is equivalent to

(1) $\tan x$ (3) $-\sin x$

(2) $\cot x$ (4) $-\cos x$

26 If $f(x) = 4 \cos 3x$, what is the value of $f\left(\frac{\pi}{4}\right)$?

(1) $-\sqrt{2}$ (3) 135

(2) $-2\sqrt{2}$ (4) 4

27 For which value of θ is the fraction $\dfrac{6}{\cos \theta}$ undefined?

(1) $0°$ (3) $60°$

(2) $30°$ (4) $90°$

28 Which equation has roots of $3 + \sqrt{2}$ and $3 - \sqrt{2}$?

(1) $x^2 + 6x + 7 = 0$ (3) $x^2 - 7x - 4 = 0$

(2) $x^2 - 6x + 7 = 0$ (4) $x^2 - 7x + 6 = 0$

29 In basketball, Nicole makes 4 baskets for every 10 shots. If she takes 3 shots, what is the probability that *exactly* 2 of them will be baskets?

(1) 0.288   (3) 0.600

(2) 0.432   (4) 0.960

30 When two resistors are connected in a parallel circuit, the total resistance is $\dfrac{1}{\dfrac{1}{R_1} + \dfrac{1}{R_2}}$. This complex fraction is equivalent to

(1) $R_1 + R_2$ (3) $R_1 R_2$

(2) $\dfrac{R_1 + R_2}{R_1 R_2}$ (4) $\dfrac{R_1 R_2}{R_1 + R_2}$

31 Which graph represents the inequality $x^2 - 4 > 0$?

(1) ◁———○———————○———▷
      −2 −1 0 1 2

(2) ◀———+———+———+———○———▶
      −2 −1 0 1 2

(3) ◀———○———+———+———○———▶
      −2 −1 0 1 2

(4) ◀———○———+———+———+———▶
      −2 −1 0 1 2

32 For which value of c will the roots of the equation $4x^2 - 4x + c = 0$ be real numbers?

(1) 1   (3) 3
(2) 2   (4) 4

33 If $\cos (2x - 1)° = \sin (3x + 6)°$, then the value of x is

(1) −7   (3) 35
(2) 17   (4) 71

34 Square $ABCD$ is inscribed in a circle with the center at O.

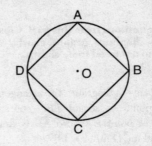

What is $(R_{-180°} \circ R_{90°})(B)$?

(1) A (3) C
(2) B (4) D

35 The graph of the equation $\dfrac{x^2 + y^2}{2} = 5$ is

(1) a circle   (3) a hyperbola
(2) an ellipse   (4) a parabola

Answers to the following questions are to be written on paper provided by the school.

Part II

Answer four questions from this part. Clearly indicate the necessary steps, including appropriate formula substitutions, diagrams, graphs, charts, etc. Calculations that may be obtained by mental arithmetic or the calculator do not need to be shown. [40]

36 In the accompanying diagram, $\overrightarrow{PA}$ is tangent to circle O at point A, secant $\overline{PBD}$ intersects diameter $\overline{AC}$ at point E, chord $\overline{AB}$ is drawn, m$\angle P$ = 40, and m$\widehat{CD}$:m$\widehat{DA}$ = 1:8.

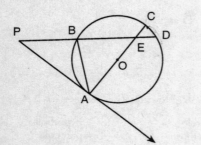

Find:

a m$\widehat{DA}$ [2]

b m$\widehat{AB}$ [2]

c m$\angle BEA$ [2]

d m$\angle BAC$ [2]

e m$\angle PBA$ [2]

37 a Solve for x: $x + \sqrt{2x - 1} = 8$ [5]

b Solve for y: $\dfrac{y}{y - 1} = \dfrac{8}{y} + \dfrac{1}{y - 1}$ [5]

38 a Find, to the *nearest degree*, all values of x in the interval $0° \leq x < 360°$ that satisfy the equation $2 \sin^2 x = 1 + \sin x$.   [5]

b For all values of x for which the expression is defined, prove that the following is an identity:

$$\cot x = \frac{\sin 2x}{1 - \cos 2x}$$ [5]

39 a On graph paper, sketch the graph of the equation $y = \tan x$ in the interval $0 \leq x \leq 2\pi$. [4]

b On the same set of axes, sketch the graph of the equation $y = 2 \sin x$ in the interval $0 \leq x \leq 2\pi$.   [4]

c Use the graphs sketched in parts *a* and *b* to determine *one* value of x in the interval $0 \leq x \leq 2\pi$ that satisfies the equation $\tan x = 2 \sin x$.   [2]

40 Two forces act on a body at an angle of 100°. The forces are 30 pounds and 40 pounds.

a Find the magnitude of the resultant force to the *nearest tenth* of a pound.   [6]

b Find the angle formed by the greater of the two forces and the resultant force to the *nearest degree*.   [4]

41 a On the same set of axes, sketch and label the graphs of the equations $xy = 8$ and $y = \log_2 x$ in the interval $-6 \leq x \leq 6$.   [8]

b Using the graphs sketched in part *a*, find an integer value of x for which $\log_2 x > \dfrac{8}{x}$.   [2]

42 a The probability of a biased coin coming up heads is $\frac{3}{4}$.

(1) When the coin is flipped three times, what is the probability of *at least* two heads?   [3]

(2) When the coin is flipped four times, what is the probability of *at most* one head?   [3]

b Find the standard deviation, to the *nearest hundredth*, for the following test scores:

100, 99, 99, 97, 96, 96, 95, 94, 93, 91   [4]

Practice Test 4

Answers

1. The correct answer is 36.

   $\overline{AB} = \overline{AC}$ tangents drawn from an exterior point

   $m\angle ABC = m\angle ACB = 72$

   $m\angle A = 180° - 2(72°) = 36°$

2. The correct answer is $a + 1$.

   Factor, then cancel common factors between numerator and denominator.

   $$\frac{(a-3)(a+3)}{a\,(a-3)} \times \frac{a(a+1)}{(a+3)} = a + 1$$

3. The correct answer is $\dfrac{5\pi}{4}$.

   $$225\left(\frac{\pi}{180}\right) = \frac{5\,\pi}{4}$$

4. The correct answer is $x = 3$.

   $\sqrt{2x-2} - 2 = 0$ Isolate radical.

   $\sqrt{2x-2} = 2$ Square both sides.

   $(\sqrt{2x-2})^2 = 2^2$

   $2x - 2 = 4$ Add 2 to both sides.

   $2x - 2 + 2 = 4 + 2$

   $2x = 6$ Divide both sides by 2.

   $x = 3$

   Check for extraneous solutions, solutions that may be produced when squaring both sides. $\sqrt{2(3) - 2} - 2 = \sqrt{4} - 2 = 2 - 2 = 0$. Thus, $x = 3$ checks.

5. The correct answer is $x = -5$.

   $T_{(x,y)}$ maps $(1, -3)$ to $(-4, 8)$. The change in the x-value is -5.

6. The correct answer is between 54 and 62.

   95 percent will be within 2 standard deviations of the mean. Thus they should fall between $58 - 2(2)$ and $58 + 2(2)$.

7. The correct answer is Quad II.

   $\sin A > 0$ in Quad I and II. $\sec A < 0$ in Quad II and III. Therefore, the terminal side of $\angle A$ lies in Quad II.

8. The correct answer is Quad III.

   $(3 + 2i) + (-4 - 5i) = [3 + (-4)] + (2 - 5)i = -1 - 3i$. Since both values are negative, it lies in Quad III.

9. The correct answer is 4.

   $2^{x+2} = (2^2)^{x-1}$ Multiply 2 times $x - 1$.

   $2^{x+2} = 2^{2x-2}$ Since bases are the same, set exponents equal.

   $x + 2 = 2x - 2$ Isolate variable

   $x + 2 - x + 2 = 2x - 2 - x + 2$

   $4 = x$

10. The correct answer is 6.

    Using the formula

    $$t^2 = a^2 + c^2 - 2ac \cos T$$
    $$t^2 = 4^2 + 5^2 - 2(4)(5)\left(\frac{1}{8}\right)$$
    $$t^2 = 16 + 25 - 5$$
    $$t^2 = 36$$

    $t = 6$ or $t = -6$ Use the positive answer, since side length must be positive.

    $t = 6$

11. The correct answer is 85.

    Replace k with the values 3, 4, 5, 6, and 7 and add them together.

    $[3(3) + 2] + [3(4) + 2] + [3(5) + 2] + [3(6) + 2] + [3(7) + 2]$

    $= [9 + 2] + [12 + 2] + [15 + 2] + [18 + 2] + [21 + 2]$

    $= 11 + 14 + 17 + 20 + 23 = 85$

12. The correct answer is $2 + i$.

    Multiply numerator and denominator by the conjugate of the denominator $2 - i$, which is $2 + i$.

    $$\frac{5}{2 - i} \times \frac{2 + i}{2 + i} = \frac{10 + 5i}{4 - i^2} = \frac{10 + 5i}{5} =$$

    $$\frac{10}{5} + \frac{5i}{5} = 2 + i$$

13. The correct answer is $y = 9$.

    Rewrite the negative exponent as a positive exponent by moving the expression to the

    denominator and then rewrite the exponent of $\frac{1}{2}$ as a square root.

    $$y^{-1/2} = \frac{1}{3}$$

    $$\frac{1}{\sqrt{y}} = \frac{1}{3} \qquad \text{Cross multiply}$$

    $$\sqrt{y} = 3 \qquad \text{Square both sides.}$$

    $$(\sqrt{y})^2 = 3^2$$

    $$y = 9$$

14. The correct answer is $\sin A = \frac{3}{7}$.

    Use the Law of Sines.

    $$\frac{\sin A}{a} = \frac{\sin B}{b}$$

    $$\frac{\sin A}{6} = \frac{\sin 30}{7} \qquad \text{Cross-multiply.}$$

    $7 \sin A = 6 \sin 30; \sin 30 = .5$

    $7 \sin A = 6(.5) = 3$. Divide both sides by 7.

    $$\sin A = \frac{3}{7}.$$

15. The correct answer is $x = 6$ or $-\frac{14}{13}$.

    There are two possibilities if the absolute value is 16. The value inside the symbols is either 16 or -16. Thus,

    $3x - 2 = 16$ or $3x - 2 = -16$. Add two to both sides of each equation.

    $3x - 2 + 2 = 16 + 2$ or
    $3x - 2 + 2 = -16 + 2$

    $3x = 18$ or $3x = -14$. Divide both sides by 3.

    $$x = 6 \text{ or } x = -\frac{14}{13}.$$

16. The correct answer is (3).

    Since $m\angle ABC = 38, \overset{\frown}{AC} = 2(38) = 76$.

    $m\angle AOC = 76$ since the measure of a central angle equals the measure of its intercepted arc.

17. The correct answer is (1).

    $CL = LD$. Any perpendicular from the center of a circle to a chord bisects the chord.

18. The correct answer is (4), because the dilation changes the size of the figure, which influences the area.

19. The correct answer is (3).

    Using the formula for the sum of sines,

    $\sin 50 \cos 40 + \cos 50 \sin 40 =$
    $\sin(50 + 40) = \sin 90$

20. The correct answer is (2).

    Because $\log_b x^2 = 2 \log_b x = 2y$.

21. The correct answer is (4).

    If y varies inversely as x there exists a constant k such that $y = \dfrac{k}{x}$. The graph of this function is (4).

22. The correct answer is (4).

    An inverse function interchanges the roles of the x and y values.

23. The correct answer is (3).

    Using the area formula, $\dfrac{1}{2} ab \sin C$,

    $\dfrac{1}{2} (6)(10) \sin 60 = 30 \times \dfrac{\sqrt{3}}{2} = 15\sqrt{3}$

24. The correct answer is (4).

    $\text{period} = \dfrac{2\pi}{b} = \dfrac{2\pi}{2} = \pi$

25. The correct answer is (2).

    $\dfrac{1 + \cos 2x}{\sin 2x} =$

    $\dfrac{1 + \cos^2 x - \sin^2 x}{2 \sin x \cos x} =$

    $\dfrac{(1 - \sin^2 x) + \cos^2 x}{2 \sin x \cos x} =$

    $\dfrac{\cos^2 x + \cos^2 x}{2 \sin x \cos x} =$

    $\dfrac{2 \cos^2 x}{2 \sin x \cos x} =$

    $\dfrac{\cos x}{\sin x} = \cot x$

26. The correct answer is (2).

    $f\left(\dfrac{\pi}{4}\right) = 4 \cos 3 \left(\dfrac{\pi}{4}\right) = 4 \cos \dfrac{3\pi}{4} = 4\left(\dfrac{-\sqrt{2}}{2}\right)$

    $= -2\sqrt{2}$

27. The correct answer is (4).

    This will be undefined when $\cos \theta = 0$ and this is when $\theta = 90$.

28. The correct answer is (2).

    $x^2 - 6x + 7$. If $3 + \sqrt{2}$ is a root, then $x - (3 + \sqrt{2})$ is a factor of $x^2 - 6x + 7$. If $3 - \sqrt{2}$ is a root, then $x - (3 - \sqrt{2})$ is a factor of $x^2 - 6x + 7$. Multiplying these gives:

    $[x - (3 + \sqrt{2})][x - (3 - \sqrt{2})] =$

    $(x - 3 - \sqrt{2})(x - 3 + \sqrt{2}) =$

    $(x - 3)^2 - (\sqrt{2})^2 =$ use difference of squares

$x^2 - 6x + 9 - 2 =$ use expansion of $(a - b)^2$

$x^2 - 6x + 7$

29. The correct answer is (1).

$_3C_2 (.4)^2 (.6)^1 = 0.288$

30. The correct answer is (4).

Multiply numerator and denominator by the Least Common Multiple which is R_1R_2.

$$\dfrac{1}{\dfrac{1}{R_1} + \dfrac{1}{R_1}} \text{ times } \dfrac{R_1R_2}{R_1R_2} = \dfrac{R_1R_2}{\dfrac{R_1R_2}{R_1} + \dfrac{R_1R_2}{R_2}} =$$

$$\dfrac{R_1R_2}{R_1 + R_2}$$

31. The correct answer is (3).

$x^2 - 4 > 0$ is equivalent to $x^2 > 4$. $x^2 > 4$ is equivalent to $|x| > 2$, which means that $x > 2$ or $x < -2$.

32. The correct answer is (1).

The value under the radical in the quadratic formula is greater than or equal to 0. So when

$(-4)^2 - 4(4)c \geq 0$

$16 - 16c \geq 0$ Add 16c to both sides.

$16 - 16c + 16c \geq 0 + 16c$

$16 \geq 16c$ Divide by 16.

$1 \geq c$

33. The correct answer is (2).

The values of sin and cos are equal for complimentary angles, angles whose sum is 90. Thus,

$2x - 1 + 3x + 6 = 90$ Combine like terms.

$5x + 5 = 90$ Subtract 5 from both sides.

$5x + 5 - 5 = 90 - 5$

$5x = 85$ Divide both sides by 5.

$x = 17$

34. The correct answer is (3).

Rotate B 90° counterclockwise to get to A, then rotate 180° counterclockwise to get to C.

35. The correct answer is (1).

Multiply both sides by 2 to get $x^2 + y^2 = 10$.

36. a. The correct answer is 160.

Let $x = m\overset{\frown}{CD}$. Since $m\overset{\frown}{CD} : m\overset{\frown}{DA} = 1 : 8$ and $m\overset{\frown}{ADC} = 180$, $x + 8x = 180$, $9x = 180$, $x = 20$. Then $m\overset{\frown}{DA} = 8(20) = 160$.

b. The correct answer is 80.

$m\angle P = \dfrac{1}{2}(m\overset{\frown}{DA} - m\overset{\frown}{AB})$

$40 = \dfrac{1}{2}(160 - m\overset{\frown}{AB})$

$80 = 160 - m\overset{\frown}{AB}$

$80 = m\overset{\frown}{AB}$

c. The correct answer is 50.

Consider right triangle PAE, where $m\angle PAE = 90$ (tangent to a radius is perpendicular at the point of tangency).

$m\angle P + m\angle PAE + m\angle BEA = 180$

$40 + 90 + m\angle BEA = 180$

$130 + m\angle BEA = 180$

$m\angle BEA = 180$

$m\angle BEA = 50$

d. The correct answer is 50.

$180 - m\widehat{BA} = m\widehat{BC}$

$180 - 80 = m\widehat{BC}$

$100 = m\widehat{BC}$

Then $m\angle BAC = \frac{1}{2}(m\widehat{BC}) = \frac{1}{2}(100) = 50$

e. The correct answer is 100.

$m\angle BAP = \frac{1}{2}m\widehat{AB} = \frac{1}{2}(80) = 40.$

Consider $\triangle PBA$.

$180 = m\angle P + m\angle PBA + m\angle BAP$

$180 = 40 + m\angle PBA + 40$

So, $m\angle PBA = 100.$

37. a. The correct answer is 5.

Isolate the radical by subtracting x from both sides.

$x + \sqrt{2x - 1} - x = 8 - x$

$\sqrt{2x - 1} = 8 - x$ Square both sides.

$(\sqrt{2x - 1})^2 = (8 - x)^2$

$2x - 1 = 64 - 16x + x^2$ Move everything to one side by subtracting.

$2x - 1 - 2x + 1$
$= 64 - 16x + x^2 - 2x + 1$ Combine like terms.

$0 = x^2 - 18x + 65$ Factor with factors of 65 that add to 18.

$0 = (x - 13)(x - 5)$ Set each factor equal to zero.

$x - 13 = 0$ or $x - 5 = 0$

$x = 13$ or $x = 5$ Check for extraneous solutions.

Check $x = 13$,

$13 + \sqrt{2(13) - 1} = 13 + \sqrt{25} = 13 + 5$
$\neq 8.$

13 is an extraneous solution.

Check $x = 5$,

$5 + \sqrt{2(5) - 1} = 5 + \sqrt{9} = 5 + 3 = 8.$

5 is a solution.

b. The correct answer is 8.

Multiply both sides by the LCM of the equation, $y(y - 1)$.

$y(y-1) \times \frac{y}{y - 1} = y(y-1) \times \left[\frac{8}{y} + \frac{1}{y - 1}\right]$

$y(y - 1) \times \frac{y}{y - 1} = y(y - 1) \times \frac{8}{y}$
$+ y(y - 1) \times \frac{1}{y - 1}$

$y^2 = 8(y - 1) + y$

$y^2 = 8y - 8 + y$

$y^2 = 9y - 8$ Move everything to one side by subtracting.

$y^2 - 9y + 8 = 9y - 8 - 9y + 8$

$y^2 - 9y + 8 = 0$ Factor with factors of 8 that add to -9.

$(y - 8)(y - 1) = 0$ Set each factor equal to zero.

$y - 8 = 0$ or $y - 1 = 0$

$y = 8$ or $y = 1$

We must check solutions to make sure they do not make the denominator equal to zero. The solution of $y = 1$ would make the denominator $y - 1 = 0$. Thus $y = 8$ is the only solution.

38. a. The correct answer is 90, 210, 330.

Set equation equal to zero and factor.

$2 \sin^2 x - 1 - \sin x = 1 + \sin x - 1 - \sin x$

$2 \sin^2 x - \sin x - 1 = 0$ Factor.

$(2 \sin x + 1)(\sin x - 1) = 0$ Set each factor equal to zero.

$2 \sin x + 1 = 0$ or $\sin x - 1 = 0$

$2 \sin x = -1$ or $\sin x = 1$

$\sin x = -\dfrac{1}{2}$ or $\sin x = 1$

$\sin x = -\dfrac{1}{2}$ when $x = 210°$ and $330°$

$\sin x = 1$ when $x = 90°$

b. $\dfrac{\sin 2x}{1 - \cos 2x} =$

$\dfrac{2 \sin x \cos x}{1 - (\cos^2 x - \sin^2 x)} =$

$\dfrac{2 \sin x \cos x}{\sin^2 x + \sin^2 x} =$

$\dfrac{2 \sin x \cos x}{2 \sin^2 x} =$

$\dfrac{\cos x}{\sin x} =$

$\cot x$

39. a.

b.

c. Since the graphs cross when $x = 0$, that is one value when $\tan x = 2 \sin x$. There will be other values at any multiple of π.

40. a. The correct answer is 45.6.

Draw the resultant using the parallelogram law.

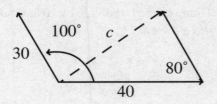

Use the law of cosines:

$c^2 = 30^2 + 40^2 - 2(3)(40) \cos 80°$

$c = 45.6$

b. The correct answer is 40.

Use the law of sines and the result from part (a).

$\dfrac{45.6}{\sin 80°} = \dfrac{30}{\sin B}$

$45.6 \sin B = 30 \sin 80°$ Cross-multiply.

$\sin B = \dfrac{30 \sin 80°}{45.6}$

$B = 40°$

41. a.

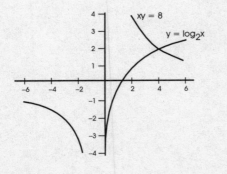

b. The correct answer is 5 or 6.

The y value of $y = \log_2 x$ when $x = 4$ is $\log_2 4$, which is 2, and the y value of $y = \dfrac{8}{x}$ when $x = 4$ is $\dfrac{8}{4}$, which is also 2. The graphs of $y = \log_2 x$ and $y = \dfrac{8}{x}$ meet at $(2, 4)$. For $x > 4$, the graph of $y = \log x$ is rising and the graph for $y = \dfrac{8}{x}$ is falling. So the graph of $\log_2 x$ is above the graph of $\dfrac{8}{x}$ for all values of x greater than 4.

42. a. (1) The correct answer is $\dfrac{27}{32}$.

At least two heads can occur in four ways, HHH, HHT, HTH and THH. The probability of HHH is $\left(\dfrac{3}{4}\right)\left(\dfrac{3}{4}\right)\left(\dfrac{3}{4}\right)$.

The probability of HHT is $\left(\dfrac{3}{4}\right)\left(\dfrac{3}{4}\right)\left(\dfrac{1}{4}\right) = \dfrac{9}{64}$.

The probability of HTH is $\left(\dfrac{3}{4}\right)\left(\dfrac{1}{4}\right)\left(\dfrac{3}{4}\right) = \dfrac{9}{64}$.

The probability of THH is $\left(\dfrac{1}{4}\right)\left(\dfrac{3}{4}\right)\left(\dfrac{3}{4}\right) = \dfrac{9}{64}$.

Thus the total probability is

$\dfrac{27}{64} + \dfrac{9}{64} + \dfrac{9}{64} + \dfrac{9}{64} = \dfrac{54}{64} = \dfrac{27}{32}$.

(2) The correct answer is $\dfrac{13}{256}$.

$_4C_0 \left(\dfrac{3}{4}\right)^0 \left(\dfrac{1}{4}\right)^4 + {_4}C_1 \left(\dfrac{3}{4}\right)^1 \left(\dfrac{1}{4}\right)^3 =$

$\dfrac{1}{256} + \dfrac{12}{256} = \dfrac{13}{256}$

b. The correct answer is 2.72.

To find $\overline{x}$ we must average the test scores.

$$\frac{100 + 99 + 99 + 97 + 96 + 96 + 95 + 94 + 93 + 91}{10}$$

$$= \frac{960}{10} = 96.$$

Using the formula we have:

$(100 - 96)^2 + 2(99 - 96)^2 + (97 - 96)^2 +$
$2(96 - 96)^2 + (95 - 96)^2 + (94 - 96)^2 +$
$(93 - 96)^2 + (91 - 96)^2 =$

$4^2 + 2(3^2) + 1^2 + 2(0^2) + (-1)^2 + (-2)^2$
$+ (-3)^2 + (-5)^2 =$

$16 + 18 + 1 + 0 + 1 + 4 + 9 + 25 = 74$

Then we need to divide by 10 and take the square root:

$$\sqrt{\frac{74}{10}} = \sqrt{7.4} = 2.72.$$

Practice Test 5

Answer 30 questions from this part. Each correct answer will receive 2 credits. No partial credit will be allowed. Write your answers in the spaces provided on the separate answer sheet. Where applicable, answers may be left in terms of π or in radical form.   [60]

1 Express 240° in radian measure.

2 In $\triangle ABC$, $a = 12$, $\sin A = 0.45$, and $\sin B = 0.15$. Find b.

3 Find the value of $\displaystyle\sum_{k=1}^{3} (3k - 5)$.

4 Solve for x: $4^{(3x+5)} = 16$

5 Express the sum of $\sqrt{-64}$ and $3\sqrt{-4}$ as a monomial in terms of i.

6 Solve for all values of x: $|2x + 5| = 7$

7 What will be the amplitude of the image of the curve $y = 2 \sin 3x$ after a dilation of scale factor 2?

8 What is the solution of the equation $\sqrt{5x - 9} - 3 = 1$?

9 In the interval $90° \le \theta \le 180°$, find the value of θ that satisfies the equation $2 \sin \theta - 1 = 0$.

10 Express in simplest form: $\dfrac{1}{\dfrac{1}{a} + \dfrac{1}{b}}$

11 If $f(x) = x^0 + x^{\frac{2}{3}} + x^{-\frac{2}{3}}$, find $f(8)$.

12 When the sum of $4 + 5i$ and $-3 - 7i$ is represented graphically, in which quadrant does the sum lie?

13 In the accompanying diagram, $\overline{AP}$ is a tangent and $\overline{PBC}$ is a secant to circle O. If $PC = 12$ and $BC = 9$, find the length of $\overline{AP}$.

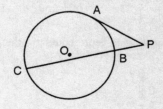

14 Circle O has a radius of 10. Find the length of an arc subtended by a central angle measuring 1.5 radians.

15 If $f(x) = 5x - 2$ and $g(x) = \sqrt[3]{x}$, evaluate $(f \circ g)(-8)$.

Directions (16–35): For *each* question chosen, write on the separate answer sheet the *numeral* preceding the word or expression that best completes the statement or answers the question.

16 For which value of x is the expression $\dfrac{1}{1 - \cos x}$ undefined?

(1) 90°   (3) 270°
(2) 180°   (4) 360°

17 The expression $\log \sqrt{\dfrac{x}{y}}$ is equivalent to

(1) $\frac{1}{2}(\log x - \log y)$ (3) $\frac{1}{2} \log x - \log y$
(2) $\log \frac{1}{2}x - \log \frac{1}{2}y$ (4) $\log \frac{1}{2}x - \log y$

18 If $f(x) = \cos 3x + \sin x$, then $f\left(\dfrac{\pi}{2}\right)$ equals

(1) 1   (3) –1
(2) 2   (4) 0

19 Expressed in $a + bi$ form, $(1 + 3i)^2$ is equivalent to

(1) $10 + 6i$ (3) $10 - 6i$
(2) $-8 + 6i$ (4) $-8 - 6i$

20 The expression $\dfrac{\tan \theta}{\sec \theta}$ is equivalent to

(1) $\cot \theta$ (3) $\cos \theta$
(2) $\csc \theta$ (4) $\sin \theta$

21 Which equation is represented by the graph below?

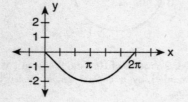

(1) $y = -2 \sin \frac{1}{2}x$ (3) $y = \frac{1}{2} \sin 2x$
(2) $y = -\frac{1}{2} \sin 2x$ (4) $y = 2 \sin \frac{1}{2}x$

22 Expressed in $a + bi$ form, $\dfrac{5}{3 + i}$ is equivalent to

(1) $\frac{15}{8} - \frac{5}{8}i$ (3) $\frac{3}{2} - \frac{1}{2}i$
(2) $\frac{5}{3} - 5i$ (4) $15 - 5i$

23 Gordon tosses a fair die six times. What is the probability that he will toss *exactly* two 5's?

(1) $_6C_5\left(\frac{5}{6}\right)^2\left(\frac{1}{6}\right)^4$ (3) $_6C_5\left(\frac{1}{6}\right)^2\left(\frac{5}{6}\right)^4$
(2) $_6C_2\left(\frac{5}{6}\right)^2\left(\frac{1}{6}\right)^4$ (4) $_6C_2\left(\frac{1}{6}\right)^2\left(\frac{5}{6}\right)^4$

24 If $\sin \theta$ is negative and $\cot \theta$ is positive, in which quadrant does θ terminate?

(1) I   (3) III
(2) II   (4) IV

25 The domain of the equation $y = \dfrac{1}{(x - 1)^2}$ is all real numbers

(1) greater than 1   (3) less than 1
(2) except 1   (4) except 1 and -1

26 In the accompanying diagram, about 68% of the scores fall within the shaded area, which is symmetric about the mean, $\bar{x}$. The distribution is normal and the scores in the shaded area range from 50 to 80.

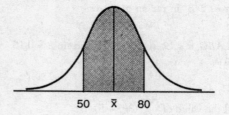

What is the standard deviation of the scores in this distribution?

(1) $7\frac{1}{2}$ (3) 30
(2) 15   (4) 65

27 The expression $2 \sin 30° \cos 30°$ has the same value as

(1) $\sin 15°$ (3) $\sin 60°$
(2) $\cos 60°$ (4) $\cos 15°$

28 In the accompanying diagram of a unit circle, the ordered pair (x,y) represents the point where the terminal side of θ intersects the unit circle.

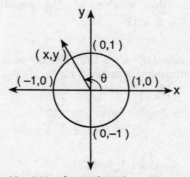

If $m\angle\theta = 120$, what is the value of x in simplest form?

(1) $-\frac{\sqrt{3}}{2}$ (3) $-\frac{1}{2}$
(2) $\frac{\sqrt{3}}{2}$ (4) $\frac{1}{2}$

29 In $\triangle ABC$, side a is twice as long as side b and $m\angle C = 30$. In terms of b, the area of $\triangle ABC$ is

(1) $0.25\, b^2$ (3) $0.866\, b^2$
(2) $0.5\, b^2$ (4) b^2

30 Which quadratic equation has roots $3 + i$ and $3 - i$?

(1) $x^2 - 6x + 10 = 0$ (3) $x^2 - 6x + 8 = 0$
(2) $x^2 + 6x - 10 = 0$ (4) $x^2 + 6x - 8 = 0$

31 Which is the fourth term in the expansion of $(\cos x + 3)^5$?

(1) $90 \cos^2 x$ (3) $90 \cos^3 x$
(2) $270 \cos^2 x$ (4) $270 \cos^3 x$

32 The graph of the equation $y = \frac{6}{x}$ forms

(1) a hyperbola   (3) a parabola
(2) an ellipse   (4) a straight line

33 The roots of the equation $-3x^2 = 5x + 4$ are

(1) real, rational, and unequal
(2) real, irrational, and unequal
(3) real, rational, and equal
(4) imaginary

34 Which equation does *not* represent a function?

(1) $y = 4$ (3) $y = x - 4$
(2) $y = x^2 - 4$ (4) $x^2 + y^2 = 4$

35 If the point $(2,-5)$ is reflected in the line $y = x$, then the image is

(1) $(5,-2)$ (3) $(-5,2)$
(2) $(-2,5)$ (4) $(-5,-2)$

Answers to the following questions are to be written on paper provided by the school.

Part II

Answer four questions from this part. Clearly indicate the necessary steps, including appropriate formula substitutions, diagrams, graphs, charts, etc. Calculations that may be obtained by mental arithmetic or the calculator do not need to be shown.   [40]

36 *a* On the same set of axes, sketch and label the graphs of the equations $y = 2 \cos x$ and $y = \sin \frac{1}{2}x$ in the interval $-\pi \le x \le \pi$.   [8]

    b Using the graphs drawn in part *a*, determine the number of values in the interval $-\pi \le x \le \pi$ that satisfy the equation $\sin \frac{1}{2}x = 2 \cos x$.   [2]

37 In the accompanying diagram, isosceles triangle *ABC* is inscribed in circle *O*, and vertex angle *BAC* measures 40°. Tangent $\overline{PC}$, secant $\overline{PBA}$, and diameters $\overline{BD}$ and $\overline{AE}$ are drawn.

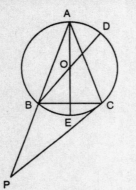

Find:

a $m\widehat{BC}$ [2]
b $m\angle ABD$ [2]
c $m\angle DOE$ [2]
d $m\angle P$ [2]
e $m\angle ACP$ [2]

38 Find, to the *nearest ten minutes* or *nearest tenth of a degree*, all values of *x* in the interval $0° \le x < 360°$ that satisfy the equation $2 \sin 2x + \cos x = 0$.   [10]

39 *a* Find the standard deviation, to the *nearest hundredth*, for the following measurements:

        24,28,29,30,30,31,32,32,32,33,35,36   [4]

    b A circle that is partitioned into five equal sectors has a spinner. The colors of the sectors are red, orange, yellow, blue, and green. If four spins are made, find the probability that the spinner will land in the green sector

        (1) on *exactly* two spins   [2]
        (2) on *at least* three spins   [4]

40 *a* Express in simplest form:

$$\frac{3y + 15}{25 - y^2} + \frac{2}{y - 5}$$ [5]

    b Solve for *x* and express the roots in simplest *a + bi* form:

$$2 + \frac{5}{x^2} = \frac{6}{x}$$ [5]

41 In $\triangle ABC$, $AB = 14$, $AC = 20$, and $m\angle CAB = 49$.

    a Find the length of $\overline{BC}$ to the *nearest tenth*.   [6]

    b Using the results from part *a*, find $m\angle C$ to the *nearest degree*.   [4]

42 Given: $f = \{(x,y) \mid y = \log_2 x\}$

    a On graph paper, sketch and label the graph of the function f.   [3]

    b Write a mathematical explanation of how to form the inverse of function f.   [2]

    c On the same set of axes, sketch and label the graph of the function f^{-1}, the inverse of f.   [3]

    d Write an equation for f^{-1}.   [2]

Practice Test 5

Answers

1. $\dfrac{4\pi}{3}$

    Since $180° = \pi$ radians

    $\dfrac{240}{180} = \dfrac{x}{\pi}$ Cross multiply.

    $240\pi = 180x$ Divide by 180.

    $\dfrac{240\pi}{180} = x$

    $\dfrac{240\pi}{180} = \dfrac{24\pi}{18} = \dfrac{4\pi}{3}$

2. 4

    $\dfrac{\sin A}{a} = \dfrac{\sin B}{b}$

    $\dfrac{.45}{12} = \dfrac{.15}{b}$ Cross multiply.

    $.45b = 1.8$

    $b = 4$

3. 3

    $[3(1) - 5] + [3(2) - 5] + [3(3) - 5]$

    $= [3 - 5] + [6 - 5] + [9 - 5]$

    $= -2 + 1 + 4$

    $= 3$

4. -1

    $4^{(3x + 5)} = 16$ Rewrite 16 as 4^2.

    $4^{3x + 5} = 4^2$ Set exponents equal.

    $3x + 5 = 2$

    $3x = -3$

    $x = -1$

5. $14i$

    $\sqrt{-64} + 3\sqrt{-4} = \sqrt{64}\cdot\sqrt{-1} + 3\sqrt{4}\cdot\sqrt{-1}$

    $= 8i + 3(2)i = 8i + 6i = 14i$

6. 1 or -6

    $|2x + 5| = 7$ so

    $2x + 5 = 7$ or $2x + 5 = -7$

    $2x = 2$ $2x = -12$

    $x = 1$ $x = -6$

7. 4

    The amplitude of $y = 2 \sin 3x$ is 2. A dilation of scale factor 2 will double the amplitude to 4.

8. 5

    $\sqrt{5x - 9} - 3 = 1$ Isolate radical.

    $\sqrt{5x - 9} = 4$ Square both sides.

    $5x - 9 = 16$

    $5x = 25$

    $x = 5$

    Check. $\sqrt{5(5) - 9} - 3$

                   $= \sqrt{25 - 9} - 3$

                   $= \sqrt{16} - 3$

                   $= 4 - 3$

                   $= 1$

9. 150°

$2 \sin \theta - 1 = 0$

$2 \sin \theta = 1$

$\sin \theta = \dfrac{1}{2}$ $\theta = 150°$

10. $\dfrac{ab}{b + a}$

$$\dfrac{1}{\dfrac{1}{a} + \dfrac{1}{b}} = \dfrac{1}{\dfrac{b}{ab} + \dfrac{a}{ab}}$$

$$= \dfrac{1}{\dfrac{b + a}{ab}}$$

$$= 1 \div \dfrac{b + a}{ab}$$

$$= 1 \times \dfrac{ab}{b + a}$$

$$= \dfrac{ab}{b + a}$$

11. $5\dfrac{1}{4}$

$f(8) = (8)^0 + (8)^{\frac{2}{3}} + (8)^{\frac{-2}{3}}$

$1 + (\sqrt[3]{8})^2 + (\sqrt[3]{8})^{-2}$

$= 1 + 2^2 + 2^{-2}$

$= 1 + 4 + \dfrac{1}{2^2} = 1 + 4 + \dfrac{1}{4} = 5\dfrac{1}{4}$

12. IV

$(4 + 5i) + (-3 - 7i) = (4 - 3) + (5 - 7)i$
$= 1 - 2i$ which will be graphed as $(1, -2)$
in quadrant IV.

13. 6

When a tangent and a secant are drawn to a circle from an outside point, the square of the tangent is equal to the product of the secant and its external segment.

$(AP)^2 = (PC)(PB)$

$(AP)^2 = (12)(3)$

$(AP)^2 = 36$

$AP = 6$

14. 15

$S = r\theta$

$= 10(1.5) = 15$

15. -12

$(f \circ g)(-8) = f[g(-8)]$

$= f[\sqrt[3]{-8}] = f(-2)$

$= 5(-2) - 2 = -10 - 2 = -12$

16. (4)

When $1 - \cos x = 0$, $\cos x = 1$, so $x = 360°$

17. (1)

$\log \sqrt{\dfrac{x}{y}} = \log \left(\dfrac{x}{y}\right)^{\frac{1}{2}}$

$= \dfrac{1}{2} \log \dfrac{x}{y}$

$= \dfrac{1}{2} (\log x - \log y)$

18. (1)

$f\left(\dfrac{\pi}{2}\right) = \cos 3\left(\dfrac{\pi}{2}\right) + \sin \dfrac{\pi}{2}$

$= \cos \dfrac{3\pi}{2} + \sin \dfrac{\pi}{2}$

$= 0 + 1$

$= 1$

19. (2)

$(1 + 3i)^2 = 1 + 2(1)(3i) + (3i)^2$

$= 1 + 6i + 9i^2 = 1 + 6i + 9(-1)$

$= 1 + 6i - 9$

$= -8 + 6i$

20. (4)

$$\frac{\tan\theta}{\sec\theta} = \tan\theta \cdot \frac{1}{\sec\theta}$$

$$= \frac{\sin\theta}{\cos\theta} \cdot \cos\theta$$

$$= \sin\theta$$

21. (1)

2π is half the period of a sine curve, so the graph is $y = a \sin\frac{1}{2}x$. Amplitude is 2, so

$y = 2 \sin\frac{1}{2}x$ or $y = -2 \sin\frac{1}{2}x$, but the

sign is changed so $y = -2 \sin\frac{1}{2}x$.

22. (3)

$$\frac{5}{3+i} \times \frac{3-i}{3-i} = \frac{15-5i}{(3)^2 - (i)^2}$$

$$= \frac{15-5i}{9-(-1)}$$

$$= \frac{15-5i}{10}$$

$$= \frac{15}{10} - \frac{5i}{10}$$

$$= \frac{3}{2} - \frac{i}{2}$$

$$= \frac{3}{2} - \frac{1}{2}i$$

23. (4)

The probability of a 5 is $\frac{1}{6}$, so the probability

of not a 5 is $\frac{5}{6}$. There are $_6C_2$ ways of

getting two 5's so the probability is

$_6C_2\left(\frac{1}{6}\right)^2\left(\frac{5}{6}\right)^4$.

24. (3)

If $\sin\theta$ is negative and $\cot\theta$ is positive, then θ is in Quadrant III.

25. (2)

$\frac{1}{(x-1)^2}$ is undefined when $(x - 1) = 0$,

that is, when $x - 1 = 0$, which is when $x = 1$.

26. (2)

68% is one standard deviation on either side of the mean. The range from 50 to 80 is 30 and this is twice the standard deviation.

27. (3)

$2 \sin x \cos x = \sin 2x$, so

$2 \sin 30° \cos 30° = \sin 60°$

28. (3)

The value of x is the same as $\cos 120° = -\frac{1}{2}$.

29. (2)

$$\text{Area} = \frac{1}{2}ab \sin C$$

$$= \frac{1}{2}(2b)b \sin 30 \qquad \text{because } a = 2b$$

$$= \frac{1}{2}(2b)b \times \frac{1}{2}$$

$$= \frac{1}{2}b^2$$

30. (1)

Factors will be $(x - (3 + i))$ and
$(x - (3 - i))$

$(x - 3 - i)(x - 3 + i)$

$(x - 3)^2 - i^2$

$= x^2 - 6x + 9 - i^2$

$= x^2 - 6x + 9 - (-1)$

$= x^2 - 6x + 9 + 1$

$= x^2 - 6x + 10$

So the equation is $x^2 - 6x + 10 = 0$

31. (3)

$_5C_3(\cos^3 x)(3)^2$

$= 10 \times \cos^3 x \times 9 = 90 \cos^3 x$

32. (1)

A hyperbola has $xy =$ number.

33. (4)

Check the discriminant $b^2 - 4ac$.

$-3x^2 = 5x + 4,$

$0 = 3x^2 + 5x + 4;\ a = 3, b = 5, c = 4$

$(5)^2 - 4(3)(4) = 25 - 48 = -23 < 0$

The roots are imaginary.

34. (4)

Because of the y^2 term more than one y can be associated with any x such that $-2 < x < 2$.

35. (3)

Interchange x and y values.

36. a.

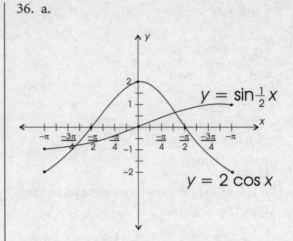

b. The graphs cross two times.

a. $m\overset{\frown}{BC} = 80$

Since $\angle BAC$ is an inscribed angle, the arc it intercepts has twice its measure.

b. $m\angle ABD = 20$

In isosceles triangle ABC, the measures angles B and C are each $\frac{1}{2}(180 - 40) = \frac{1}{2}(140) = 70$.

$m\angle ABD = \frac{1}{2}m\overset{\frown}{AD} = \frac{1}{2}(m\overset{\frown}{BD} - m\overset{\frown}{AB}) =$

$\frac{1}{2}([180 - 2(70)] = \frac{1}{2}(180 - 140) = \frac{1}{2}(40)$

$= 20$

c. $m\angle DOE = 140$

In $\triangle AOB$, the sum of the angles is 180. From part (b), $m\angle ABD = 20$. Since $m\angle ABO = m\angle ABD$, $m\angle ABO = 20$. In isosceles triangle AOB, $m\angle OAB = m\angle ABO$. So $m\angle OAB = 20$. Then

$m\angle AOB = 180 - m\angle ABO - m\angle OAB =$
$180 - 20 - 20 - 140$. Since $\angle AOB$ and
$\angle DOE$ are vertical angles, $= 140$

d. $m\angle P = 30$

An angle formed by a secant and a tangent
is equal to half the difference of the intercepted arcs.

$m\widehat{ADC} = 2m\angle ABC = 2(70) = 140$

$m\widehat{BEC} = 2m\angle BAC = 2(40) = 80$

So $m\angle P = \frac{1}{2}(140 - 80) = \frac{1}{2}(60) = 30$

e. $m\angle ACP = 110$

$m\angle ACP = m\angle ACB + m\angle BCP$

$= 70 + 40 = 110$

38. 90, 194.5, 270, 345.5

$2\sin 2x + \cos x = 0$

$2(2\sin x \cos x) + \cos x = 0$

$4\sin x \cos x + \cos x = 0$

$\cos x(4\sin x + 1) = 0$

$\cos x = 0 \qquad\quad 4\sin x + 1 = 0$

$x = 90°, 270° \qquad 4\sin x = -1$

$\sin x = -\frac{1}{4}$

$x \approx 345.5°, 194.5°$

39. a.   3.06

$\text{Mean} = \dfrac{372}{12} = 31$

$\sigma = \sqrt{\dfrac{1}{12}[(24-31)^2 + (28-31)^2 + (29-31)^2 + 2(30-31)^2 + (31-31)^2 + 3(32-31)^2 + (33-31)^2 + (35-31)^2 + (36-31)^2]}$

$= \sqrt{\dfrac{1}{12}[(-7)^2 + (-3)^2 + (-2)^2 + 2(-1)^2 + (0)^2 + 3(1)^2 + (2)^2 + (4)^2 + (5)^2]}$

$= \sqrt{\dfrac{1}{12}(49 + 9 + 4 + 2 + 3 + 4 + 16 + 25)}$

$= \sqrt{\dfrac{1}{12}(112)}$

$= \sqrt{9.33} = 3.06$

b. (1) $\dfrac{96}{625}$

Probability of green $= \dfrac{1}{5}$

Probability of not green $= \dfrac{4}{5}$

There are $_4C_2$ ways of getting two green.

$_4C_2\left(\dfrac{1}{5}\right)^2\left(\dfrac{4}{5}\right)^2 = 6\left(\dfrac{1}{25}\right)\left(\dfrac{16}{25}\right) = \dfrac{96}{625}$

b. (2) $\dfrac{17}{625}$

Need probability for 3 greens and 4 greens.

P(3 greens) =

$_4C_3\left(\dfrac{1}{5}\right)^3\left(\dfrac{4}{5}\right) = 4\left(\dfrac{1}{125}\right)\left(\dfrac{16}{125}\right) = \dfrac{16}{625}$

P(4 greens) = $_4C_4\left(\dfrac{1}{5}\right)^4 = 1\left(\dfrac{1}{625}\right)$

$\dfrac{16}{625} + \dfrac{1}{625} = \dfrac{17}{625}$

40. a. $\dfrac{1}{5-y}$

$\dfrac{3y+15}{5-y(5+y)} + \dfrac{-2}{(5-y)}$

LCD $(5-y)(5+y)$

$= \dfrac{3y+15}{5-y(5+y)} + \dfrac{-2(5+y)}{(5-y)(5+y)}$

$= \dfrac{3y+15}{5-y(5+y)} + \dfrac{-10+2y}{(5-y)(5+y)}$

$= \dfrac{\cancel{y+5}}{(5-y)\cancel{(5+y)}} = \dfrac{1}{(5-y)}$

b. $\dfrac{3}{2} \pm \dfrac{i}{2}$

$2 + \dfrac{5}{x^2} = \dfrac{6}{x}$ Multiply by x^2

$2x^2 + 5 = 6x$

$2x^2 - 6x + 5 = 0$ $a = 2$ b -6 $c = 5$

$x = \dfrac{6 \pm \sqrt{(6)^2 - 4(2)(5)}}{2(2)}$

$= \dfrac{6 \pm \sqrt{36 - 40}}{4}$

$= \dfrac{6 \pm \sqrt{-4}}{4} = \dfrac{6}{4} \pm \dfrac{2i}{4} = \dfrac{3}{2} \pm \dfrac{i}{2}$

41. a. 15.1

$BC^2 = AB^2 + AC2 - 2(AB)(AC) \cos A$

$= (14)^2 + (20)^2 - 2(14)(20) \cos 49°$

$= 196 + 400 - 367.393$

$BC^2 = 228.607$

$BC = 15.1$

b. 44

$\dfrac{\sin A}{BC} = \dfrac{\sin C}{AB}$

$\dfrac{\sin 49}{15.1} = \dfrac{\sin C}{14}$

$\sin C = \dfrac{14 \sin 49°}{15.1} = .699$

$C = 44.4 \approx 44$

42. a.

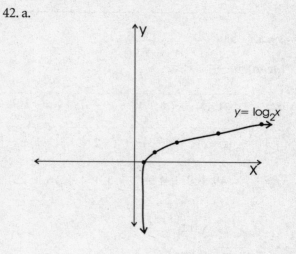

$y = \log_2 x$ is the same as $2^y = x$.

x	y
1	0
2	1
4	2
8	3
16	4

b. Reflect the graph in the line $y = x$. To get values, interchange x and y values.

x	y
0	1
1	2
2	4
3	8
4	16

c.

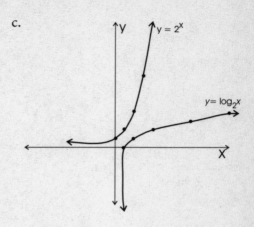

d. $f^{-1}(x) = 2^x$

Subject Index

A

Absolute value, 43

   absolute value inequalities, 49–50

Acute angle, 105

Addition

   adding like algebraic fractions, 42

   adding radicals, 41

   addition method, 45

   addition with complex numbers, 53

Algebra operations, 40–43

Algebraic fractions, 42–43

Amplitude, 130

Angle, 103

   acute angle, 117

   angle measure, 104

   angle measurement theorems, 109–110

   central angle, 105–106

   double angle formula, 147–148

   geometric (static) concept of angles, 117

   half angle formula, 149

   inscribed angle, 106

   negative angle, 118

   obtuse angle, 117

   positive angle, 118

   reference angles, 124–126

   reflex angle, 117

   right angle, 117

   sides of the angle, 103

   static concept of angles, 117

   straight angle, 117

   sums and differences, 146–47

Applications to graphing, 71–74

Arc, 106

Arccos function, 134

Arcsin function, 133

Arctan function, 134

Notes

Notes

Notes

Notes

Notes

Notes

Notes

Notes

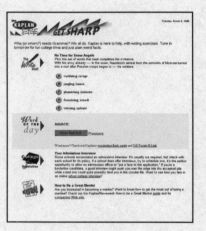

How Did We Do? Grade Us.

Thank you for choosing a Kaplan book. Your comments and suggestions are very useful to us. Please answer the following questions to assist us in our continued development of high-quality resources to meet your needs.

The Kaplan book I read was: _____

My name is: _____

My address is: _____

_____

My e-mail address is: _____

What overall grade would you give this book? Ⓐ Ⓑ Ⓒ Ⓓ Ⓕ

How relevant was the information to your goals? Ⓐ Ⓑ Ⓒ Ⓓ Ⓕ

How comprehensive was the information in this book? Ⓐ Ⓑ Ⓒ Ⓓ Ⓕ

How accurate was the information in this book? Ⓐ Ⓑ Ⓒ Ⓓ Ⓕ

How easy was the book to use? Ⓐ Ⓑ Ⓒ Ⓓ Ⓕ

How appealing was the book's design? Ⓐ Ⓑ Ⓒ Ⓓ Ⓕ

What were the book's strong points? _____

How could this book be improved? _____

Is there anything that we left out that you wanted to know more about?

Would you recommend this book to others? ☐ YES   ☐ NO

Other comments: _____

_____

_____

Do we have permission to quote you? ☐ YES   ☐ NO

Thank you for your help. Please tear out this page and mail it to:

Dave Chipps, Managing Editor
Kaplan Educational Centers
888 Seventh Avenue
New York, NY 10106

Or, you can answer these questions online at www.kaplan.com/talkback.

Thanks!

KAPLAN

Want more information about our services, products or the nearest Kaplan center?

 Call our nationwide toll-free numbers:

1-800-KAP-TEST for information on our courses, private tutoring and admissions consulting
1-800-KAP-ITEM for information on our books and software
1-888-KAP-LOAN* for information on student loans

 Connect with us in cyberspace:

On AOL, keyword: kaplan
On the World Wide Web, go to: www.kaplan.com
Via e-mail: info@kaplan.com

 Write to:

Kaplan Educational Centers
888 Seventh Avenue
New York, NY 10106

About

KAPLAN
Educational Centers

Kaplan Educational Centers is one of the nation's leading providers of premier education and career services. Kaplan is a wholly owned subsidiary of The Washington Post Company.

TEST PREPARATION & ADMISSIONS

Kaplan's nationally recognized test prep courses cover more than 20 standardized tests, including secondary school, college and graduate school entrance exams and foreign language and professional licensing exams. In addition, Kaplan offers private tutoring and comprehensive, one-to-one admissions and application advice for students applying to graduate programs. Kaplan also provides information and guidance on the financial aid process.

SCORE! EDUCATIONAL CENTERS

SCORE! after-school learning centers help K-8 students build confidence, academic and goal-setting skills in a motivating, sports-oriented environment. Its cutting-edge, interactive curriculum continually assesses and adapts to each child's academic needs and learning style. Enthusiastic Academic Coaches serve as positive role models, creating a high-energy atmosphere where learning is exciting and fun. SCORE! Prep provides in-home, one-on-one tutoring for high school academic subjects and standardized tests.

KAPLAN LEARNING SERVICES

Kaplan Learning Services provides customized assessment, education and professional development programs to K-12 schools and universities.

KAPLAN INTERNATIONAL PROGRAMS

Kaplan services international students and professionals in the U.S. through a series of intensive English language and test preparation programs. These programs are offered at Kaplan City Centers and four new campus-based centers in California, Washington and New York via Kaplan/LCP International Institute. Kaplan and Kaplan/LCP offer specialized services to sponsors including placement at top American universities, fellowship management, academic monitoring and reporting, and financial administration.

KAPLAN PUBLISHING

Kaplan Publishing produces books, software and online services. Kaplan Books, a joint imprint with Simon & Schuster, publishes titles in test preparation, admissions, education, career development and life skills; Kaplan and Newsweek jointly publish guides on getting into college, finding the right career, and helping your child succeed in school. Through an alliance with Knowledge Adventure, Kaplan publishes educational software for the K-12 retail and school markets.

KAPLAN PROFESSIONAL

Kaplan Professional provides recruitment and training services for corporate clients and individuals seeking to advance their careers. Member units include Kaplan Professional Career Services, the largest career fair provider in North America; Perfect Access/CRN, which delivers software education and consultation for law firms and businesses; HireSystems, which provides web-based hiring solutions; and Kaplan Professional Call Center Services, a total provider of services for the call center industry.

DISTANCE LEARNING DIVISION

Kaplan's distance learning programs include Concord School of Law, the nation's first online law school; and National Institute of Paralegal Arts and Sciences, a leading provider of degrees and certificates in paralegal studies and legal nurse consulting.

COMMUNITY OUTREACH

Kaplan provides educational resources to thousands of financially disadvantaged students annually, working closely with educational institutions, not-for-profit groups, government agencies and other grass roots organizations on a variety of national and local support programs. Kaplan enriches local communities by employing high school, college and graduate students, creating valuable work experiences for vast numbers of young people each year.